How to Retire Prosperously and Gracefully

C. Colburn Hardy

J.K. Lasser Institute
NEW YORK

J.K. LASSER INSTITUTE

Simon & Schuster, Inc.
Gulf + Western Building
One Gulf + Western Plaza
New York, NY 10023

J.K. Lasser, the J.K. Lasser Institute, and Colophon
are trademarks of Simon & Schuster, Inc.

DISTRIBUTED BY PRENTICE HALL TRADE SALES

Manufactured in the United States of America

1 2 3 4 5 6 7 8 9 10

ISBN 0-13-510587-0

Library of Congress Cataloging-in-Publication Data

Hardy, C. Colburn.
    How to retire prosperously and gracefully : the comprehensive
guide to retirement planning and living / C. Colburn Hardy.
        p.   cm.
    Includes index.
    ISBN 0-13-510587-0 : $16.95
    1. Finance, Personal. 2. Retirement income. 3. Retirees—
Finance, Personal.   I. Title.
HG179.H282 1989
332.024'01—dc20

Publisher's Note: *J.K. Lasser's How to Retire Prosperously and Gracefully* is published in recognition of the great need for clarification of personal retirement planning for millions of men and women. We believe the research and interpretation by the author and the J.K. Lasser Institute to be authoritative and will be of general help to readers. Readers are cautioned, however, that this book is sold with the understanding that, although every care has been taken in the preparation of the text, the Publisher is not engaged in rendering legal, accounting, financial, or other professional service. Readers with specific problems are urged to seek the professional advice of a certified financial planner, an accountant, or lawyer.

Foreword

Decisions about one's retirement are often made without a blueprint for success. Each of us needs useful information and examples to make well-informed and meaningful decisions about our retirement future.

My father has been both thoughtful and successful. From his personal involvement with aging programs and public officials in Florida and in Washington, and through his extensive knowledge of pension and retirement policies, he continues to provide significant advice and counsel.

This book comes at a time when our nation is paying greater attention to retirement issues. And, as we look ahead to the 21st century, this kind of information will become ever more valuable. Each of us should be conscious of the need to make early decisions on long-range planning for our future well-being; wise and practical advice is essential.

I am confident that *How to Retire Prosperously and Gracefully* will make a difference for many Americans, both those preparing for the "Golden Years" and those already benefitting from Social Security.

Dorcas R. Hardy, *U.S. Commissioner of Social Security*

Acknowledgments

pg. vii Data on percentage of elderly facing financial problems furnished courtesy of State of Florida Aging and Adult Services State Advisory Council.

pg. 47 Table 3-1, Effect of Early Retirement on Pension, furnished courtesy of Hewitt Associates, Lincolnshire, Illinois.

pg. 65 Table 4-6, Limits of Defined Benefit Pension Plan Payment, furnished courtesy of Hewitt Associates, Lincolnshire, Illinois.

pg. 73 Table 4-8, Quality Rating: Minimum Criteria for Investments, furnished courtesy of Wright Investors Service.

pg. 80 Table 4-9, Tax-Exempt vs. Taxable Bonds: Comparative Yields, furnished courtesy of Research Institute of America, New York, NY.

pg. 82 Table 4-11, Duration Years of Bonds: AAA-rated Municipals, furnished courtesy of Hugh R. Lamle, M.D. Sass Investors Service Inc., New York, NY.

pg. 128 Table 6-1, Calcium Content in Various Foods, reprinted with permission of Macmillan Publishing Company from *LifeSpan Plus* by Sigmund Stephen.Miller, Julian Asher Miller and Don Ethan Miller. Copyright © 1986 by Sigmund Stephen Miller, Julian Asher Miller and Don Ethan Miller.

pg. 130 List of exercise benefits from *The Senior Citizen Handbook* by Marjorie Stokell and Bonnie Kennedy. Copyright © 1985. Reprinted by permission of the publisher, Prentice-Hall, Inc., Englewood Cliffs, NJ.

pg. 134 Table 6-4, Recommended Daily Dietary Allowances for Retirees, reprinted with permission of Macmillan Publishing Company from *LifeSpan Plus* by Sigmund Stephen Miller, Julian Asher Miller and Don Ethan Miller. Copyright © 1986 by Sigmund Stephen Miller, Julian Asher Miller and Don Ethan Miller.

pg. 135 Table 6-5, Ideal Weights for Older Adults, reprinted courtesy *Statistical Bulletin*, Metropolitan Life Insurance Company, New York, NY.

pg. 140 The ten amendments for widows reprinted with permission of Virginia Graham from *Life After Harry* by Virginia Graham. Copyright © 1988 by Virginia Graham.

pg. 147-148 Table 6-6, Cholesterol, Saturated Fat, and Calories in Different Foods, reprinted with permission of The Lancet, Ltd., London, U.K. CSI used with permission of the Oregon Health Sciences University, Portland, Oregon.

pg. 149 Table 6-7, Caffeine Level in Different Foods and Beverages, reprinted with permission of Macmillan Publishing Company from *LifeSpan Plus*, by Sigmund Stephen Miller, Julian Asher Miller and Don Ethan Miller. Copyright © 1986 by Sigmund Stephen Miller, Julian Asher Miller and Don Ethan Miller.

pg. 150-151 Table 6-8, High-Fat, Low-Fat Menus, reprinted with permission of The Cooper Clinic from "Cholesterol," Nutrition Tips series, by Georgia Kostas, M.P.H., R.D., Cooper Clinic Nutrition Program, Dallas, Texas. Copyright © 1986 by The Cooper Clinic.

pg. 153 Table 6-9, Sodium Content of Different Foods and Beverages, reprinted with permission of Macmillan Publishing Company from *LifeSpan Plus* by Sigmund Stephen Miller, Julian Asher Miller and Don Ethan Miller. Copyright © 1986 by Sigmund Stephen Miller, Julian Asher Miller and Don Ethan Miller.

pg. 155 Table 6-10, Fiber Content of Different Foods and Beverages, reprinted with permission of Macmillan Publishing Company from *Lifespan Plus* by Sigmund Stephen Miller, Julian Asher Miller and Don Ethan Miller. Copyright © 1986 by Sigmund Stephen Miller, Julian Asher Miller and Don Ethan Miller.

pg. 189 Table 8-1, Top Retirement Communities, adapted from *Retirement Places Rated* by Richard Boyer and David Savageau. Copyright © 1987 by Rand McNally and Company. Reprinted by permission of the publisher, Prentice Hall Press, New York, NY.

pg. 191 Table 8-2, How States Rate As Retirement Havens, furnished courtesy of WEFA, Inc. (formerly Chase Econometrics, Inc. and Wharton Econometrics Forecasting Associates, Inc.).

pg. 192 Table 8-3, Consumer Price Index: Comparative Cities, adapted in part from *Home Sales* (February 1989), copyright © 1988 by the National Association of Realtors. Reprinted by permission of the National Association of Realtors.

pg. 202 Table 8-6, Living Costs Around the World, adapted from *The Book of World City Rankings* by John Tepper Marlin (copyright © 1986 by Council on Municipal Performance; reproduced by permission of The Free Press, a Division of Macmillan, Inc.) and from *Executive Living Costs Worldwide* (BI/COL) by Business International Corporation, 1988.

pg. 218 Example 8-1, on shared equity, furnished courtesy of Karen DeVost Rollings, American Venture Realty, Silver Spring, MD.

Contents

Introduction vii

Chapter 1 Financing Your Lifestyle—
Sources of Retirement Income 1

Chapter 2 Financing Your Lifestyle—
Using Your Retirement Income Efficiently 27

Chapter 3 Financing Your Lifestyle—
Making Early Retirement Work 45

Chapter 4 Creating Wealth to Enhance Your Retirement 51

Chapter 5 Planning Your Estate—
Balancing Your Needs With Those of Your Heirs 95

Chapter 6 Your Health—How to Keep It Up 121

Chapter 7 Your Health—How to Pay for the Care You Need 169

Chapter 8 Housing—Meeting Your Lifestyle
Needs for the Rest of Your Life 187

Chapter 9 Moving Into Retirement 229

Chapter 10 Using Your Time—Making the Most
of the Opportunities that Retirement Offers 235

Index 259

Introduction

America's New Breed of Retirees: Planning Younger, Retiring Richer, Living Longer

About 2 million Americans turn 65 every year. With age 65 still the traditional gateway to retirement, this means that, every month, over 165,000 Americans must decide how to spend their years after work. This involves deciding how to support yourself once the paycheck stops coming in, and also what to do when you don't have to go to work anymore.

Why You Need To Plan Now (No Matter How Young You Are)

You can expect to live nearly a quarter of your life as a retiree. Think about what that means. You spent anywhere from 12 to 20 years (about a quarter of your life) preparing for your working career, a period that probably covered 40 years, about half of your life. Doesn't it make sense to take some time, over the next few years, to prepare for such a significant part of your life, a period where you have the potential to achieve so much? Considering that, once you're retired, you won't be able to accumulate further wealth, isn't it wise to make sure that your financial affairs are taken care of, so you get the best of care when you need it?

Essentially, planning for your financial needs after you retire is just like planning for your current financial needs. After you retire, you'll still need food, shelter, health care, and clothing. And you'll want to be able to afford the things in life that you enjoy. But there are these complicating factors:

(1) You won't be earning any more wages from your job. Apart from losing that source of income, stopping work means no extra cash from working overtime or moonlighting, and no expectation that your wages will more or less keep up with inflation.

(2) You can't tell for sure what anything will cost in the future. Inflation, over a period of 20 years, has varied between 4% and 14%. Future inflation cannot be predicted with any certainty; its course will probably turn on the occurrence of events that probably could not have been reasonably forecast at this point in time. (Who in 1964, for example, could have forecast the inflation that resulted from the oil embargoes of the 70s?) Worse, the price of individual items can vary greatly from the general trend of inflation.

(3) People who have relied on government programs (be they farmers, welfare recipients, or even the Government of South Viet Nam) have eventually come to a bad end when the public support, and increased funds to match inflation, ran out for the program in question. Perhaps no group is a bigger recipient of government funding than the elderly. Although the fact is that funding for Social Security is as safe as can reasonably be anticipated, given the current conditions, it's also true that predicting 20 and 30 years into the future is inherently hazardous. Think you can predict the political climate 20 years from now? Would you have predicted, in 1964, that the Republicans would control the White House for 20 out of 24 years, **beginning in 1968, just four years later?**

Long Life: A Personal Blessing, A Financial Nightmare

Thanks to higher Social Security checks, employer and personal pension plans, and savings and investments, Americans are beginning retirement more affluent than ever. However, the percentage of elderly who face financial problems rises sharply with age:

Percentage of Elderly Facing
Financial Problems

Age	Percentage
55-64	40.9%
65-74	48.9%
75 and over	62.5%

SOURCE: State of Florida Aging and Adult Services State Advisory Council.

As retirees grow older, and unforeseen events force sale of personal assets and future losses of income, they have to accept ever-lower standards of living just to survive. Their financial security may begin to erode from inflation and health care costs. And as more people outlive their actuarial life expectancies, some retirees will have to help support their parents as well as their children and grandchildren. For the typical retiree, expenses will begin to outstrip income by age 75. By age 80, most people will have to invade capital, and by age 85, there will probably be one survivor who will need support systems within the family, from friends and from community services.

Most people have lived longer than experts expected them to when they were younger. If this trend continues, you will too. If you don't take this into account in your retirement planning, the likelihood of your ending up living a life of poverty before you die is much greater.

Statistics aren't available for unhappiness among retirees, but the level of misery among retired Americans probably matches the level of poverty. Indeed, poverty and misery often go together. Therefore, it's never too early to begin preparing for your retirement. You'll need to save as much as you can to provide for your future needs, and the earlier you start, the less you'll have to save each year. Start early enough, plan wisely enough, and you can even retire early.

Whether you retire early or late, start your planning five years before you actually retire. And start implementing those plans two years before you retire, such as making major purchases (a new car, appliances and furniture), developing specific financial plans, setting up reserves, and, when there are special responsibilities (such as a troubled child or failing parent), putting away extra savings.

Plan to review your plans regularly. You've got to be flexible enough to cope with any resurgence in inflation, investments that go sour, pension plans that go bust, and any cutbacks in the real (that is, taking inflation into account) income you may receive from Social Security. Being flexible means having alternatives available, and planning for possible future difficulties by having hedging strategies in place before those problems occur.

I am not persuaded that saving for your retirement is, or will be, as traumatic as many fear. It's a matter of priorities. If you are still trying to balance your budget, it's time to shift your financial emphasis: whittle down loans, boost your savings, and set specific goals. If you already have plenty of money, concentrate your efforts developing hobbies, skills, and interests that can make after-work living more enjoyable.

What too many fail to realize is that planning what to do with your time is as important as planning what to do with your money. Once you retire, you will not be the same person you were while working. In projecting life in retirement, you may assume that the major changes will be in the pace of life, the lack of pressures and the opportunity to set your own priorities. Don't anticipate that you will keep old friends and will do many of the same things to which you have been long accustomed. Although retirement life may start that way, it will seldom last.

Already, younger seniors view retirement as another phase of active living. And why not? As one gerontologist tells me, we realize now that many conditions, previously thought characteristic of old age, are actually the result of poor nutrition, lack of exercise and self-excess. "Many of the presumed psychological deficits of old age," says he, "occur to people of any age when deprived of loved ones, close friends, meaningful involvement and intellectual stimulation."

Consider these seniors who remained vital and made some of their greatest achievements after they were supposed to have retired.

- At 71, Golda Meir became prime minister of Israel and served for five years.

- At 73, Pablo Picasso completed some of his greatest works and continued to paint until age 90.

- At 77, John XXIII was elected Pope and brought a new regime to the Catholic Church.

- At 80, Voltaire led France's struggle for greater respect for the rights of man.

- At 83, Barbara McClintock won the Nobel Prize for research in genetics.

- At 89, Frank Lloyd Wright completed the famous Guggenheim Museum.

- At 96, Pablo Casals was staging cello recitals.

A meaningful, joyful retirement can provide the opportunity to engage in activities missed or not fully utilized while working. "The world is your oyster," says Peter Schwed, an octogenarian who still writes amusing books—when he isn't playing tennis.

Another way to look at retirement is expressed by this successful small businessman who fled the city, in his late 50s, to remodel an old farm and mill in New Hampshire:

> "To enjoy retirement, the most important factor is a positive, optimistic, realistic outlook; to learn how to accept things as they are and to have the most fun with what you have in hand or can find/create on your own."

And this, from a social worker turned volunteer in aging programs:

> "Living, really living, with your spouse becomes a challenge. No matter how much you love each other, no matter how congenial,

how good the companionship and sense of security, it's a new kind of relationship that requires tact, patience, tolerance and many forms of love.

"If you must keep busy and active and involved, so be it, but now, perhaps for the first time in your life, you can heed the words of John Burroughs, 'I still find each day too short for all the thoughts I want to think, all the walks I want to take, all the books I want to read and all the friends I want to see. The longer I live, the more my mind dwells on the beauty and wonder of the world.' "

The goal of this book is not only to show you how to plan your retirement better in terms of personal finances, but also in terms of personal satisfaction. This book will show you how to make the necessary plans to retire prosperously—and gracefully!

CHAPTER 1

Financing Your Lifestyle— Sources of Retirement Income

Before determining what you'll need to live on, you should first examine what you can anticipate in income. Generally, retirees earn income from five sources:

Social Security, available to almost all working Americans with benefits tied to work credits and earnings—jointly financed by the employer and employee;

Employer-funded pension plans (often with provisions for employee contributions), with payouts based on the amount of contributions and years of eligible service;

Personal pension plans, where the benefits are paid from your own savings;

Savings/investments such as bank accounts, pooled funds, securities, real estate, etc.—based on individual savings directly or through inheritances.

Post-retirement employment

In this chapter, we'll examine all of these.

SOCIAL SECURITY

Social Security is the foundation on which all after-work income is built. The monthly checks will be welcome, but, alone, will never be enough to assure a financially secure retirement—unless you opt to live in the Falkland Islands or Mexico.

Basically, Social Security is a form of replacement income. Before anyone receives a benefit check, there has to be a loss: by disability, by death or by cessation of normal working income. Retirees can collect Social Security checks as early as age

1

62, but, usually, only retirees who delay drawing Social Security until age 65 draw full benefits.

A Coming Crisis?

Until recently, Social Security was politically untouchable. Now there are signs that this unique status is changing. Young people are worried about the long-term solvency and are aggressively discussing reducing benefits for affluent retirees. In the next several years, expect major changes to the Social Security system that will result in lower net benefits to retirees.

As a nation, the United States spends a disproportionate share of its national income on its senior citizens. For the 12% of the population age 65 and over, the Federal Government allocates 27% of its budget and, with major corporations, one third of total wages goes for retirement/health benefits. Furthermore, the payments of pensions and benefits reduces the money available to the rest of the population. Here are some things to think about and take into account in long-term planning:

(1) To continue to pay all the benefits promised to those entering the work force today, projections indicate that the combined employer/employee Social Security taxes will eventually have to be raised to 37.5% compared to 15.3% (1990): a deduction of $15,000 on a $40,000 salary.

(2) In counting on higher Social Security and health care benefits, the elderly are betting that young Americans will be richer, less healthy and more inclined to raise large families (to pay more Social Security taxes).

(3) The elderly, as a group, have gotten richer. On the other hand, the young have become poorer with a poverty rate six times that of older Americans.

Benefits

At normal retirement age of 65 (67 in 1991 and rising to 70 in the next century), the benefits are calculated by a complex formula: (1) based on average earnings in counted years since 1951 with the elimination of the five years with the lowest income; (2) indexed upward annually when the cost of living rises more than 3.1% a year but subject to revision by Congress.

In 1989, the fully qualified new retiree gets $899 per month plus $449 for a non-working, or lower-benefit, spouse: a welcome total of $1,348 per month or $16,176 a year. (Table 1-1). And if the retiree's spouse has worked and receives a pension that is greater than $429 a month, that partner qualifies for a higher check. A spouse who qualified for maximum benefits will get $899 for a total of $21,576 a year for a qualified couple.

Beware of Social Security Hustlers

Certain hustlers are trying to exploit the fear many retirees have over the safety of their Social Security benefits. You may receive an "official" looking envelope, perhaps mentioning Social Security. Inside, perhaps you'll even find a form authorizing the organization to, say, get a statement of your earnings from the Social Security Administration. Perhaps you'll find dire warnings of an impending end to Social Security, and a request for funds to "help oppose this trend."

Fact is, you can get a copy of your Social Security records (including an estimate of your benefits) yourself—for free. (To see how, see page 7.) And if you want to contribute to organizations that will fight for your rights, contribute to organizations (such as the AARP, the NRTA, and others) that have actually testified and lobbied in Washington. Don't trust anyone "masquerading" as the Social Security Administration, or some other government agency. If you suspect something's fishy, contact your local Post Office.

For surviving spouses, whether female or male, there are special benefits. When the surviving spouse is age 60 or over, the benefit is 100% of the partner's Primary Insurance Amount (PIA)—more if the deceased was entitled to a delayed retirement credit—but when the primary wage earner retired early, the benefit is reduced by 19/40ths of 1% for each month before age 65 to a maximum cut of 28.5%.

A divorced spouse qualifies if married for 10 years and may be entitled to benefits as early as age 60. Remarriage, over age 60, allows the choice of the higher benefit: as a surviving, divorced spouse or as the spouse of the new partner. The original benefit terminates when the divorced spouse remarries unless the new partner is receiving Social Security benefits as a widow, widower or parent of a disabled child. *Be smart— If you are a 59-year-old widow and planning to marry, wait until you're 60!*

A person who has been married more than once is entitled to the highest benefit payable on the earnings record of ANY spouse. That equals 71.5% of the deceased spouse's PIA at 60; at 62, 75%. That person can switch to the best deal at any time.

A disabled surviving spouse who cannot work because of a severe mental or physical disability qualifies for benefits at age 50 to 59: 71.5% of the partner's PIA after a five-month waiting period. The disability must have occurred within seven years of the spouse's death or last entitlement to benefits.

Effect of Early Retirement. To compute your Social Security benefits available before age 65, when fully qualified, subtract the number of months before age 65 from 180; then, multiply this result by the primary benefit payable at age 65 and divide by 180.

TABLE 1-1   Examples of Monthly Payments of Social
Security (based on 4% COLA in 1989)

	Payments	
Age 65 (1989)	*Monthly*	*Annually*
Worker retiring		
Maximum	$899	$10,788
Non-working spouse	449	5,394
Total	1,348	16,176
Average	545	6,528
Non-working spouse	272	3,264
Total	817	9,804
Aged couple, both with benefits	911	10,932
Widow(er) and 2 children	1,120	13,440
Disabled worker with spouse and		
children	956	11,742
All disabled workers	528	6,336

SOURCE: Social Security Administration

Example: at age 65 in 1989, the maximum benefit is $899 per month. You are age 62 and one month, so you're eligible for Social Security. Subtract 36 months from 180 to get 144. Multiply 144 by $899 to get $129,456. Divide this by 180 to determine the monthly benefit of $719. This is 20% less than received by those turning 65.

Your 62-year-old, non-working spouse's benefit would be 50% of the primary benefit: at age 65, $449 per month. To find your spouse's Social Security at age 62 (and one month), use 144. Subtract 36 months from 144 to get 108. Multiply this by $449 to get $48,492. Divide this by 144; your spouse will receive $337 monthly at age 62.

For projections of Social Security benefits for those who work past age 65, the payments rise 3% annually to age 70 until 1990 when, under current law, the increase will begin to rise gradually to a maximum of 8% annually.

Eligibility

To qualify for Social Security retirement benefits, the individual must have 36 work credits today and 40 in 1991. This means earnings of $440 for employment covered by Social Security in one quarter whether paid for work for one hour, one day, one week or three months.

To be eligible for Social Security, a surviving spouse must have been married nine months before the death of the covered spouse, unless the death was due to an accident or military duty or the surviving spouse was the parent of a child (natural or adopted). If the surviving spouse was married for one year and caring for an eligible child under age 16 or a child disabled before age 22, that spouse is entitled to 75% of the covered spouse's Primary Insurance Amount (PIA).

Once you're eligible, you will get benefits related to your age at retirement and earnings over the years. If you become injured and cannot work for at least one year, you are eligible for disability benefits and, in certain cases when you have received such payments for 24 months, may be eligible for Medicare even though you are under age 65.

Other Benefits

When anyone covered by Social Security dies, there's a lump sum death payment of $255. This is payable to a surviving spouse who was living with the deceased at the time of death. If there's no spouse, payment will be made to the children who are eligible for benefits in the month of death. Otherwise, there's no payment.

For more information, consult your local Social Security office.

Records Needed for Social Security

Since you are dealing with a governmental agency with its thousands of rules, regulations and requirements, you must have proper proof of your eligibility:

- Your own Social Security cards or a record of that number.

- Proof of age: a public or religious record of birth or a baptismal certificate made before fifth birthday. This should be certified bearing the official seal of the agency or organization from which obtained. Photocopies are not acceptable unless certified by the custodian of the original document or submitted with the original record. If these are not available, other proven data may be acceptable.

- Proof of marriage when applying for a wife's, widow's or widower's benefits. This should be the original or a certified copy. Depending on state law, a common-law marriage may be recognized when substantiated by statements from relatives.

- Your W-2 Form for the last year or a copy of your last Federal income tax return if you are self-employed. Without this, there can be a long delay because those earnings may not be in Social Security records.

For survivor benefits you'll need:

- Proof of death, usually made available by the funeral director.
- Social Security numbers of both deceased and spouse.
- Proof of marriage of widow or widower.

Payment Date and Terms

Social Security checks are mailed to be received on the third day of each month. If that day is a holiday or on a weekend, the check is mailed earlier.

Each check represents the benefit for the previous month. For instance, one dated November 3 is for October. When both husband and wife are eligible, the check is usually made out to them jointly. However, separate checks can be requested.

If the check is cashed before the death of the beneficiary, no repayment is required. If it arrives after the death, this may be considered an overpayment and subject to recovery by the government. This possibility can be avoided by direct deposit in a financial institution as authorized by signing Form SF-1199A. This eliminates the possibility of theft from a mailbox and minimizes the problems at death because the check is considered cashed at receipt.

At all times, the beneficiary, or authorized representative, should keep the local Social Security office and bank informed of change of address or death, as well as when a check is lost, destroyed or forged.

Information on Earnings, Benefits and Errors

For earnings, periods of self-employment or employment, with names and addresses of reporting employers, contact your local office or write Social Security Administration, Office of Central Records Operation, Baltimore, MD 21235. If you find an error, submit proof on Form 1040. Make this check every three years because only data for that period is broken down.

For information on the status of your Social Security, call this toll-free number—1-800-937-2000—and ask for PEBES (Personal Earnings and Benefit Estimate Statement) Form SSA-7004. This is a free report that, when properly filled out, will provide you with

- your own earnings history
- how much you've paid in
- and an estimate of your future Social Security protection—retirement, disability and survivors' benefits

If you have trouble getting through, call late at night—the line can handle up to 10,000 calls per hour, 24 hours per day. If you prefer, you can contact your local Social Security office or write to Consumer Information Center, Dept. 60, Pueblo, Colo., 81009. If you go to your local office, call first to make sure they have the form.

If the data are to be sent to someone else, you'll be billed when the cost is more than $5.00.

Working After Retirement

When you work after age 65 without taking benefits, your income will be subject to Social Security taxes and your benefits, when taken, will be greater.

If you opt to accept the pension and still earn a paycheck, however, you will be subject to penalties: a reduction of $1 for every $2 earned over $6,480 in 1989 for those who retire at ages 62-64; over $8,880 for quit-at-65ers. In 1991, the reduction will be $1 for every $3 in excess earnings.

Exception: for the first six months after retirement, you can collect Social Security as long as you do not earn more than $510 per month. This is a one-time deal.

Over age 70, earnings are not penalized. There is a small break in that, in the year that you become 70, the earnings limit applies only to income in the months before your birthday.

TABLE 1-2   How Earnings Affect Social Security Benefits (1989)

Above $6,480 at ages 62-64 and above $8,880 at ages 65-69, $1 is deducted from Social Security for every $2 in excess earnings.

At age 70, there are no penalties. In 1990, the FICA tax, under current legislation, will rise to 7.65% and the earnings test changes to a deduction of $1 for every $3 of excess earnings for beneficiaries age 65-69.

Post Retirement Wages	$ 10,000	$ 15,000	$ 20,000
At age 62:			
Excess over $6,480	$ 3,520	$ 8,520	$ 13,520
Reduction in SS benefits*	1,760	4,260	6,760
FICA tax (7.51%)	751	1,127	1,502
Total deductions	2,511	5,387	8,262
Net before income taxes	7,489	9,614	11,738
At age 65:			
Excess over $8,880	1,120	6,120	11,120
Reduction in SS benefits*	560	3,060	5,560
FICA tax (7.51%)	751	1,127	1,502
Total deductions	1,311	4,187	7,062
Net before income taxes	8,689	10,813	12,938

* Assumes that amount of benefits payable before the effect of the earnings test is at least as great as the reduction shown.

SOURCE: Social Security Administration

Caution: before you continue to work after age 65, calculate your net income. For example, someone age 65, receiving $10,000 in primary benefits (with the spouse receiving an additional $5,000) who took a part-time job at $10,000 a year, would be penalized $560 (since this is $1,120 above the $8,880 limit). Take away another $751 in FICA (Federal Insurance Contributions Act) and $2,800 income tax, and take-home pay would be just $5,889.

TAXATION OF SOCIAL SECURITY BENEFITS

This invasion of traditional Social Security started in the early 1980s when taxes were increased for retirees whose income was over $25,000 for a single, or

$32,000 for joint filers. The tax base includes interest from tax-exempt securities when they total more than 50% of Social Security. Social Security benefits subject to tax include your monthly retirement, survivor, or disability benefits. Monthly Tier 1 Railroad Retirement benefits are divided into two parts. One part may be treated as Social Security benefits and is identified on Form RRB-1099 as the Social Security equivalent portion of the Tier 1 benefit; the other part is treated as pension income and like Tier 2 Railroad Retirement benefits is not treated as Social Security benefits subject to tax.

If any part of your Tier 1 benefits is equivalent to Social Security benefits, you should receive Form 1099 from the government by February 1 of the following year. Otherwise, you should receive Form RRB-W-2P.

Social Security benefits are not reduced by withholdings for supplementary medical insurance. Your Form SSA-1099 includes the withholdings in total benefits.

Benefits paid on behalf of child or incompetent. If a child is entitled to Social Security benefits, such as after the death of a parent, the benefit is considered to be the child's regardless of who actually receives the payment. Whether the child's benefit is subject to tax will depend on the amount of the child's income.

Workmen's compensation. If you are receiving Social Security disability payments and Workmen's Compensation for the same disability, your Social Security benefits may be reduced by the workmen's compensation. For example, you are entitled to Social Security disability benefits of $5,000 a year. After receiving a $1,000 workmen's compensation award, your disability benefits are reduced to $4,000. For purposes of the 50% of benefits rule, you treat the full $5,000 as Social Security benefits.

Repayment of benefits. If you forfeit part of your Social Security benefits because of excessive outside income, the forfeited amount reduces your benefits for purposes of the 50% inclusion rule. You make the reduction even if the forfeit relates to benefits received in a prior year. For example, your regular 1987 benefit of $5,000 is reduced by $1,000 because of earnings of the prior year. For tax purposes, your 1987 benefits are considered $4,000.

If you must repay Social Security benefits that were subject to tax and you must repay benefits that were taxed, you must first reduce current year benefits by the amount of repayment. If the repayment exceeds current year benefits, you may claim the excess as an itemized deduction. If the repayment exceeds $3,000, you may recompute your tax for the year in question by claiming a credit for the amount of tax overpaid on your current year tax return.

Nonresident aliens. A special rule applies to Social Security and Tier 1 Railroad Retirement benefits received by nonresident aliens. Unless provided otherwise by tax treaty, one half of a nonresident alien's Social Security benefits will be subject to the 30% withholding tax imposed on U.S. source income that is not connected with a U.S. trade or business.

In the following chart, the second column lists how much income (*including tax-exempt interest*) you may receive before benefits become taxable. The last column lists the levels at which 50% of benefits become taxable.

TABLE 1-3   Effect of Other Income on Taxable Benefits—
Single

Monthly Social Security benefits	No benefits taxed unless other income exceeds—	50% of benefits taxed if other income is at least—
$300	$23,200	$26,800
350	22,900	27,100
400	22,600	27,400
450	22,300	27,700
500	22,000	28,000
550	21,700	28,300
600	21,400	28,600
650	21,100	28,900
700	20,800	29,200
750	20,500	29,500
800	20,200	29,800
850	19,900	30,100
900	19,600	30,400
950	19,300	30,700
1,000	19,000	31,000

TABLE 1-4 Effect of Other Income on Taxable Benefits—
Married Filing Jointly

Monthly Social Security benefits	No benefits taxed unless other income exceeds—	50% of benefits taxed if other income is at least—
$700	$27,800	$36,200
750	27,500	36,500
800	27,200	36,800
850	26,900	37,100
900	26,600	37,400
950	26,300	37,700
1,000	26,000	38,000
1,050	25,700	38,300
1,100	25,400	38,600
1,150	25,100	38,900
1,200	24,800	39,200
1,250	24,500	39,500
1,300	24,200	39,800
1,350	23,900	40,100
1,400	23,600	40,400

Examples:

(1) You are married and have dividend and interest income of $28,000 and tax-exempt interest of $2,000. Your net Social Security benefits are $4,000 and you file a joint return.

Adjusted gross income		$28,000
Plus: Tax-exempt interest	$2,000	
50% of benefits	2,000	+4,000
		$32,000
Less: Base amount		32,000
		0

None of your benefits are taxable.

(2) Same as in (1) above except your Social Security benefits are $8,000.

Adjusted gross income		$28,000
Plus: Tax-exempt interest	$2,000	
50% of benefits	4,000	+6,000
		$34,000
Less: Base amount		32,000
Excess		$2,000

Part of your benefits are subject to tax. The amount of benefits subject to tax is 50% of the excess over the base amount or 50% of benefits, whichever is less.

Therefore, $1,000 of benefits are subject to tax because 50% of the excess over the base amount (50% of $2,000) is less than 50% of benefits (50% of $8,000).

PENSION INCOME

You'll find complete information on pension plans in Chapter 4. For now, let's concentrate on how to calculate what you can expect to receive in annual pension income.

You should be able to obtain information about what you can expect in pension income from your employer's pension administrator or human resources office. Individual plans have different terms, conditions, and benefits, and should be consulted when planning for retirement.

Different categories of pension plans have differing characteristics which affect payouts. In general terms, there are these categories of pension plans:

(1) *Employer plans* of large companies or governments where all or a large portion of contributions are paid as part of compensation. Generally, total benefits from most private pension plans, plus Social Security, amount to 50% to 70% of the employee's last working year's compensation. This figure is generally lower for hourly workers and those with limited service, and somewhat higher for executives and long-timers.

With most plans, the payouts are made monthly as an annuity to the employee and spouse as long as either lives. Workers can also take benefits in a lump sum, fully when vested and always with distributions of voluntary contributions.

(2) *Keogh and Professional Corporation plans*—used primarily by small groups such as physicians, dentists, lawyers, architects and so on.

(3) *Special plans such as 401(k)s, 403(b)s, SEP* where you make or direct contributions. The savings are limited but permit tax savings and can be matched by the employer.

(4) *Personal pension plans,* primarily the Individual Retirement Account (IRA) where you make contributions and select the investments. The savings represent your earnings and the withdrawals are at your direction, within IRS regulations.

If the participant dies before age 55, his widow gets lifetime benefits starting in the year the deceased worker would have reached age 65.

These are the most common formulas used by private employers to determine pension benefits:

Flat Amount Per Year of Service: a plan that pays $30 per month for each year of employment would pay $810 a month to an employee who worked for 27 years. Social Security is separate. This formula is not widely used.

Percentage of Earnings Per Year of Service: based on time and compensation. The participant receives credit equal to a percentage of earnings for each year enrolled in the plan. This would be 1% to 2%, so, after 25 years of toil, the worker would get a pension of one quarter to one half of pay, usually calculated as average compensation over the three or five years your income was highest.

Integrated Formula: Since the employer bears part of the cost of Social Security, he might wish to recognize these benefits in his calculations and reduce the company payout in line with the government benefits.

How does integration work? For *defined-benefit* plans (where contributions are geared to provide a fixed level of benefits at retirement), the employer can basically reduce his monthly pension benefits by the amount of your Social Security checks. For *defined-contribution* plans (where the level of contributions is fixed, and benefits depend on the size of contributions and the number of years before retirement), the employer may include his Social Security contributions attributable to your retirement benefits (known as old-age, survivor, and disability insurance, or OASDI) in contributions on your behalf. For example, under a plan that promises contributions of 10% of salary, the employer may include its OASDI contribution (currently 5.7% of earnings up to the Social Security wage base) in that 10% contribution. Employers who integrate Social Security with a defined-contribution plan are limited in their ability to make contributions for earnings that exceed the Social Security wage base.

The above generalizations are limited by complex rules, including application of IRS anti-discrimination rules, which are designed to keep highly paid employees from getting unfair benefits. Furthermore, tax reform affected the integration rules; one set of rules applied from 1984 to 1988, and another set applies from 1989 on.

Government Pensions

In most cases, pensions for federal government employees are more generous than those of private industry: the *time* for reasonable benefits is shorter (20 years for 50% of pay and 30 years for 75% for military personnel and many police/firemen); the *calculations* more rewarding (for instance, a soldier who retired at age 51 after 30 years of active duty, at $15,000, receives about $22,500 at age 65); and, in many cases, when the worker took early retirement, he or she can count on Social Security benefits from working in private industry.

As a rule of thumb, long-time civil servants will receive a pension of 60% of the last working year's salary.

To an increasing degree, the formulas used by state and local governments have been and are, similar to those of the Federal Government (but not always). In many areas, especially rural states and small communities, pension benefits are not overly generous.

Withdrawals

At retirement, the distribution of pension assets can be made in these ways: as an annuity where there's a monthly payment for as long as either partner lives; as a lump sum where all of the assets are paid out and spent or reinvested; or a combination.

Each method has its advantages, but, usually, the determining factors will be: (a) how much other income is available; and (b) the impact of taxes. At all times, the payout of the assets representing tax-deductible dollars (but not voluntary contributions made with after-tax dollars) is taxable and subject to withholding tax unless you notify the trustee, in writing, that you want to receive the full benefits and pay the taxes yourself. If you fail to do this, the withholding will be based on the tax to be paid by a married individual claiming three exemptions.

With most employer plans, there's little choice unless you are an executive and can make special arrangements. The monthly payments will be paid for life and will be calculated on the basis of the vested assets and your age at retirement.

With other types of plans, employer-paid or self-directed, the minimum withdrawals must be under IRS regulations: (1) the percentage method whereby the distribution is

10% of the aggregate amount of the balance. This will exhaust the fund quickly; (2) the life expectancy schedule where the payout reflects the ages of the participant and spouse. ***Withdrawals May Be Complex.*** To understand how much money you will get from your pension savings, how it can be paid out and what may be the tax consequences, consult a knowledgeable adviser well before retirement: the Personnel Director of your employer, the trustee of your personal pension plan or, when substantial sums are involved, a tax adviser. There are strict rules and numerous options. The magic ages are 59^{1}/2 and 70^{1}/2; you *may* start withdrawals without penalty at age 59^{1}/2, and you *must* start withdrawals by age 70^{1}/2.

Warning

Start planning withdrawals of pension assets a year before you expect to make the first withdrawal. With multi-employer-involved plans, you should be able to get full explanations from publications, seminars and personal interviews. With plans of smaller companies and a self-directed IRA, you will have to do most of the work.

All payouts must be approved by IRS. This is usually no problem with large firms, with professional trustees such as banks, insurance companies and mutual funds, but can be slow and exasperating with Defined Benefit Plans where: (a) assets must be certified by an actuary; (b) a lawyer must make sure all details conform to the trust agreement and federal regulations—for hefty fees, of course.

Calculating Your Pension Plan: What You Will Have

Use Table 1-5 to determine: (1) the total amount of saved dollars, in a pension plan, at different rates of return and periods of savings; (2) the annual contributions needed to fund a set retirement assets goal.

Use Table 1-6 to calculate the future value of a single sum investment, in a pension plan, at various rates of return over a different number of years.

A note about using these tables—if you want to calculate the nominal value of what your pension savings will be (that is, how many dollars you'll have), use the column that corresponds to your expected rate of return. However, if you want to calculate what the real value, after discounting for inflation, of what your pension savings will be (that is, what the dollars that you will have will be worth in today's dollars), use the column that corresponds to your real rate of return. Your real rate of return equals your expected rate of return, less the inflation rate. Generally, you can expect your real rate of return to be about 2% over an extended period of time.

TABLE 1-5   Compounding Factor with Same Annual Contribution

Rate	5	10	15	20	After Year 25	30	35	40
-4%	4.43	8.04	10.99	13.39	15.35	16.95	18.25	19.31
-3%	4.57	8.49	11.86	14.75	17.23	19.37	21.20	22.77
-2%	4.71	8.96	12.81	16.29	19.43	22.27	24.84	27.16
-1%	4.85	9.47	13.85	18.03	22.00	25.77	29.36	32.77
0%	5.00	10.00	15.00	20.00	25.00	30.00	35.00	40.00
1%	5.15	10.57	16.26	22.24	28.53	35.13	42.08	49.38
2%	5.31	11.17	17.64	24.78	32.67	41.38	50.99	61.61
3%	5.47	11.81	19.16	27.68	37.55	49.00	62.28	77.66
4%	5.63	12.49	20.82	30.97	43.31	58.33	76.60	98.83
5%	5.80	13.21	22.66	34.72	50.11	69.76	94.84	126.84
6%	5.98	13.97	24.67	38.99	58.16	83.80	118.12	164.05
7%	6.15	14.78	26.89	43.87	67.68	101.07	147.91	213.91
8%	6.34	15.65	29.32	49.42	78.95	122.35	186.10	279.78
9%	6.52	16.56	32.00	55.76	92.32	148.58	235.12	368.29
10%	6.72	17.53	34.95	63.00	108.18	180.94	298.13	486.85
11%	6.91	18.56	38.19	71.27	127.00	220.91	379.16	645.83
12%	7.12	19.65	41.75	80.70	149.33	270.29	483.46	859.14
13%	7.32	20.81	45.67	91.47	175.85	331.32	617.75	1145.49
14%	7.54	22.04	49.98	103.77	207.33	406.74	790.67	1529.91
15%	7.75	23.35	54.72	117.81	244.71	499.96	1013.35	2045.95
16%	7.98	24.73	59.93	133.84	289.09	615.16	300.03	2738.48
17%	8.21	26.20	65.65	152.14	341.76	757.50	1668.99	3667.39
18%	8.44	27.76	71.94	173.02	404.27	933.32	2143.65	4912.59
19%	8.68	29.40	78.85	196.85	478.43	1150.39	2753.91	6580.50
20%	8.93	31.15	86.44	224.03	566.38	1418.26	3538.01	8812.63

To find the total worth of a set number of dollars savings, in a tax-deferred pension plan, for a set number of years, find where the anticipated rate of return crosses the number of years to retirement and multiply this figure by the dollars to be contributed each year. At age 25, Sue starts her IRA with $1,000 and plans to continue these savings until retirement in 40 years. She projects an annual yield of 8% so multiplies 279.78 by $1,000 to get a nest-egg target of $279,780. At a real rate of return (earnings less inflation) of 2%, her $279,780 nest egg will be worth $61,610 in today's dollars ($1,000 times 61.61).

To determine the annual contributions needed to fund a set retirement goal, find where the year column crosses the yield column and divide this figure into the projected assets. At age 35, Antonio sets his pension plan goal at $500,000 at age 65. He anticipates an average annual rate of return of 10%. He checks where the 30 year and 10% columns cross in Table 1-5: 180.94, then divides this into $500,000 to get $2763.35, the dollars he must invest each year in his retirement plan. With compounding over three decades, total savings of $82,900 will grow to half a million.

TABLE 1-6   Compounding Factor for Single Sum Investment

Rate	5	10	15	20	After Year 25	30	35	40
-4%	0.82	0.66	0.54	0.44	0.36	0.29	0.24	0.20
-3%	0.86	0.74	0.63	0.54	0.47	0.40	0.34	0.30
-2%	0.90	0.82	0.74	0.67	0.60	0.55	0.49	0.45
-1%	0.95	0.90	0.86	0.82	0.78	0.74	0.70	0.67
0%	1.00	1.00	1.00	1.00	1.00	1.00	1.00	1.00
1%	1.05	1.10	1.16	1.22	1.28	1.35	1.42	1.49
2%	1.10	1.22	1.35	1.49	1.64	1.81	2.00	2.21
3%	1.16	1.34	1.56	1.81	2.09	2.43	2.81	3.26
4%	1.22	1.48	1.80	2.19	2.67	3.24	3.95	4.80
5%	1.28	1.63	2.08	2.65	3.39	4.32	5.52	7.04
6%	1.34	1.79	2.40	3.21	4.29	5.74	7.69	10.29
7%	1.40	1.97	2.76	3.87	5.43	7.61	10.68	14.97
8%	1.47	2.16	3.17	4.66	6.85	10.06	14.79	21.72
9%	1.54	2.37	3.64	5.60	8.62	13.27	20.47	31.41
10%	1.61	2.59	4.18	6.73	10.83	17.45	28.10	45.26
11%	1.69	2.84	4.78	8.06	13.59	22.89	38.57	65.00
12%	1.76	3.11	5.47	9.65	17.00	29.96	52.80	93.05
13%	1.84	3.39	6.25	11.52	21.23	39.12	72.07	132.78
14%	1.93	3.71	7.14	13.74	26.46	50.94	98.10	188.88
15%	2.01	4.05	8.14	16.37	32.92	66.21	133.18	267.86
16%	2.10	4.41	9.27	19.46	40.87	85.85	180.31	378.72
17%	2.19	4.81	10.54	23.11	50.66	111.06	243.50	533.87
18%	2.29	5.23	11.97	27.39	62.67	143.37	328.80	750.38
19%	2.39	5.69	13.59	32.43	77.39	184.68	440.70	1051.67
20%	2.49	6.19	15.41	38.34	95.40	237.38	590.67	1469.77

To calculate the future value of a single sum investment, at a set rate of return over a set number of years, find where the yield and year columns cross, then multiply this figure by the dollars invested.

At age 50, Phil changes jobs. He receives a lump sum payment of $50,000 from the pension plan of the old company and rolls this over into an IRA. At age 65, when he plans to start withdrawals, with a projected 12% average annual rate of return, the figure is 5.47 (15 years and 12% in Table 1-6). He multiplies 5.47 by $50,000 to get $273,500, a welcome addition to his new retirement plan.

Let's see what a single investment will be worth when left in a tax-deferred pension plan. With $10,000 in a Rollover IRA, for example, over 20 years, with a 12% yield: 9.65 × $10,000 = $96,500.

Now, let's see how to calculate a combination: $30,000 in a frozen pension plan plus $2,000 a year contributed for 20 years.

TABLE 1-7   Calculating Retirement Income

Karen, age 45, plans to retire at 65. She has $30,000 in a corporate retirement plan from a previous employer. She sets up an IRA to which she will contribute $2,000 a year. With all holdings, she projects a annual real rate of return of 2%. The current life expectancy for a 65-year-old female is 83.2, or 18.2 additional years; Karen is planning on living 22 years after turning 65. Here's how she calculates her pensions:

1. Current value of existing pension plan		$30,000
2. Number of years to retirement	20	
3. Estimated real annual rate of return	2%	
4. Growth factor of fixed sum (Table 1-6)		1.49
5. Value of assets at age 65 (line 1 × line 4)		44,700
6. Annual contributions to IRA	2,000	
7. Growth factor of IRA (Table 1-5)	24.78	
8. Value of IRA at age 65 (lines 6 × 7)		49,560
9. Total value of pension plans (line 5 + line 8)		94,260
10. Lump-sum payout: after 28% tax of $26,393		69,867

If invested at 2% real interest, this will yield $1,397 annually and the principal will go to heirs.

11. Annuity payout (assuming same age spouse):

Year 1:

1/22nd of $69,867	$ 3,176
minus 28% tax	−889
net of taxes	2,287
Principal remaining ($69,867 − 3,176)	66,691
Interest over year one on remaining principal	1,334
Balance at beginning of year two	67,480

Year 2:

1/21st of $68,025	$ 3,239
minus 28% tax	−907
net of taxes	2,332
Principal remaining ($68,025 − 3,239)	64,786
Interest over year one on remaining principal	1,296
Balance at beginning of year two	66,081

Payouts for year 3, 4, and so on are calculated similarly.

If the annuity payout schedule is used, and both are age 65, the first withdrawal will be 1/22nd: $3,176 minus the 28% tax will net $889 the first year. From then on, since the payouts will be greater: 1/21st in Year 2; 1/20th in Year 3, etc. Meantime,

TABLE 1-8   Savings Needed to Finance Y Years of Monthly $100 Withdrawals at X Rate of Interest

				Rate			
Year	2%	4%	6%	8%	10%	12%	14%
1	$ 1,189	$ 1,178	$ 1,168	$ 1,157	$ 1,147	$ 1,137	$ 1,127
2	2,355	2,311	2,268	2,226	2,185	2,146	2,107
3	3,497	3,398	3,304	3,213	3,126	3,041	2,961
4	4,618	4,444	4,279	4,124	3,976	3,836	3,703
5	5,715	5,448	5,199	4,965	4,746	4,541	4,348
6	6,791	6,413	6,064	5,742	5,443	5,166	4,910
7	7,846	7,340	6,880	6,459	6,074	5,722	5,398
8	8,879	8,231	7,648	7,121	6,645	6,214	5,824
9	9,893	9,088	8,371	7,733	7,162	6,652	6,194
10	10,887	9,910	9,053	8,297	7,630	7,040	6,516
11	11,860	10,701	9,694	8,819	8,054	7,384	6,796
12	12,815	11,460	10,299	9,300	8,438	7,691	7,039
13	13,750	12,190	10,868	9,744	8,785	7,961	7,252
14	14,667	12,891	11,405	10,155	9,100	8,202	7,436
15	15,566	13,566	11,910	10,534	9,384	8,416	7,597
16	16,447	14,212	12,386	10,884	9,641	8,605	7,737
17	17,311	14,834	12,833	11,208	9,874	8,774	7,858
18	18,158	15,431	13,257	11,506	10,086	8,923	7,964
19	18,987	16,006	13,654	11,781	10,276	9,055	8,056
20	19,801	16,557	14,028	12,035	10,449	9,173	8,136
21	20,598	17,088	14,381	12,270	10,606	9,277	8,205
22	21,379	17,597	14,713	12,488	10,747	9,370	8,266
23	22,146	18,087	15,026	12,688	10,876	9,452	8,319
24	22,896	18,557	15,321	12,873	10,992	9,525	8,365
25	23,633	19,009	15,599	13,043	11,097	9,590	8,405
26	24,354	19,443	15,860	13,201	11,192	9,647	8,440
27	25,061	19,860	16,106	13,347	11,278	9,699	8,470
28	25,755	20,261	16,339	13,481	11,357	9,744	8,496
29	26,434	20,646	16,557	13,605	11,427	9,784	8,519
30	27,100	21,016	16,763	13,720	11,490	9,820	8,539

WORKSHEET 1-1

1. Current value of existing pension plan _____
2. Number of years to retirement _____
3. Estimated real annual rate of return _____
4. Growth factor of fixed sum (Table 1-6) _____
5. Value of assets at age 65 (line 1 × line 4) _____
6. Annual contributions to IRA _____
7. Growth factor of IRA (Table 1-5) _____
8. Value of IRA at age 65 (lines 6 × 7) _____
9. Total value of pension plans (line 5 + line 8) _____
10a. After 28% tax _____
10b. Lump-sum payout: _____
11. Annuity payout:

Annuity withdrawal
   ([1/(remaining life expectancy*)] times line 9)   11a_____
Minus 28% tax   11b_____
   11c_____
Principal remaining (line 9 − line 11a)   11d_____
Interest over year one on remaining principal (rate of   11e_____
return times line 11d)
Balance at beginning of year two (11d plus 11e)   11f_____

* The period of years that you should use is the number of retirement years that you and your spouse (if married) can be expected to live. If you're married and, under current actuarial tables, your spouse is expected to survive you, add the years by which your spouse is expected to survive you to your life expectancy. (You'll find an actuarial table on page 40.) For instance, if your life expectancy is 17 years and your spouse is expected to survive you by 3 years, use 20 years as the life expectancy.

the assets will keep growing tax deferred. Three months before the end of the 22nd year, there will be a lump sum withdrawal.

If you desire a constant annual payout over a number of years, and are willing to invade your principal to achieve it, Table 1-8 will enable you to calculate what you can afford to withdraw each month.

The dollar figure is the amount you need to have saved to allow $100 withdrawals each month for the stated period of years. For example, if you want to be able to withdraw $100 for 15 years, and you anticipate an 8% rate of return, you should have $10,534 saved.

If you divide your savings by the dollar figure indicated, and then multiply the result by $100, you can determine how much you can withdraw each month before your savings are exhausted. For example, if you have $400,000 saved up, you could withdraw (based on the above assumptions) $3,797.00 each month.

($400,000/$10,534 = 37.97; $100 × 37.97 = $3,797.00)

Worksheet 1-1, on page 20 will enable you to calculate your retirement income.

WORKING AFTER RETIREMENT

Whether for necessity or for pleasure, you may look forward to working after you retire. With all types of businesses and second careers, be cautious, be conservative and be careful. Keep your cash investments at a minimum; lease rather than buy; set up an office in your home until more space becomes essential; and never commit more capital than you can afford to lose. To minimize the effect on your Social Security, if you must work, try to postpone receiving your monthly benefit. You'll get bigger checks when you do stop all work, and you'll save the money that your checks would be reduced by (see page 7).

Unless you have special skill or experience or have close contacts within your industry or with family and friends, getting a full-time job after age 55 will be difficult. Most major employers are reluctant to accept the high costs of benefits such as a pension plan, life and health insurance.

Usually, the best bet for a well-paying job will be a temporary arrangement, directly, or as a consultant. Both are stop-gaps and worthwhile only when you face a challenge, are well compensated and have reasonable assurances that the job will last until you have earned enough to afford that long-anticipated leisure.

Recognize that work, of almost any type, will affect retirement plans and lifestyle. Employment involves responsibilities—the very pressures that many people want to avoid after a lifetime of toil. The opportunities will be primarily with smaller organizations where you will probably have to learn to adapt to new philosophies, policies and procedures . . . not always easy for some older folks.

In most cases, the greatest financial rewards will come from utilizing your working experience. Plans can be developed while still working as long as you do not violate confidentiality or corporate rules. If large sums are involved, consult an attorney and get written approval from your employer. Look for precedents within your industry and recognize that, unless these plans are handled carefully, you could be fired or blackballed.

Most companies and many governments have special projects that can benefit from your experience. If the company has a plant in Arizona and you are willing to move from Chicago, ask about part-time opportunities. Your experience and loyalty could be valuable.

Find out about retirement-training courses, especially if you are considering moving into a new area of work. IBM Retirement Education Assistance program provides tuition aid to potential retirees and their spouses for three years before, and two years after, retirement. Usually, the employer pays for college or vocational courses to learn special skills such as auto repair, photography, retail selling, electronic programming, etc.

Even when there are no financial incentives, both partners should attend courses at local institutions to learn new skills, to sharpen old hobbies, to update business fundamentals or to prepare for examinations to be a real estate salesperson, financial adviser or teacher.

Finding a Job

If you stay in the same area: start building a network of contacts before you retire with family, friends, work associates directly or through professional associations, union or church. After you retire, network through AARP chapters and retiree groups such as Telephone Pioneers or job committee at senior centers.

If you relocate: check out local employment opportunities with the Chamber of Commerce, personnel placement agencies, directors of technical courses at junior colleges, and state employment centers. You may qualify for Job Training Partnership Act which finances training for displaced workers and those faced with discrimination—in your case, probably, age.

Advice: If you are looking for a real position, full or part-time, prepare a one page resume that lists your skills and accomplishments. The degree of explanation will depend on the type of position you seek—detailed when you are shooting for a key position, summarized if you are willing to accept a minor role.

Send this in answer to newspaper classified ads, to employment agencies, to friends and to people who make decisions on hiring. With large companies, mail with a personal note to the president. When you follow up, call his office. The secretary will probably refer you to the personnel manager so you can honestly say that you were referred by ''the president's office.'' I'd say the odds are 10 to 1 you will get an appointment for an interview.

Identify your interests. What would you really like to do? What are the chances of getting along happily with this employer?

What sacrifices are you willing to make? Will you work nights? Weekends? Are you prepared to accept a job that's below your capabilities?

Getting a job at age 66 requires tact, patience and persistence. And when you find a position, get ready for snubs, subtle pressures and harassment. Some of your colleagues will resent your age and experience and feel that you are taking a job that should have gone to their friend.

Define your capabilities. Many skills are transferable and can be used in a variety of activities and places: accounting, computer programming, interpreting languages; researching or writing reports; driving a car; training other employees. Always relate them to the prospective employer and, when possible, explain how your experience can benefit his operations.

Follow up every interview, even if you're scheduled to play golf or expect a visit from your in-laws. Write a thank-you note and request that if things can't work out at this time, please keep your availability in mind and your resume on file.

Although these suggestions sound elementary, an ex-personnel manager says, "Most retirees haven't applied for a job in 30 years and find it easy to forget the fundamentals."

At the interview: be neatly dressed and groomed with a briefcase of records/samples of successful projects. Use them to illustrate your skills. You may consider yourself retired and relaxed but the interviewer wants to hire the best person for the job.

Don't be defensive about your age. Discrimination is illegal. If the company is worth working for, management will look for quality and experience that can improve profits.

Don't push too hard. Mentally, change places with the interviewer and ask yourself how you would handle the application from someone your age. Relax and enjoy. You're retired, so you have plenty of time.

Do listen and ask questions that will force the interviewer to talk to you about the company, its products, its services and its people. The best way to make a friend is to make the other person feel important.

Don't take the first job offer unless it's exceptionally attractive. Survey the field and narrow down your options so that you understand the alternatives.

Avoid hazardous jobs, such as clerking in a liquor store, especially at night. Avoid jobs that might be boring to you, too. Boredom creates stress, and stress can kill you (see Chapter 6). For instance, working as a teller in a bank where your co-workers will be probably be much younger than you may be boring, with few concerns of interest to you, and will keep you on your feet all day— seldom a welcome situation.

Don't be too proud to take a "menial" job. Forget about dignity and have fun, meet people, get out from under your spouse's feet and become involved.

Many businesses, throughout the nation, are recruiting elders back to part-time work. They recognize that mature men and women can be excellent employees: patient, dedicated, loyal, and reliable. Locally, department and discount stores welcome sales clerks on weekends and holidays. They pay a minimum wage plus commission and offer discounts on personal purchases.

This trend is likely to accelerate because: (1) with the slowing birthrate since the 1970s, there are fewer young people of working age; (2) more businesses are turning to part-time help.

Job Training?

When you're retired and decide you want to work, ask your local Area Agency on Aging or community Aging Department if there is a job-training program. These are designed to help seniors brush up on resumes, follow-up letters and interviewing techniques. They boost students' confidence and help veterans to get over the point that they can be gold mines of experience and skill plus being more reliable and dedicated than their younger counterparts.

In Palm Beach County, Florida, for example, there's a Job Workshop sponsored by a Private Industry Council, free to those over age 55. With experienced teachers, from local industry, governments and colleges, the retirees learn of job opportunities, what employers want and how best to make presentations. There are mock interviews and plenty of repartee on problems and solutions.

Special Assignments

In major communities, temporary help agencies look for seniors with special skills. Many stand ready to train and place workers with local businesses. Kelly Services sponsors *Encore,* a recruitment drive aimed exclusively at adults 55 or older. They look for retirees with specific experience but also offer training courses in computers, research and office management. The seniors are interviewed, tested for skills, coached for special projects and rated on the basis of experience and grades. They pay weekly and also offer health insurance at group rates.

In West Palm Beach, the local office has been most successful with: (a) men with backgrounds in accounting, tax preparation, sales, management and engineering; (b) women with secretarial, office and retail sales experience. Some of the jobs last for the ''season''—from November to May; others involve a flexible work week or weeks.

Running Your Own Business

Everyone wants to be his or her "own boss." But be slow to consider any concept that will require substantial financing which could cut into your reserves. No matter how able or confident you are, you will soon learn that it takes twice as long and three times as much capital as anticipated. And, in most cases, you will not be able to rely on the support services to which you have become accustomed nor have ready access to potential customers.

There are two options:

To **BUY** a business or service, store, agency or franchise. Hopefully, this will be an established, growing, profitable enterprise available on favorable terms: small cash down and easy payments.

Unless you are financially knowledgeable, hire an accountant to:

a) check all receipts and costs for the past two years;

b) review the lease and future commitments such as rent increases, responsibility for such tangential items as snow removal, painting, parking, rubbish disposal, etc.;

c) break down the inventory and services according to their profits and losses;

d) examine such obligations as funding pension plans, paying employee benefits and meeting special taxes and assessments.

Then, on your own, project the probable future with the same volume and the steps needed to make the enterprise a worthwhile investment. Keep in mind that, with age, there can be temporary illness or even death so that the responsibility for operations will fall to your widow or children. You did not retire to become a slave!

To **START** a business: to expand a hobby, to open an office as a consultant or salesperson, to become a writer, to provide a needed service such as repairing appliances, shopping for shut-ins or offering financial counsel.

Build Knowledge and Background

Starting any type of business and keeping it on course demands planning and analysis, skill and experience, lots of patience and knowledge of some of the fundamentals that, in a large organization, are handled by someone else. Even with the help of a sharp accountant, it's difficult to learn how to fill out governmental forms, meet tax deadlines, set up pension and savings plans and file reports.

Many colleges and some high schools have adult education courses designed to train entrepreneurs. In New York City, for example, The New School for Social Research offers an eight-week program on *"Your Own Business: How To Run It Profitably,"* for $150. The classes cover business planning, goals, business advisory teams and maintaining business records.

Similar programs are available through trade associations, chambers of commerce and city and state development agencies. Other sources:

Management Assistance Publications (115A) and *Business Development Booklets (115B).* U.S. Small Business Administration lists publications on topics ranging from financial management to small business decision-making. Call the nearest office or write to 1725 I Street, NW, Washington, DC 20416.

Business Information Guide (American Institute of Certified Public Accountants, 1211 Avenue of the Americas, New York, NY 10036: $5 plus $2 postage). This explains and illustrates business records, how to select and use computers, etc.

How To Set Up Your Own Small Business (American Institute of Small Business, 7515 Wayzata Blvd., Minneapolis, MN 55426). Two-volume loose-leaf handbook: $99.95.

CHAPTER 2

Financing Your Lifestyle—Using Your Retirement Income Efficiently

THE PLIGHT OF THE OLD-OLDS

America is growing older. The number of those over age 65 is increasing at twice the rate of the overall population. In 1987, according to the Census Bureau, about 12% of the nation's total population (29.2 million citizens) were over 65. By the year 2000, more than 35 million will be 65 or older, and in 2030, the post-World War II baby boomers will have increased the number of Americans over 65 to 64 million, 21% of America's population.

Life expectancy continues to gain at an amazing rate. An American born in 1910 had an actuarial life expectancy of 49 years. That same American, graduating from college in 1931, could expect to live to age 59. If that same American were alive today, his life expectancy would be age 85, 73% longer than the experts predicted when he was born. Put another way, the odds of living to 100 were 400 to 1 100 years ago; today, those odds are just 87 to 1.

Each week, 200 more Americans celebrate their 100th birthday. The number of centenarians, now 35,000, will rise to over 100,000 by the year 2000 and to 1 million by 2050.

Lifespans once remarkable for their longevity are becoming almost commonplace. The over 85s are growing fast: 2 million now; 5.4 million by the year 2000 and 8.4 million by 2030. The majority of people over age 60 will live into the 21st century and can look forward to being self-supporting for at least 20, probably 25, and, possibly, 30 years. On the average, the new retiree can expect to live at least 10 years longer than his or her parent. Remember that when you make projections.

This increasing longevity is due to the startling improvements in nutrition, health care and lifestyle plus the financial security that most retirees now enjoy. However, the longer the life, the more likely they will need support services. Of all retirees, regardless of age:

- 7 million (of 28 million) need some care.

- 1.5 million live in an institutional setting. That number is expected to double by the turn of the century, and double again every 25 years.

With age, health care costs soar. For those over age 65, these expenses, on a per capita basis, are 250% more than those under 50. Of those over age 75, 6.4% are in nursing homes; over 85, it's 21.6%.

As the statistics above indicate, a growing number of you will become what I call Old-Olds (OOs): those who outlive their life expectancies, roughly past age 80. The majority of people who will live to be OOs will be those who look at longevity as a challenge. They will learn to:

(1) cope with a changing society;

(2) build personal protective aids through friends and neighbors;

(3) make better use of available community resources;

(4) invest more profitably to increase income;

(5) take care of body and mind, with regular exercise, proper nutrition, minimum use of pills and powders and organized emphasis on mentally stimulating reading and conversation.

(6) remain vital by caring for others: people and pets, family and friends, and devoting service to others who need consolation or inspiration.

Being an OO doesn't mean being in ill health. Although almost all OOs have some physical disabilities, 75% feel that their health is "good, considering," and 50% are living what they describe as "active lives."

For OOs, it's the consequences of ill health that are more serious than for younger retireds. Once the health of OOs begins to fail, the chances of full recovery are not good. In most cases, the need for care and support starts as a temporary situation but the odds of recovery keep falling and those of new ailments rising. At 85, however, over half need help in walking, bathing or dressing, even though 50% of these insist they are "neither ill nor handicapped."

Often, the increasing disability is a worsening of an existing condition, or an increase in the frequency and severity of illness. For instance, arthritis may shift from merely becoming an irritation to a crippling ailment, or hearing and vision, once aided by artificial means, may begin to falter completely.

In spite of the reduced incidence of chronic illness and the growing sophistication of medical care, almost inevitably, the time will come when you will face a medical or financial crisis. That's why it is essential to review your retirement plans frequently, particularly when ill health begins to set in. Plans that made sense at age 65 are seldom suitable when you're in your 80s, due to changes in the investment horizon and in your personal circumstances.

One of the reasons for this is the steady decline of the purchasing power of fixed income dollars. The buying power of every $1,000, in 10 years, drops to $737 with 3% inflation, and to just $665 with a 4% annual rate. In 20 years, the original worth is cut about in half: to $544 at a 3% annual increase in the cost of living; to $442 at 4%. In effect, if you live to be 85, your income will have to double to maintain the same standard of living.

Another reason for reviewing your retirement plans is the cessation of payments from personal pension plans such as an IRA, 401(k), SEP. It sounds comforting to know that, if you start withdrawals at age 65, these savings will last until you reach the age of 87. But this is a minimum and, according to pension experts, 60% of retirees take their money out faster. After 15 years, just as they become OOs, there's no more money from this source!

OOs are usually asset-rich and income-poor. The average income of 85-year-olds is 33% below the average income of 70-year-olds. Therefore, planning is important to ensure that any asset liquidation necessary to provide for your support is anticipated.

Later, you'll consult an actuarial table to determine your life expectancy for retirement planning purposes. When you do, keep in mind that there's a significant chance (especially if you anticipate retiring in good health with no chronic, potentially fatal, illnesses) that you will live far in excess of the actuarial limits. Plan accordingly.

WHAT WILL IT COST YOU TO LIVE?

There are two ways to plan for your retirement. You can figure out how to have enough money to live the way you want, or you can figure out how to live on the money you will have. Obviously, it's better to be able to plan how to finance the lifestyle you desire than to be forced to figure out how to make ends meet. The farther away your retirement is (in other words, the more time you have), the easier it will be to meet this planning ideal. If retirement is imminent, you'll be forced to plan how to fit your expenses into your available cash flow.

As a rule of thumb, if your retirement income equals at least 75% of your preretirement income, you'll be able to retire comfortably. But if your retirement income is less than 50% of your pre-retirement income, retirement will probably be difficult financially.

First, let's size up what you spend your after-tax income on now. What people spend on food, shelter, clothing and the other necessities of life (as well as its luxuries) can vary greatly. See how what you spend in these categories measures up to what the U.S. Commerce Department says Americans spend, on average. (Allocate debt service to the category that pertains to the good borrowed for. For example, attribute mortgage payments to housing, car payments to transportation, etc.):

WORKSHEET 2-1

Item	Average Percentage	What You Spend Total	Percent
Food and Beverages	20.6%		
Home consumption	13.3%	___	___
Dining out	4.8%	___	___
Alcoholic beverages	2.5%	___	___
Housing	16.5%	___	___
Transportation	14.1%		
Vehicle purchase	4.2%	___	___
Operating/maintenance	8.7%	___	___
Other	1.2%	___	___
Household Expenses	13.7%		
Furniture and appliances	2.1%	___	___
Utilities	6.8%	___	___
Other	4.8%	___	___
Medical Care	10.4%	___	___
Clothing and Jewelry	7.4%	___	___
Recreation	6.3%	___	___
Personal Business	5.3%	___	___
Private Education	1.5%	___	___
Philanthropy	1.4%	___	___
Personal Care	1.4%	___	___
Tobacco	1.2%	___	___
Other	0.2%	___	___

To get a good idea of what you spend money on, go through your checkbook. Allocate any checks written to "cash" or to yourself to what you ordinarily spend the cash on. If you can't tell what you're spending in a given area, keep better records. You'll probably find you're spending too much in that area.

If you're spending a greater percentage of your after-tax income than the national average in any category other than housing, you're probably spending too much. You should examine your expenditures in this area, and see if you can eliminate some expenditures to live within the general national averages.

HOW MUCH SHOULD YOU SPEND ON HOUSING?

Housing is a special area. Generally, devoting 20% to 30% of your after-tax income to housing is acceptable. If you're a renter, you should try to spend about 20% of your after-tax income on housing; up to (but not over) 30% is acceptable for homebuyers. (See page 211 for more information.)

With all housing that you buy, keep a 10-year frame in mind. For most dwellings, that's about the time when appliances will need repairs, plumbing will leak, the air conditioner or heating unit will conk out and the roof will begin to sag. These extra expenses will, inevitably, occur just when you've taken the last installment from your pension plan or savings account.

If your income cannot support paying for the house you want without exceeding 30% of your sure income, first try to use the savings or profits from the sale of your home to make up the difference. If you plan to purchase a new home, look at lowering the down payment (so you will have more money to earn income), or stretching out the terms of the mortgage from a 15-year mortgage to a 25- or 30-year loan.

If you choose a good house in a good location, it's value should appreciate so that you can recast the loan or take out a reverse annuity mortgage. (See Chapter 8 for information.) If interest rates drop 2% in the future, refinancing may create a better cash flow. And if one spouse dies, that spouse's life insurance should provide an extra cushion to replace inflation-eroded income. *Be conservative:* lengthen the payout only when the income is sure. After the spouse's death, Social Security may be one-third less!

If you are close to, or over, the limit, and you plan to live in your old home, consider selling or taking in boarders.

Always review future housing costs. Don't go overboard with a new house, just because you are retired and want to make all your dreams come true immediately. Remember, if things are tight at the start, they will seldom ease over the years. If problems develop, you may have to get a job. That's not what most retirees want to be forced to do.

BRINGING YOUR BUDGET UNDER CONTROL

If you're spending too much money in any one area, debt is the first place to look to cut expenses. Suppose you earn $2,000 each month in after-tax income, and you spend $500 each month on car payments, insurance, and maintenance. That's too much—you've probably got more car than you can afford. You could try to sell the car and buy a less expensive model. However, if your loan payments alone are $350, retiring the debt (perhaps by cutting out entertainment costs for a few months) will cut your monthly car costs to just $150, bringing your transportation costs to an acceptable level. We'll examine ways to retire debt in the next chapter.

Assuming you've fixed your monthly expenses, and you're not overspending in any areas, what's likely to change when you retire? Anticipate spending less on:

- Work-related costs, such as commuting and lunches away from home

- Payments to retirement plans

- Federal and state income taxes

- Mortgage payments; at some point, the mortgage will be paid off

- Savings

Anticipate spending more on:

- Health care costs—plan on spending twice as much as you do now

- Recreational expenses

- Taxes

Historically, retirees could count on lower tax rates after retirement. Today, things are different. With just three tax brackets (15%, 28%, and 33%), and imposition of the 28% rate at relatively low income levels, many (if not most) retirees won't qualify for the lowest 15% bracket even after retirement.

Meanwhile, taxes for retirees have increased recently. Social Security benefits, once tax-free income, are now taxed in certain circumstances. And the catastrophic health insurance legislation will impose heavy new taxes on those that qualify for Medicare Part A benefits. A tax surcharge will cost senior taxpayers up to $800 in 1989, and will go up to $1,050 in 1993. (For married taxpayers, double these maximum amounts.)

Now that you know what you'll spend less on, and what you'll be buying more, let's take another look at your budget. Adjust what you spend now to determine what you'll need to spend when you retire (if already retired, you won't need to fill out this worksheet; you can use the figures you used on page 30):

WORKSHEET 2-2

Item	What You Spend Now	What You'll Probably Spend When Retired	Usual Change
Food and Beverages	_____	_____	
Home consumption	_____	_____	Same
Dining out	_____	_____	Less
Alcoholic beverages	_____	_____	Less
Housing	_____	_____	Less
Transportation			
Vehicle purchase	_____	_____	Same
Maintenance	_____	_____	Same
Other	_____	_____	Same
Household Expenses			
Furniture	_____	_____	Same
Utilities	_____	_____	More
Other	_____	_____	
Medical Care	_____	_____	More
Clothing and Jewelry	_____	_____	Less
Recreation	_____	_____	More
Personal Business	_____	_____	Same
Private Education	_____	_____	Less
Philanthropy	_____	_____	More
Personal Care	_____	_____	More
Tobacco	_____	_____	Less
Other	_____	_____	Less

YOUR INFLATION WEAKNESS WORKSHEET

You can't adequately project your expenses and income requirements into the future without taking inflation into account. If your income is fixed, rising costs will erode your purchasing power. And compounding annual inflation rates can result in a much greater erosion than you might expect. For example, here's what an object that costs $100 today would cost in the future, at an inflation rate of just 4% per year.

In one year	$104
In three years	112
In five years	122
In ten years	148
In twenty years	219

Over the past 20 years, we've seen inflation rates ranging from virtually nil to over 12%. Other countries have seen even higher inflation. When it comes to inflation, and predicting future rates, you can count on these things to be true:

- The government will come to grips with the staggering federal deficit, at least to a partial extent; the growing interest rates threaten Congress' ability to fund politically popular programs

- At least part of the solution will be the politically easy way out of permitting higher inflation; this enables Congress to pay the interest on the deficit at lower real rates

- Future inflation rates will probably be higher than the rates we saw in the 80's, which were generally between 4 and 6 percent

You always have to reevaluate your financial projections in light of changing inflation rates. You should also keep an eye on the costs of items that you need to get by; rates of price increases can vary greatly between products. It would be reasonable to presently anticipate inflation to average 5% or more in the future.

Your vulnerability to inflation depends on whether or not your income will grow with inflation, or if you will otherwise be able to compensate for inflation (such as dipping into savings). Social Security will probably keep pace with inflation; private pensions won't. Income from investments will probably exceed inflation by 2% (that is, if inflation is 6%, you'll probably be able to earn 8% on your money). The greater the portion of your total income that is fixed, the more severe the effect of inflation will be.

WORKSHEET 2-3   INFLATION EROSION IN FIRST YEAR OF RETIREMENT

	Today (a)	*Rate* (b)	(c)	*One Year Later* (a) − (c) for fixed (a) + (c) for other
Total Fixed income	_____ ×	____ =	_____	_____
Total Investment Income	_____ ×	____ =	_____	_____
Total COLA Income	_____ ×	____ =	_____	_____
Total	_____			_____

Inflation erosion for first year of retirement = today's income − income one year later _____

Your inflation erosion in first year divided by $1000 _____

Multiplied by figure in Table 2-1 (see page 37) corresponding to your life expectancy and average annual inflation rate _____

Your anticipated average yearly inflation shortfall _____

Here's how to figure how inflation will affect you:

(1) First, classify your planned income in terms of fixed income, investment income, and COLA (cost of living adjustment) income that will keep pace with inflation. Most private pensions are fixed income. So is income from long-term fixed interest rate investments. Although investment income is fixed to the extent that the interest rate is fixed for the life of the investment, you can expect that, once your invested principal is returned, you'll have investment options that will allow you to earn real income at about 2% above the prevailing inflation rate at that time. Plan on investment income equalling 2% of your liquid investment capital; that is, the funds you have available for investment that can be moved from one form of investment to another easily to stay ahead of inflation. This DOESN'T include capital placed in long-term fixed rate investments. Social Security income and income from most public employee pensions are COLA income.

(2) Next, multiply each category of income by the degree that it will be affected by inflation. Fixed income will be reduced by the inflation rate. COLA income will not be affected by the inflation rate. Investment income will be increased by 2% (although you may want to adjust this, depending on your success in investing at a rate that exceeds inflation).

(3) Add up each row to get the anticipated value (in today's dollars) of your projected income in one year. Then add your income class totals to get your overall anticipated value of your projected income.

(4) Divide your answer from step 3 (the overall anticipated value of your projected income) by your current income. Subtract 1 from this number; that's the percentage by which you can expect your buying power to increase from year to year. If the percentage is negative (which it will be if your answer to step 3 is less than your current income), you will lose buying power thanks to inflation.

Example: Ted anticipates that, in his first year of retirement, he will receive $25,000 in a pension from his company and $10,000 from Social Security. The pension doesn't allow for cost of living allowances. He has $50,000 in a savings account earning 5% (that's $2,500 each year), and $25,000 in a bond maturing in 20 years that pays $2,000 in interest annually. Inflation in Ted's first retired year is 3%.

Ted's total income is $39,500. He should be able to move his $50,000 savings account around to find investments that will pay 2% over the prevailing inflation rate. The pension and bond earnings that he receives will be eroded by inflation. After one year, the value of Ted's income in today's dollars will be

	Today	Inflation Erosion	Value in Today's Dollars One Year Later
Pension	$25,000	−3% (−$750)	$24,250
Social Security	10,000	0%	10,000
Investment Income	2,500	2% (+$50)	2,550
Bond Interest	2,000	−3% (−$60)	1,940
Total	$39,500		$38,740

Net erosion = $38,740/$39,500 = 98%.

In other words, the net effect of inflation on Ted's overall income is a loss of 2% of buying power every year. That 2% loss will be compounded annually; Ted's buying power will be just 90% of what it is today after 5 years ($.98 \times .98 \times .98 \times .98 \times .98 = .90$). Put another way, Ted will have just $35,705 in today's dollars (a decrease of $3,795) to spend in five years.

The effect of inflation is compounded as the years go on. What's important to you, as you plan your retirement, is how much inflation will cost you each year. Inflation is like a tax—it robs you of monetary value that you could otherwise use to buy goods and services. Therefore, it's best to think of inflation as an expense. You can use Table 2-1 to discover the average cost of inflation over your life expectancy.

TABLE 2-1   Average Anticipated Yearly Shortfall at Varying Inflation Rates Over Life
Expectancy Based on $1000 Shortfall In First Year

				Average Annual Inflation Rate				
Year	1%	2%	3%	4%	5%	6%	7%	8%
0	$1,000	$1,000	$1,000	$1,000	$1,000	$1,000	$1,000	$1,000
1	$1,010	$1,020	$1,030	$1,040	$1,050	$1,060	$1,070	$1,080
2	$1,015	$1,030	$1,045	$1,061	$1,076	$1,092	$1,107	$1,123
3	$1,020	$1,041	$1,061	$1,082	$1,103	$1,125	$1,147	$1,169
4	$1,025	$1,051	$1,077	$1,104	$1,131	$1,159	$1,188	$1,217
5	$1,030	$1,062	$1,094	$1,127	$1,160	$1,195	$1,231	$1,267
6	$1,036	$1,072	$1,110	$1,150	$1,190	$1,232	$1,276	$1,320
7	$1,041	$1,083	$1,127	$1,173	$1,221	$1,271	$1,323	$1,377
8	$1,046	$1,094	$1,145	$1,198	$1,253	$1,311	$1,372	$1,436
9	$1,051	$1,106	$1,163	$1,223	$1,286	$1,353	$1,424	$1,499
10	$1,057	$1,117	$1,181	$1,249	$1,321	$1,397	$1,478	$1,565
11	$1,062	$1,128	$1,199	$1,275	$1,356	$1,443	$1,535	$1,634
12	$1,067	$1,140	$1,218	$1,302	$1,393	$1,490	$1,595	$1,708
13	$1,073	$1,152	$1,237	$1,330	$1,431	$1,540	$1,658	$1,786
14	$1,078	$1,164	$1,257	$1,359	$1,470	$1,591	$1,724	$1,868
15	$1,084	$1,176	$1,277	$1,388	$1,510	$1,645	$1,793	$1,955
16	$1,089	$1,188	$1,298	$1,419	$1,553	$1,701	$1,865	$2,047
17	$1,095	$1,201	$1,318	$1,450	$1,596	$1,759	$1,941	$2,144
18	$1,101	$1,213	$1,340	$1,482	$1,641	$1,820	$2,021	$2,247
19	$1,106	$1,226	$1,362	$1,515	$1,688	$1,883	$2,105	$2,356
20	$1,112	$1,239	$1,384	$1,548	$1,736	$1,950	$2,193	$2,471
21	$1,118	$1,252	$1,407	$1,583	$1,786	$2,019	$2,286	$2,593
22	$1,123	$1,266	$1,430	$1,619	$1,838	$2,091	$2,383	$2,722
23	$1,129	$1,279	$1,453	$1,656	$1,891	$2,166	$2,486	$2,859
24	$1,135	$1,293	$1,477	$1,694	$1,947	$2,244	$2,594	$3,004
25	$1,141	$1,307	$1,502	$1,732	$2,005	$2,326	$2,707	$3,158
26	$1,147	$1,321	$1,527	$1,772	$2,064	$2,412	$2,826	$3,321
27	$1,153	$1,335	$1,553	$1,814	$2,126	$2,501	$2,952	$3,494
28	$1,159	$1,350	$1,579	$1,856	$2,190	$2,594	$3,084	$3,677
29	$1,165	$1,364	$1,606	$1,899	$2,257	$2,692	$3,223	$3,872
30	$1,171	$1,379	$1,633	$1,944	$2,325	$2,793	$3,369	$4,078
31	$1,177	$1,394	$1,661	$1,990	$2,397	$2,900	$3,523	$4,297
32	$1,183	$1,410	$1,690	$2,038	$2,471	$3,011	$3,685	$4,530
33	$1,190	$1,425	$1,719	$2,087	$2,547	$3,127	$3,856	$4,777
34	$1,196	$1,441	$1,749	$2,137	$2,627	$3,248	$4,036	$5,039
35	$1,202	$1,457	$1,779	$2,189	$2,710	$3,375	$4,226	$5,317

To use Table 2-1, find the number where your life expectancy and the expected average inflation rate for that period intersect. Then, multiply that figure by your figure for inflation erosion, and divide the result by $1,000. For example, suppose you expect inflation to cost you $3,000 in lost buying power in your first year of retirement. If your life expectancy is 20 years, and you anticipate inflation to average 5% over that 20-year period, the number you should get using Table 2-1 is $1,736. Multiplying $1,736 by $3,000 gives you $5,208,000; $5,208,000 divided by $1,000 equals $5,208. In other words, although in the first year of retirement inflation will cost you $3,000 in lost buying power, over the 20 years that you will live as a retired citizen, the average cost (in today's dollars) of inflation will be $5,208 each year.

MEETING YOUR RETIREMENT EXPENSES

There's no big secret to funding your retirement. You should have sufficient positive cash flow to meet your annual living expenses. You can generate cash flow through two sources: income and savings/asset liquidation. Put another way, you will have to dip into savings, or sell off assets (your house, business, or other property you can sell) to make up any difference between what you receive each year in income, and what you spend. (A word here: another way to offset income shortfalls is through after-retirement employment. However, for planning purposes, you should never count on after-retirement employment as an income source. Obtaining worthwhile employment may be difficult, significantly adding to your income in light of the Social Security benefit offset and income taxes may be difficult and, with your increased susceptibility to illness, you may become disabled precisely when your income needs are greatest.)

By now, you should know how much you expect to spend in your first year of retirement, how much income you'll take in in your first year of retirement, and how much inflation will erode your total annual income. Hopefully, your income will cover your annual living expenses. But if you have sufficient savings put away, or own sufficient assets, to offset this shortfall over your life expectancy, you will be okay.

The key is in determining what a sufficient amount of assets and savings constitutes for you. Essentially, assets you're not willing to part with will be unavailable for asset liquidation. If you want to live in your house for the rest of your life (which may be unwise, see Chapter 8), you must plan on not being able to sell your house. If you own valuables you want to leave to others after you're gone, those are also "off the table." Particularly critical are assets that your spouse would need to survive after you're gone.

List all of the savings and assets that you have at your disposal that you do not expect to leave to anyone after you are gone, and the asset's current value. Savings accounts, CDs, and other liquid assets should be valued at their full value; other assets should be valued at 80% of what you think you could sell them for within 30 days. (For example, a $100 savings account is valued at $100, but a $100 stamp collection should only be valued at 80%.)

WORKSHEET 2-4

Item	Value
Total Value of Assets	

IMPORTANT: Do not include assets you would turn over to relatives if you anticipated becoming impoverished by being forced into nursing home care (see page 186.)

Next, you should determine the life expectancy for a person at the age you plan to retire at. (This is not your present life expectancy which, unless you are already retired, will be shorter; use Table 2-2 if single, or Table 2-3 if married). Whatever your life expectancy is, less your retirement age, are the years of income shortfall that your savings will have to finance. For example, suppose you're a man who is going to retire at 64. Your life expectancy at 64 will be 79.6, so you should be able to finance 15.6 years of your anticipated shortfall from inflation and lack of income. Be conservative. Feel free to add years to this period. After all, if you don't live that long, your heirs will receive what's left over. On the other hand, if you live longer than you anticipated (and the chances are good that you will), your last years may be miserable: filled with worry over money, perhaps forced to live off of the kindness of others.

TABLE 2-2   Life Expectancy—Single

| If you are | *You Can Expect To Live To Be* | | If you are | *You Can Expect To Live To Be* | |
	Male	*Female*		*Male*	*Female*
35	73.2	77.8	61	78.5	82.0
36	73.3	77.9	62	78.9	82.3
37	73.5	78.0	63	79.2	82.6
38	73.6	78.0	64	79.6	82.9
39	73.7	78.1	65	80.0	83.2
40	73.8	78.2	66	80.4	83.5
41	74.0	78.3	67	80.8	83.9
42	74.1	78.5	68	81.2	84.2
43	74.2	78.6	69	81.6	84.6
44	74.4	78.7	70	82.1	85.0
45	74.6	78.8	71	82.6	85.4
46	74.7	79.0	72	83.0	85.8
47	74.9	79.1	73	83.5	86.2
48	75.1	79.2	74	84.1	86.6
49	75.3	79.4	75	84.6	87.1
50	75.5	79.6	76	85.1	87.6
51	75.7	79.7	77	85.7	88.0
52	76.0	79.9	78	86.3	88.5
53	76.2	80.1	79	86.8	89.1
54	76.4	80.3	80	87.5	89.6
55	76.7	80.5	81	88.1	90.1
56	77.0	80.7	82	88.7	90.7
57	77.3	81.0	83	89.3	91.3
58	77.6	81.2	84	90.0	91.8
59	77.9	81.4	85	90.7	92.5
60	78.2	81.7	86	91.4	93.1

TABLE 2-3   Joint Life Expectancy for Withdrawing Pension Assets

Age Male	Female Same	Female Younger by Years				Female Older by Years		
		1	*2*	*3*	*5*	*1*	*2*	*3*
59	26.9	27.4	27.9	28.5	29.6	26.4	25.9	25.4
60	26.0	26.5	27.1	27.6	28.8	25.5	25.1	24.6
61	25.2	25.7	26.2	26.8	27.9	24.7	24.3	23.8
62	24.4	24.9	25.4	25.9	27.1	23.9	23.5	23.0
63	23.6	24.1	24.6	25.1	26.2	23.1	22.7	22.2
64	22.8	23.3	23.8	24.3	25.4	22.3	21.9	21.5
65	22.0	22.5	23.0	23.5	24.6	21.6	21.1	20.7
66	21.3	21.7	22.2	22.7	23.8	20.8	20.4	20.0
67	20.5	21.0	21.4	21.9	23.0	20.1	19.6	19.2
68	19.8	20.2	20.7	21.2	22.5	19.3	18.9	18.5
69	19.0	19.9	19.9	20.4	21.5	18.6	18.2	17.8
70	18.3	18.3	19.2	19.7	21.2	17.9	17.5	17.1

SOURCE: Internal Revenue Service. Publication 575.

WORKSHEET 2-5

1. Your anticipated annual Social Security benefits—see page 4 for a rough estimate, or get estimate from Social Security Administration (see page 7 for details) _____
2. Your anticipated pension income _____
3. Annual interest income from investments _____
4. Total annual estimated income (add lines 1, 2, and 3) _____
5. Your anticipated retirement expenses, as listed on page 33 (if you haven't retired yet) or page 30 (if you have retired) _____
6. Taxes on income listed on lines 1-3 (for rough estimate, use 40% of amount on line 4) _____
7. Average annual effect of inflation (from worksheet on page 35) _____
8. Total yearly expenses, including average annual inflation effect (line 5 plus line 6 plus line 7) _____
9. Your surplus (line 4 minus line 8) _____
If line 9 is less than zero, you have a shortfall that must be made up.
10. Value of assets available for liquidation (from page 39) _____
11. Interest earned by assets available for liquidation _____
12. Net income available from asset liquidation _____
13. Yearly income available from asset liquidation (line 12 divided by your life expectancy) _____
14. Line 9 plus line 13 _____

Now it's time to put everything together. If you fill out the following worksheet, using your expected income and expenses (in today's dollars) for your first year of retirement, you'll discover how you stand in terms of your financial ability to retire.

If line 14 is still less than zero, you still have a gap between anticipated income and anticipated expenses. As you have presumably exhausted all sources of funds, you must look to cutting your living expenses in retirement.

MANAGING YOUR MONEY

If you can't make ends meet, you suffer from one of three problems:

You carry too much debt.

You waste too much money.

You don't produce enough income.

Let's examine some solutions to each of these problems.

Too Much Debt: If you spend more than 10% of your after-tax income on debt payments (not including your mortgage, which shouldn't be greater than 30% of your income), you're carrying too much debt. And if that percentage is greater than 20%, you're carrying a dangerous amount of debt.

Debt is always troublesome, but it's especially critical for retirees because, as their income is basically fixed, debt doesn't become any easier to pay. Wage earners, on the other hand, can expect raises that will cut the percentage of income that they devote to debt.

When planning for retirement, resolve to pay off as much debt as you can. List your outstanding accounts, in the order of the interest rate charged. Set aside a portion of your income for debt retirement. Economizing 10% in other areas can create a sizable amount for debt retirement! Pay off outstanding accounts early, in the order of the interest rate charged. (Make sure you won't pay a prepayment penalty.) The idea is to save interest charges, and free up that debt payment for things you'll enjoy more. Make your goal 100% consumer debt retirement by age 65.

If you're having trouble paying your debts, write the National Foundation for Consumer Credit, 8701 Georgia Ave., Silver Spring, MD 20910. This nonprofit organization will put you in touch with a local office that can help you draw up a budget and institute a payment plan to pay off your debts for a small monthly fee. Avoid for-profit debt counselors, or people who promise to "clean up your credit overnight." The only way to fix your credit is to pay your creditors. If you fall for any of this hooey, you deserve to be parted from your money (which you soon will be).

Wasting Money: In this consumer society of ours, it's easy to spend. But you've got to face facts: being broke is tough, and if you don't want to risk being homeless, you'd better learn to control your spending. If you think I'm exaggerating, just remember—no one tries to become homeless. Among the tens of thousands of homeless people in New York City alone, there's probably one who had a family, a good job, and position in the community just like you. There are many reasons why the homeless become homeless—drug and alcohol abuse, a lack of employable skills—but for the many elderly among the homeless, poverty is probably the biggest cause.

For starters, try to cut out just $20 from what you spend each month. Many people could save that much by not purchasing that magazine they never get around to reading, or ''brown-bagging'' it to work a couple of days a week. If you saved just $20 a month each month for 10 years, and deposited that money in a passbook account at 5%, you'd have over $3,100—real money, not pin money—at the end of that period. You could take out $20 each month for the next 20 years if you desired!

Next time you go shopping, check over your receipt. Ask yourself, ''If my spouse were in the hospital, and I had to get by on as little as I could, what could I have done without?'' Then, add up how much you spent for these goods. You'll be surpised how much you could have saved. Now ask yourself—do I want to scrimp now—when I'm healthy and working, or later, when I might not be so well off? Because sooner or later, you are going to be in a position where medical expenses for yourself or your spouse threaten your financial security.

Making saving money a challenge. When you can get by with less, you'll soon feel superior to the wastrels who pay too much. Saving money can have other benefits. If you're spending too much for junk food, for instance, saving money by buying the right kinds of food can result in a trimmer waistline and better health. Or you could quit smoking. And you'll have more money for the things that make life truly enjoyable.

Not Enough Income: If your problem really is that you're not making enough money, the only solution is to make more. This isn't the place to discuss strategies for getting a raise, or a better-paying new job; there are many good books in your library for that. (For some solid advice on applying for a new job, however, see pages 21–24.) You might consider, however, getting a second job. As America gets older, there's a shortage of workers for available jobs. Working at a fast-food restaurant, for example, might not be what you'd like. On the other hand, you can probably get a free meal, and, with your experience and work habits, you might soon rise to shift manager. Don't be ashamed to take any legitimate job if you need the income.

If your spouse isn't working, try to get him/her to find work. Even part-time work will bring in welcome income, and will possibly help the spouse qualify for bigger Social Security checks.

CHAPTER 3

Financing Your Lifestyle— Making Early Retirement Work

Early retirement isn't just a dream limited to the very rich. The majority of new retirees start taking Social Security at age 62, the first year of eligibility.

Most early retirees say early retirement was as good, or better, than they had anticipated. And financing early retirement is easier than ever. Most pension plans allow payments (albeit reduced ones) after 10 or 15 years of service; that's short enough to allow participants to retire in their 50s. Tax-favored pension and profit-sharing plans can be drawn against at age 59½ without penalty. Add this to Social Security benefits that commence at age 62, and early retirement may become a viable financial proposition.

Unless you're in a mandatory retirement situation, choosing when to retire is a personal decision that involves your job satisfaction, your health, and your financial capability to retire. Whether or not to choose early retirement also involves these factors. Increased self-employment and higher wages due to the shrinking labor pool, according to Jon Moen, economist with the Federal Reserve Board, are resulting in an increasing number of older males staying on the job.

Deciding on Early Retirement

In deciding whether to take early retirement, on your own or as the result of special inducements, consider these factors:

- You may leave work behind but you are not leaving reality. Life goes on. You have to keep busy and interested; bills have to be paid; your health is likely to falter; and either or both of you can become bored and irritable.

- Surviving is not enough. Once you leave the safe harbor of regular employment, you need to establish yourself as a somewhat different person. Now, you must make most of the decisions and can no longer toil in a structured, controlled environment.

- Freedom can be wonderful for those who can handle it. But some folks, especially those who have enjoyed little autonomy, may find that the new, self-controlled responsibilities can be overwhelming.

- Make your decisions logically and factually, not emotionally because of frustration, fear or anger. Have a solid base, financially and mentally, and, most important, a clear, viable idea of what you want to do and how you want to do it. Too many people become so concerned about getting out of what they feel is a work-trap that they fail to think through their future.

- Be sure that your spouse agrees with, or at least accepts, your decision. Too often, early retirement means half the income and twice the time.

Personally, I am leery of recommending early-out unless there are compelling reasons of health, extra benefits, a strong desire to retire into something new and a financial situation that allows you to count on ample income for as long as you both live. However, there are reasons other than financial considerations that can affect your decision.

Here's why early retirement can make sense for many:

Financial cost of early retirement isn't so severe. At age 62, you can start collecting Social Security benefits that will be 20% less than at age 65 (a deduction of 5/9 of 1% for each month before age 65). Thus, if you are entitled to $10,926 at age 65, you will get $8,741 when you quit three years earlier. Add half of that for the non-working spouse and the couple will receive $13,111 compared to $16,389 at normal retirement age. Ignoring COLAs and discounting factors, the early-out will be ahead of the 65-year-old until both are over 75. (The effect of early retirement on Social Security is fully discussed on page 4.)

The impact of early retirement with company pensions, however, can be severe, due to the probability of higher earnings and the compounding of vested assets. At age 50, with an average five-year high pay of $40,000, the retiree would receive $7,200 a year. At age 62, with a wage base of $56,284 (5% annual raises), the pension would be $20,060. At age 65, the assumed salary would be up to $65,156 and the annuity to $29,320: over four times that of the earliest out and one-third more than that of the 62-year-old (Table 3-1). Even if raises are less, there will be a lot more lifetime income when work continues.

TABLE 3-1   Effect of Early Retirement on Pension

Age	Average Pay Last 5 Years	Years Service	Typical Pension Benefit Early	Age 65
50	$40,000	20	$ 7,200	$12,000
56	42,000	21	8,467	13,230
57	44,100	22	9,896	14,553
58	46,305	23	11,502	15,975
59	48,620	24	13,302	17,503
60	51,051	25	15,315	19,144
61	53,604	26	17,561	20,906
62	56,284	27	20,060	22,795
63	59,098	28	22,835	24,821
64	62,053	29	25,913	26,993
65	65,156	30	29,320	29,320

Assumptions: Pay increases of 5% each year of work

Pension formula: 1.5% of final five-year average pay times years of service

Pension reduced 4% a year for retirement before age 65

SOURCE: Hewitt Associates

However, many plans effectively penalize employees who work past age 60, or work for more than 20 years, by cutting back the rate of increase in their pension benefits. In these situations, leaving early makes more sense, because it costs less in reduced pension benefits. And thanks to the two-paycheck household and the increased value of the home, many couples can afford to retire early despite reduced Social Security and pension income.

Why Work at a Job You Don't Like? Surveys show that 40% of men and 26% of women retire early because they are tired of working or unhappy with their job. If you can afford to retire financially, this is a valid reason: stress can kill, and job dissatisfaction is a major cause of stress. However, be sure that you really are ready to leave your job. Are you sure that you're dissatisfied with your job, or is some other reason the cause of your unhappiness? If your problem isn't with what you do, but who you do it with, or where you do it, investigate changing those circumstances to your satisfaction before you quit. You're probably at your peak in terms of earnings, and unless you have an attractive alternative, it may make sense for you to hold on a few more years.

If you like the company and have confidence in its future, discuss your fears with your immediate boss, or, in a large organization, with the Personnel Director. Most firms, mindful that it is expensive to hire and train new workers, are anxious to keep competent employees. Usually, your position will be reviewed and adjustments made to provide less pressure and greater rewards.

Still, if you are convinced that the company is headed for trouble and that you may be stuck, start looking for another job and hope to be able to have your pension benefits grow until you are age 65.

Health Problems . . . listed by 30% of early-outs. If you are so sick that you can't continue to work, you may be eligible for disability payments which, when from Uncle Sam, turn into Social Security at age 65. On the other hand, if your spouse is the ill one, continuing to work can enable you to qualify for group health plan coverage. Individual coverage is expensive.

If you decide to retire, and you do have such company protection, find out if it can be maintained: by the employer or, personally, at the lower group rate. Under federal law, you have the right to continue health coverage, at your own expense, for up to 18 months after retirement. However, there's no requirement to continue dental care (which can be expensive for retirees—according to my dentists, the annual cost of dental care doubles after age 65 and triples for those over 75 . . . if they have any teeth left).

Special Benefits: to encourage older workers to quit early. The employer saves money by shifting payrolls from operating budgets to pension plans. Under DuPont's Early Retirement Opportunity plan (typical of proposals made by major employers), the worker added five years of service and five years of age to his or her current pension. Thus, a 53-year-old with 27 years of service qualified as a 58-year-old with 32 years of employment: a whopping increase in benefits for real veterans.

With these early-out deals, the payouts vary widely but, according to one pension adviser, the average worker who retires before age 60 with 25 years of work credit, can count on 50% of his most recent annual compensation. Usually, the payout is in the form of an annuity but it can also be taken in a lump sum: a welcome opportunity for those who plan to start their own business or buy into a going concern. Be careful, though, about lump sums or plans requiring you to receive more than $117,529 in benefits (in 1989 dollars); they're subject to a 15% tax.

In most cases, the employee must accept or reject the offer within a month or so . . . not easy unless you have started retirement planning. Obviously, if you feel your job will not be assured after the offer is withdrawn, that's a reason to accept the offer. If the offer is limited to employees in your class (for instance, middle managers), consider this a warning flag for your job security. But before accepting or rejecting an early retirement offer, calculate whether or not it is worth it to accept. Offers can be complex, so if you can't figure it out, consult your accountant.

Financing Your Early Retirement

If you'd like to retire early, go through Chapters 1 and 2, using the income and life expectancy assumptions that would apply to the age that you'd like to retire at. If, when you complete Worksheet 2-5, you can make ends meet, economically, you can afford to retire early.

If you have a shortfall, early retirement may not be for you right now. But there are ways to achieve it, especially if you're still young.

Here's the easy way to early retirement:

(1) Compute Your Net Worth. In Chapter 4, you'll see how to calculate your net worth. Calculate what this amount could earn if invested.

(2) Establish a solid income base. A source of income that doesn't require much work (that is, an income source that is capital-intensive, not labor-intensive) can produce income that will let you afford to retire early, pension income or no. If you have a talent (such as a hobby) that can enable you to dominate a local market niche, get started in that line now. The key is to become proficient producing goods that people are willing to consistently pay premium prices for. One person I know creates custom-made bathroom tiles. Other people have invested in rental real estate. Once the mortgages are paid off, these can produce steady income that, combined with interest from investments, can make early retirement feasible. Chapter 4 contains information to help your investments, and your net worth, grow.

(3) Develop an after-retirement career. One common theme among early-retirees, particularly younger ones, is a post-retirement career. Typically, these careers are self-employment deals where you set the hours. It's best if not much capital is involved; if your investment is too great, you'll have to spend a considerable amount of time (and worry) making sure your investment isn't lost. One good idea: learn to prepare taxes. Tax computer software (such as *J.K. Lasser's Your Income Tax* program) make preparing federal tax returns easier, the pay is good, and you can work as much as you like. Chapter 1 contains solid advice on getting a job or starting your own business.

(4) Scale back your lifestyle. If it's worth it to you to retire early, it's worth it to you to sacrifice the extra pension dollars postponing retirement would earn, and the more opulent lifestyle those dollars would finance. Cutting back on expenses now allows you to set aside more cash for investment, which allows you to build up wealth to finance your early retirement. If early retirement is important to you, look to shifting half of your non-essential expenses (food, health care, shelter, and clothing) to investments to fund your early retirement. Of course, debt retirement is a must. (See Chapter 2 for details on how to cut your expenses and pay off debt.) Cutting back also acclimates you to life as a retired person with a fixed income. You can move to a less expensive locale, and save significantly on your living expenses. (You'll find information on where you can live inexpensively in Chapter 8.)

A Disappearing Opportunity?

Early retirement will become more difficult to achieve in the future, at least with the help of pension plans and Social Security. In 1986, Congress imposed age-based limits on pension payouts that discriminate against early retirees. Persons retiring at 55 are limited to $38,000 in yearly benefits from pension plans; that limit increases to $72,000 for 62-year-old retirees, and $90,000 for 65-year-old retirees. And as it gets harder to obtain new employees, companies can be expected to make early retirement less attractive. As for Social Security, the standard retirement age is scheduled to increase to 67; this means that your benefit will be less than it is today if you retire at 62.

Despite present and future financial obstacles, if retiring early is important to you, and you're willing to cut back your living expenses, you can probably put together a financial plan that will make early retirement work. Don't be discouraged! Set your goal, stick with it, and you'll enjoy the reward of living life on your own terms when you want, while many of your peers are still slaving away.

Chapter 4

Creating Wealth to Enhance Your Retirement

Saving—it's one of those things that are supposed to be good for you, like castor oil. And like taking castor oil, it's not much fun to do. But almost everyone wants to be rich (few of us enjoy poverty), and savings is a reliable path to greater affluence, if not wealth.

People pay to use two things in this life—your labor, and your money. There's only so much you can be paid for your labor, because there's only so much labor you can produce. So if you want to make more than what you're paid for your labor, you've got to put aside money that you can put to work to earn income for you.

As we've seen, you can't live well on Social Security alone. And if you have a pension plan, you could live comfortably. But you'd have no defense against a renewed spurt of inflation that would make mincemeat of your fixed income. Ultimately, if you want to protect against being impoverished should you be fortunate enough to beat the actuarial tables, you've got to have some reserves—your savings.

Calculating Your Net Worth

What are you worth? You've studied and worked all of your life—what has it amounted to? If you don't know what you're worth, chances are that you are worth less than many of your peers. The following table lists several characteristics of wealth; see how you measure up.

TABLE 4-1   Asset Ownership by Age Group

Asset	National Average	Average Age 55-64	Average Age 65-69	You
Own your own home	64.3%	80.2%	78.7%	_____
Own other real estate	10.0%	15.9%	12.0%	_____
Own stocks/mutual fund shares	20.0%	25.5%	22.9%	_____
Passbook savings	62.9%	65.0%	60.8%	_____
Certificates of Deposit	19.1%	28.2%	34.5%	_____
Have IRA/Keogh	19.5%	38.9%	17.5%	_____

Source: U.S. Dept. of Commerce

Now, here's asset ownership broken down by income:

TABLE 4-2   Asset Ownership by Income Group

	Monthly Household Income			
Asset	under $900	$900-$1,999	$2,000-$3,999	$4,000 and over
Own your own home	42.5%	60.4%	76.4%	88.7%
Own other real estate	4.1%	8.1%	12.5%	20.6%
Own stocks/mutual fund shares	6.4%	13.5%	26.1%	49.2%
Passbook savings	40.0%	61.0%	76.2%	81.9%
Certificates of Deposit	11.6%	20.0%	20.5%	28.5%
Have IRA/Keogh	4.5%	11.7%	26.4%	52.8%

Source: U.S. Dept. of Commerce

The conclusion to be drawn from these two tables is this: if most people in your age group, or in your income class, tend to own particular assets, and you don't, you're probably not paying enough attention to accumulating assets.

Now let's see what your net worth is. Net worth, simply, is the value of the assets that you own reduced the by amount of the debts that you owe. In other words, if you cashed everything in, and paid off everyone you owe, how much would you have?

WORKSHEET 4-1   Calculating Your Net Worth

Assets

Value of home owned _____

Value of other homes owned _____

Value of rental property owned _____

Passbook savings account _____

Money market deposit account _____

Certificates of deposit _____

Interest-earning checking accounts _____

Money market funds _____

U.S. Govt. securities _____

Municipal or corporate bonds _____

Other interest earning-assets _____

Stocks and mutual fund shares _____

Amount owed to you by others _____

Regular checking accounts _____

U.S. Savings Bonds _____

IRA/Keogh _____

Motor Vehicles _____

Other Assets _____

Total Assets (1) _____

Liabilities   _____

Mortgages on your home _____

Mortgages on other real estate _____

Mortgages on rental property _____

Motor vehicle loans _____

Loans from financial institutions _____

Educational loans _____

Credit card and store bills _____

Medical bills _____

Amount you owe to others _____

Other liabilities _____

Total Liabilities (2) _____

Net Worth (Line 1 minus Line 2) _____

BUILDING WORTHWHILE NET WORTH

The more you make, the more you should add to your net worth each year. And the older you are, the greater you net worth should be. The average annual income for Americans between 35 and 65 is $25,764, based on Commerce Department figures. Since these are 1984 figures, I add another 17% to account for inflation, resulting in an estimate of $30,140. If we use the net worth of the average 65-year-old as the net worth of the average American at the end of his or her working career, we can say that the net worth of the average American worker at the end of his or her working career is about $122,000 (again, based on Commerce Department figures). Obviously, someone halfway through their working career (that is, a 45-year-old, assuming the career started at age 25) can only be expected to have accumulated half as much net worth as someone who has completed their working career. It's also obvious that someone making twice as much money should accumulate wealth twice as fast (at least).

Worksheet 4-2 tells you where you stand in relation to the average American, taking into account your income and your age. If your actual net worth is less than it should be, you should concentrate on building it up.

Arlene discovers that, at her present rate, she will have a net worth of $130,435 (line 7) at age 65. Given her higher-than-average income, however, her target at age 65 should be $141,672 (line 9), which is another $11,237 (line 10). In order to make this target, she should try to budget another $661 (line 11) each year towards savings and investments.

If early retirement's your goal, you can still use this worksheet. Your answer to line 4a, though, won't be 65 minus your age—it will be the age that you wish to retire minus your age. And line 6 won't be line 4 divided by 40—instead, subtract the number of years you wish to retire in advance of age 65, and divide line 4 by that number. For example, suppose you wish to retire at 58. That's seven years before age 65, so you would divide line 4 by 33 (40 minus 7).

Remember, net worth is only a guideline because, in retirement, income becomes paramount. But if you do not increase your assets steadily, you probably will not have the income you need. The more of those assets that can provide income, the more financially secure your retirement years will be. This leads us to a subject related to net worth—asset accumulation.

Part of accumulating net worth involves debt retirement. That improves your future cash flow because money once used to repay debts can be used for other purposes. But when you compiled your net worth, you listed the equity in your home.

WORKSHEET 4-2

1. Estimated Average Annual Income, 35-65-year-olds _____
    Your annual income _____
3. Your age —
4. Line 3 minus 25 —
4a. Years to 65 (65 minus line 3) —
5. Your net worth _____
6. Line 4 divided by 40 _____
7. Line 5 divided by line 6 _____
8. Line 2 divided by line 1 _____
9. Target net worth
    Line 8 times $122,000 _____
10. Ahead of target (line 7 minus line 9) _____
11. Additional amount to devote to savings (if line 10 is negative, line 10 _____
    divided by line 4a)

Example: Arlene is 48; she earns $35,000 a year, and is single. Her net worth is $75,000. Here's how she filled out this worksheet:

1.	Estimated Average Annual Income, 35-65-year-olds		$ 30,140
2.	Your annual income		$ 35,000
3.	Your age	48	
4.	Line 3 minus 25	23	
4a.	Years to 65 (65 minus line 3)	17	
5.	Your net worth		$ 75,000
6.	Line 4 divided by 40		0.575
7.	Line 5 divided by line 6		$130,435
8.	Line 2 divided by line 1		1.16
9.	Target net worth		
	Line 8 times $122,000		$141,672
10.	Ahead of target (line 7 minus line 9)		($ 11,237)
11.	Additional amount to devote to savings (if line 10 is negative, line 10 divided by line 4a)		$ 661

Your home isn't particularly liquid or available to sell to produce income, so, in terms of generating everyday retirement income, it really isn't an asset available to you. Therefore, you should concentrate on accumulating liquid assets. These include:

Rental property and other real estate

Interest-bearing savings and checking accounts

Money market account

Certificates of deposit

U.S. Govt. securities

Municipal or corporate bonds

Stocks and mutual fund shares

U.S. Savings Bonds

How much is enough? Take a look at these Commerce Department figures:

TABLE 4-3   Median Net Worth by Age Group, Excluding Home Equity

	Average	55-64	65-69
All incomes	7,783	22,073	21,502
Monthly income under $900	1,386	2,470	2,468
Monthly income between $900 and $1,999	6,329	14,983	22,412
Monthly income between $2,000 and $3,999	11,437	30,452	73,618
Monthly income over $4,000	44,860	88,437	156,751

Now let's see where you stand:

WORKSHEET 4-3   Net Worth (Not Including Home Equity and Mortgage)

1.   Your Net Worth (from worksheet 4-1)   _____
2.   Your Home Value   _____
3.   Line 1 minus line 2   _____
4.   Home mortgage outstanding   _____
5.   Net worth excluding home (line 3 plus line 4) _____
6.   Line 5 divided by 1.17 (allowing for inflation since 1984) _____

If line 5 from this worksheet is less than the figure indicated for your age and earning range in Table 4-3, that's another sign that you should concentrate on accumulating more liquid assets.

Not only should you worry with keeping up in asset accumulation with others like you, you should also make sure that you'll have sufficient liquid assets to ensure that you'll be comfortable in retirement. In Chapter 2, you completed Worksheet 2-5. If line 9 of that worksheet was less than zero, you stand to not have enough total retirement income to live in the manner you've become accustomed to. One answer is to accumulate sufficient liquid assets in advance of your retirement that will allow you to make up the difference through additional interest income, or at least withdrawals of interest and principal over your expected retirement lifespan.

How much is that? On line 13 of Worksheet 2-5, you calculated what you could expect in yearly withdrawals based on assets you already own. If line 14 of that worksheet is still less than zero, you need to acquire more assets that will allow you to make up the difference.

Example: Ted's line 14 on Worksheet 2-5 is $3,000. He anticipates that he can earn 10% overall on his savings and other liquid assets. He should increase his liquid assets by $30,000 by retirement ($3,000 divided by 0.1 (10%)).

In summary, you should concentrate on paying off debt and saving or investing more income if

- your net worth is less than it should be (Worksheet 4-2)

- you have less liquid assets than you should (Worksheet 4-3), or

- you don't have sufficient liquid assets to live in the manner you're accustomed to (Worksheet 2-5).

Investing: What's Right for You?

Managing investments is fun for some, nervewracking for others. Avenues for you to invest in depend primarily on your tolerance for risk, and your ability to withstand swings in the value of your investment. You have to manage your investments for the long term, and if you're likely to bail out when the going gets rough, you're likely to bail out when your investment has bottomed out, which is the worst way to invest. The solution, then, is to invest in less risky, more stable avenues.

Safety is particularly important to people saving for their retirement. Your investment goals for retirement should first be

(1) preservation of capital

(2) income

(3) growth.

The older you are, the less time you have to recover a loss of investment capital before you need that capital for your retirement. What's more, the closer you are to retirement, the closer you are to being unable to replace lost investment capital from wages or salary.

The following questionnaire, excerpted from *J.K. Lasser's Personal Investment Annual 1989-1990*, by Judith Headington McGee and Jerrold Dickson, will help you discover how risk-averse an investor you are.

WORKSHEET 4-4   Discovering Your Investor Type

Instructions: In front of each item below, enter number from the following scale that best reflects your answer. If you do not currently invest, imagine how you might feel or behave in the situation described.

Very Much Like Me		Sometimes Like Me		Not Like Me at All
5	4	3	2	1

_____ 1. The money I invest should earn superior returns, even if I stand a chance of losing some or all of my principal.

_____ 2. I take the time to learn about an investment before I put down my money.

_____ 3. I don't mind making a quick investment decision if the payoff is high enough.

_____ 4. Financial recordkeeping is a chore, but it's important that I do it myself.

_____ 5. My motto is "Don't worry, it's only money."

_____ 6. I believe that nobody looks after my money as well as I do.

_____ 7. I believe in the old saying "Nothing ventured, nothing gained."

_____ 8. My motto is "If you want something done right, do it yourself."

_____ 9. I never second-guess a spending or investment decision after I've made it.

_____ 10. I believe in the saying "An investor who runs with the herd is bound to get trampled!"

_____ 11. I don't mind taking big risks when the reward is great enough.

_____ 12. I like to draw my own conclusions about spending and investing.

_____ 13. Most investments are a crap shoot anyway, so why not bet high and enjoy the game?

_____ 14. I'm pretty good at interpreting information about the economy.

_____ 15. If I know enough about an investment and can afford the possible losses, I'm willing to take a chance.

_____ 16. I have trouble trusting experts with my money.

Scoring Your Answers

To discover your investor type, add the numbers you entered for each odd-numbered item and enter the sum in Space A below. Now add the numbers you entered for each even-numbered item and enter that sum in Space B.

A. Total for odd-numbered items: _____

B. Total for even-numbered items: _____

If your total for A and your total for B above are *both* greater than 24, you are a Type I investor. If your total for A is greater than 24 but your total for B is 24 or less, you are a Type II investor. If your total for A is 24 or less, but your total for B is greater than 24, you are a Type III investor. If your total for A is 24 or less, *and* your total for B is also 24 or less, you are a Type IV investor.

These investor types will give you a good clue about your tolerance for risk and the most appropriate ways for you to manage your money and your investments.

Type I: Risk Tolerant/Active. These investors prefer to manage their own high-potential investments and make timing or reallocation decisions themselves. They typically prefer to own portfolios of individual high-growth stocks, operate their own income property, and maintain individual options or future accounts.

Type II: Risk Tolerant/Passive. These investors prefer to pay someone else to make market timing and reallocation decisions for their speculative or high-growth vehicles. This type of investor often feels comfortable with aggressive growth mutual funds, hedge funds, and managed options accounts.

Type III: Risk Averse/Active. These investors prefer to supervise their own portfolio of safer investments. They feel comfortable with switching funds, short-term CDs, and more liquid group real estate investments.

Type IV: Risk Averse/Passive. These investors prefer to pay someone else to manage a portfolio of safer investments or buy and hold investments of long duration. They feel comfortable with balanced mutual funds, REITs, and debt instruments such as long-term U.S. Treasury issues.

TABLE 4-4   Risk, Income and Growth Ratings for
                 Common Investment Avenues (0
                 lowest, 10 highest)

	Risk	*Income*	*Growth*
Stocks	6	4	10
Bonds	4	8	4
Money market funds	2	8	1
Stock mutual funds	4	5	8
Certificates of deposit	2	8	1
Treasury bills	0	9	5
Short-term bond funds	3	8	5
U.S. Savings Bonds	0	6	1
Savings accounts	2	4	1
Rental real estate	5	5	7
Raw land	6	1	7

Source: *J.K. Lasser's Personal Investment Annual 1989-1990*

You could conclude from the above table that there's no reason for anyone to invest in anything besides treasury bills. They combine superior income with minimal risk and average growth prospects. But it's also true that some investors can beat the averages and, if you're willing to accept the additional risk, you could be one of them. For example, we'll show you how to cut the risk, and increase the prospects of growth in investing in certain stocks.

Pension Plans: The Best Way to Build Retirement Security

The most important, most rewarding, and most tax-beneficial way to build a financially secure retirement is by means of a pension plan or profit-sharing program. In most cases, the contributions are tax deductible by the company (and sometimes by the individual). And in almost all IRS-approved plans, the income appreciation is tax-deferred until withdrawn.

Types of Pension Plans

In broad terms, there are four categories of these save-for-the-future opportunities:

(1) *Employer* plans of large companies and governments where all or a large portion of contributions are paid as part of compensation.

(2) *Keogh and Professional Corporation* plans—used primarily by small groups such as physicians, dentists, lawyers, architects and so on.

(3) *Special plans such as 401(k)s, 403(b)s, and SEPs* where you make or direct contributions. The savings are limited but permit tax savings and can be matched by the employer. Within IRS guidelines, you are, or can be, in control.

(4) *Personal pension* plans, primarily the Individual Retirement Account (IRA) where you make contributions and select the investments. The savings represent your earnings and the withdrawals are at your direction, within IRS regulations.

Employer Pension Plans

Generally, annual payments from private pension plans plus Social Security equal to 50% to 70% of the employee's last working year's compensation (lower for hourly workers and those with limited service, higher for executives and long-timers).

Checkpoints for Corporate Pension Plans

By law, all participants in employer pension plans must have access to the rules, regulations and rewards of their retirement savings that involve company contributions.

Periodically, and especially when nearing retirement, ask the plan administrator for: (a) answers to any questions or provisions you do not understand; (b) the projected value of your pension at a future age; and (c) the tax consequences of various types of withdrawal. By law, the employer must provide full information.

What Happens When Your Employer Goes Broke

These days, with takeovers and competition, some companies will go out of business and some of these failures could include the assets of your retirement fund. Fortunately, there is a last resort: the Pension Benefit Guaranty Corporation (PBGC).

Despite a sharp increase in PBGC premiums, it is currently running a deficit of $4 billion. Take my advice: if your company is shaky and the pension plan permits you to withdraw a lump sum, take it and run! However, assuming the PBGC can make good its promises, here's a summary of what it will protect:

- An insured worker can count on getting a vested pension up to a ceiling of $1,857.75 a month (adjusted upwards annually) when retired at age 65. This pension covers only the individual. It will be less when the spouse is included or with early retirement. So far, about 85% of workers in failed plans have received their full benefits.

- PBGC insures "shutdown benefits" promised to workers if the plant closes. That action must come before the pension plan fails.

What the PBGC Doesn't Cover

The PBGC doesn't protect health insurance benefits, executive pensions and deferred pay. Executive pensions and deferred pay can be secured against bankruptcy through a secular trust but the rules are not yet finalized. With this, all of the money is shifted into an irrevocable trust, usually taxable to the executive.

The PBGC also doesn't protect employee profit-sharing plans, 401(k) plans and company thrift plans from bankruptcy. These are supposed to be funded by separate trusts. But you could still lose if some of their assets are invested in corporate stock.

Government Pensions

In most cases, pensions for government employees are more generous than those of private industry. As a rule of thumb, long-time federal civil servants will receive a pension of 60% of the last working year's salary. However, in many areas (especially rural states and small communities), pension benefits are not overly generous.

Military Pensions are being revised. In 1987, Congress changed the rules for those attaining regular or reserve status on or after August 1, 1986. Those serving before that date will receive retirement pay under the old system. For instance, those with 20 years service receive benefits that equal the basic pay of the final grade times $2^{1/2}$ the years of credited service. The pension starts at 50% of final compensation and rises, annually, to 75%.

Under the new schedule, the formula is the same except that 1% is deducted for each year fewer than 30. Thus, the 20-year veteran gets 40% of his last pay.

Military pay is subject to federal and most state income taxes. Six states exempt it totally; 25 partially.

Civil Service Retirement System (Federal Government CSRS). The base salary upon which benefits are calculated is the employee's highest three-year average compensation and years of employment. The basic annual pension equals:

1.5% of the high three-year earnings for the first five years of service

plus 1.75% for each of the next five years
plus 2% for each year of service over 10.

IMPORTANT: The pension of a retiree electing a survivor's annuity is calculated by reducing the base annuity by 2.5% of the first $3,600 of the annuity and by 10% of the amount over $3,600. All CSRS benefits are adjusted for inflation.

Example: Sally, age 62, has 30 years of service with a high three-year average pay of $50,000 (not counting sick leave, disability, etc.).

Base	=	$50,000
5 years × 1.5% × $50,000	=	3,750
5 years × 1.75% × $50,000	=	4,375
20 years × 2% × $50,000	=	20,000
Total yearly benefit	=	$28,125

Her annuity will be $28,125. If she includes her husband as co-beneficiary:

Total yearly benefit	=	$28,125
$28,125 − $3,600	=	24,525
10% of $24,525	=	2,453
2.5% of $3,600	=	90
$2,453 + $90	=	2,543
Survivor's annuity	=	$25,582

TABLE 4-5   Federal Civil Service Retirement Benefits: 30 Years Service

	Estimated Annual Pension	
Highest 3-Year Average Compensation	*No Survivor's Annuity*	*Survivor's Annuity*
$40,000	$22,500	$20,520
45,000	25,312	23,050
50,000	28,125	25,582
60,000	33,750	30,645
70,000	39,375	35,707
80,000	45,000	40,770

Under recent changes in the Federal system, participants in the Federal Employees' Retirement System (FERS) can raise their after-work benefits by employee contributions which will be matched up to 7% of compensation.

There are a number of variables that influence the level of government pensions, such as the extent of participation in the Thrift Savings Plan, investment results, and

Social Security coverage outside of Government employment. FERS benefits are not adjusted for inflation except under limited circumstances and, then, not before age 62.

Keogh and Professional Corporation Plans

Although Keogh and Professional Corporation plans differ in some aspects, as the result of recent legislation, the pension terms are similar. Contributions by the employer are tax deductible as business expenses, the allocations are limited and the withdrawals subject to IRS regulations.

Keogh plans are concerned only with pensions and do not affect business operations. Professional Corporations, however, have advantages in other areas: company-paid life insurance, deferred compensation, tax savings and so forth. With both, there are two types of pension plans:

- *Defined Contribution Plan (DCP).* The annual allocation must be the same percentage for all qualified participants: up to 25% of compensation or $30,000 (whichever is less). With Keoghs, the contributions are net of retirement allocations so that, with a salary of $100,000, the annual set-aside would be $20,000: 25% of $80,000.

  When the DCP is integrated with Social Security (and thus lowers employer contributions), there are restrictions that require all participants to be treated uniformly.

  If you leave before retirement, you are entitled to all of your contributions plus earnings and matching employer funds when you are fully vested: 100% after three years of service or 20% each year after two years' service with full ownership after six years.

- *Defined Benefit Plan (DBP).* Here, you start with the projected retirement income, determine the assets needed to furnish such an amount and then calculate the employer contribution that will compound to that sum at retirement at age 65 or at age 70$^{1}/_{2}$ if the participant has been in the plan for five years.

  Under IRS rules, these projections must be made by an actuary (for a hefty fee) and, typically, assume a 6% annual yield. If the assets grow faster, the contribution must be decreased. The same maximum of 25% of compensation or $30,000 applies.

In 1988, the maximums were annual benefits of 100% of compensation to $94,023 and total pension assets of $562,500 with these restrictions:

(1) a 15% penalty on annual distributions from ALL of the individual's pension-related plans (company sponsored savings, personal pensions, including IRAs and tax-sheltered annuities/insurance) when the totals are over $150,000 or the lump sum payouts are more than $750,000;

(2) annual benefits are lower and related to age at retirement: at 60, the maximum annuity is $72,000 a year for those born before 1938 and $67,500 for those born later (Table 4-6).

(3) special "grandfathering" provisions for accounts that were over $562,500 as of August 1, 1986.

Both contributions and benefits will be adjusted for inflation.

The employer can make up the difference between the old and new benefits but these dollars are not tax deductible and, in some cases, require payment of taxes on the income of the special investment.

Special provisions limit salary base and contributions of highly compensated personnel. Therefore, if you are thinking of instituting a plan, consult a competent adviser first.

Profit-Sharing Plans. These can be used with Keogh and corporate plans. The annual contributions reflect the financial success of the business: no profits, no contributions. The maximum allocation, per participant, is still $30,000 but not more than 15% of compensation. These contributions are also deductible as business expenses.

Beginning in 1989, under the vesting provisions for pension plans to which the employer contributes, the employee "owns" the savings made for his/her benefit after working five years with the same organization or, after three years, 20% vesting with a 20% annual increase for each added year to full ownership after seven years.

TABLE 4-6   Limits to Defined Benefit
Pension Plan Payment*

| | Date of Birth | |
Retire at age	Pre-1938	1938-54
55	$35,800	$33,600
57	43,300	40,600
60	58,400	54,700
62	72,000	67,500
65	90,000	84,000
66	99,600	90,000

* Subject to indexing

SOURCE: Hewitt Associates

Personal Pension Plans

These are do-it-yourself pension opportunities that permit individual savings while working and, in a special format, to set up tax benefits for the assets withdrawn from other types of retirement plans.

Individual Retirement Account (IRA). This is funded by savings from earned income: to an annual maximum of $2,000 for one worker, $2,250 with a non-working spouse. Contributions, in many cases, are no longer tax-deductible for everyone. However, because income can build up tax-free within the IRA, they are still an attractive form of a tax-favored investment.

Contributions are deductible only when neither spouse is covered by an employer-paid retirement plan and, then, only when adjusted gross income is: (a) for a single, below $25,000; (b) for marrieds, below $40,000. Above that, the available tax break drops $200 for each $1,000 added income up to a maximum of $35,000 for singles and $50,000 for marrieds (See Table 4-7).

TABLE 4-7   Allowable Tax Deductions for IRAs

Filing Status	Adjusted Gross Income*	Allowable IRA deduction
Single	Up to $24,999	Full amount, up to $2,000
	$25,000-$34,999	Deduction reduced by $200 for every $1,000 over $25,000***
	$35,000 & above	No deduction
Married/	Up to $39,999	Full amount
Joint**	$40,000-$49,999	Deduction reduced by $200 for every $1,000 over $40,000***
	$50,000 & above	No deduction
Married/Separate Returns	Up to $9,999	Deduction reduced by $200 for every $1,000 income***
	$10,000 & above	No deduction

* Adjusted Gross Income, determined before reduction for any deductible contributions to IRA

** Married/joint, where either spouse is active participant

*** When applying calculation to determine deductible limit, any amount greater than $0 but less than $200 is rounded up to $200.

If you have both an IRA and another tax-favored plan that permits exclusion/deduction of contributions, that should be the first place you put away cash for retirement. But don't abandon your IRA; the tax-free compounding that it offers can pay off. For instance, at an 8% yield, 20 years of $2,000 annual contributions

($40,000 total) will grow to $91,520. If these same sums were taxed at the 28% rate, the total would be about $61,000.

IRA Rollover. A participant in a pension or profit-sharing plan may keep control of vested assets and continue tax deferral until age 70$^{1}/_{2}$ by rolling over, into a new retirement account, a lump sum of 50% or more of pension savings.

This shift can be made once a year, must be from plan to plan (never to your own savings account) and must be completed within 60 days. Otherwise, IRS will levy a 10% penalty on the full amount plus immediate payment of all taxes.

An IRA Rollover is: (1) sort of a portable pension when you change jobs. You can freeze the original pension and start a second retirement plan with your new employer; (2) a reserve savings account when you take early-out under a favorable severance offer and, with ample other income, can watch your savings grow tax-free until the ultimate payout. And rolling over assets from your business' Defined Benefit Plan can save actuarial approval and legal fees.

Special Group Pension Plans

These plans are available through employers, but aren't subject to the requirements stated previously:

Simplified Employee Pension Plan (SEP). This permits the employer with fewer than 25 workers to make contributions for employees up to the lesser of 15% of compensation or $30,000 a year. Each participant has a choice: to take the money in cash (as taxable income) or to have the money invested in the SEP where it is excluded from gross income and thus tax-free until withdrawal.

SEPs are kind of an IRA under a company umbrella. The contributions are turned over to a single administrator such as a bank or mutual fund but each employee establishes his/her own plan. Vesting is immediate and, at withdrawal, the contributions and earnings on them are taxed as ordinary income. The contributions can be integrated with Social Security, thus reducing the amount the employer puts in by the old age disability portion of what the employer pays in Social Security taxes.

401(k) Plan. This involves a salary reduction where the annual contribution (up to $7,313 now and indexed for inflation) is made by the employer and is not counted as income to the employee. Thus, an individual earning $50,000 each year can have $7,313 allocated to his/her account and only have to report $42,687 in taxable income. At the 28% tax rate, that cuts the tax bill by $2,048.

The big benefit is that the employer can contribute up to 25% of compensation (maximum $30,000) as long as the same percentage applies to all employees. Most firms limit that extra to 6% or 10%.

403(b) Plan. This is a form of 401(k) for eligible employees of public schools and non-profit organizations such as hospitals. Contributions, up to an annual maximum of $9,925 (indexed for future inflation) are made under a salary reduction program that lowers income taxes. The participants can choose the type of investment vehicle and when there's a job change, transfer the balance to another employer's 403(b) plan or roll over into an IRA.

Withdrawals May Be Complex

Withdrawals before age 59½ are subject to a 10% penalty plus taxes on the payout, unless withdrawn for purposes of death, disability, to pay for catastrophic medical expenses (in excess of 7.5% of adjusted gross income) or "hardship." At age 70½, the savings must start to be distributed and, in most cases, contributions are no longer permitted.

Loans With Retirement Plans

Many people are reluctant to contribute adequately to pensions plans because they fear they may need these savings in an emergency when withdrawals, before age 59½, usually trigger penalties. However, many plans allow you to borrow the vested assets. This enables you to fully participate without worry that the funds won't be available in an emergency. See your pension plan administrator for details.

All loans to married participants must have written consent of the spouse. Generally, interest charges on loans from retirement plans aren't deductible.

Comment: with any type of loan from a pension or profit-sharing plan, go slow. If you leave the company and cannot repay the loan, the shrinkage will be permanent and there will be a 10% early withdrawal penalty. Still, in most cases, these loans are safer and less expensive than borrowing on your home equity.

Lump Sum Payment: Immediate Cash, Possible Tax Savings

With this option, you can take out all or part of the vested assets, if the trust agreement permits, under one of these terms:

(1) *Roll the funds over into an IRA.* This makes sense when the continuation of the old plan becomes expensive. For instance, with a Defined Benefit Plan of a Professional Corporation, there must be annual reports to IRS with certification by actuaries. This can be much more costly than the few dollars required to maintain the IRA. The income in the trust continues to be tax-deferred.

(2) *Pay the taxes immediately* and use the balance for pleasure, to buy a house, start or buy a business or make investments.

Again, the wisdom of this choice will depend primarily on how much outside income you have at that time. If it's modest, averaging will probably be wise. For details, see IRS Publication 575.

Except with an IRA, you can reduce the tax bite by using five-year averaging: paying taxes as a single person with no exemptions.

With all lump sums, check the tax laws.

- For people born before 1932, when their tax rate is 28% or 33%, five-year averaging can be used.

- For those born between 1932 and 1935, the same option is available but there's an extra 10% levy on the total.

- For those born after 1935, an extra 10% must be added when five-year averaging is used.

Caveat: before you make any decision with a lump sum withdrawal, check your tax adviser. Congress may make further revisions.

How Divorce Affects Pensions

With divorce, as long as the decree or separation agreement meets several requirements, the assets of the retirement plan must be available for family support.

Usually, the pension assets become part of the bargaining process, so that one spouse might say, ''Give me a share of your pension and I'll take less cash.'' At this point, that spouse is treated as a separate participant in the employer pension plan, and can start collecting once the employed ex-spouse qualifies for early retirement, normally at age 55, even if the ex-spouse keeps on working. The non-employed ex-spouse can also preserve his/her right to survivor's benefits should the employed ex-spouse expire before retirement. In effect, the rule is that anyone who depends on their spouse's earnings during marriage can count on them when retired. All decisions must be made at the time of divorce.

With an IRA established by a former spouse, the divorced individual can make her/his own contribution up to $1,125 a year when the pension plan was established for five or more years before the final decree and the contributions were deductible in three of those five years.

Pensions for Those Who Work after Age 65

Companies are not required to make pension contributions for workers over 65, but, if the plan permits accruals, pensions can swell. A $500 a month benefit at age 65 will grow to $750 at age 70 and, in some cases, there may be an actuarial increase to $900 to compensate for the fact that the benefits were not paid for this period.

Supplementary/Alternative Retirement Benefits

By law, qualified retirement plans have limits in contributions and benefits. But there are also non-qualified plans that are more flexible, permit greater savings and benefits and provide tax breaks. Here are some of the most widely used:

Deferred Compensation where the participant takes a lower salary while working and receives extra income after retirement. This works best with executives of small companies or professional corporations where only a few people are involved.

Stock Options instead of extra compensation in salary or pension benefits. With a $10,000 bonus, you are offered a choice between immediate cash and options on 1,000 shares of stock, now trading at $10 each. Since no money changes hands, there's no immediate tax.

When you need money, before or after retirement, exercise the option. If the stock is at $50 per share, you get $50,000 and pay taxes on the $40,000 capital gain. This makes sense only when you have confidence in the future of the company.

Rabbi Trust. Named after an IRS ruling on money deposited by a synagogue on behalf of a rabbi, this permits deferral of taxes with limitations on the beneficiary's access to the fund: no loans, pledges or transfers of interest or protection from creditor claims.

Non-funded compensation. No money is set aside while the participant is working. At retirement, the corporation pays the benefits from current earnings. Since there is no money involved at the outset, there are no taxes to be paid until the checks are received. If you agree to such a proposal, be sure to have the contract approved by your attorney and the corporate board of directors. You are betting that your associates will honor the commitment.

Investing for Rewarding Returns

Successful investing is easy when you insist on quality, look for value and manage your savings: buying when the securities are undervalued and prospects bright; selling when the shares become fully priced. Strive for total returns (income plus appreciation) that average +10%-+15%. In a bull market, these figures should be higher; in a bear market, they will be lower . . . but not by much.

Since all investments should be for the long term—at least three, preferably five, and, often 10 years—the results will be very worthwhile. A slightly higher rate of return can make a whopping difference: in a tax-deferred pension plan, with an annual contribution of $5,000 over 20 years (total investment of $100,000), these savings will compound to $247,115 at an 8% yield, $315,012 at a 10% yield and $403,494 at 12%!

As we have seen, there are many available investment alternatives. No one chapter—no one book—can make you an expert in all of them, or even one of them. Three areas deserve concentration, however, due to their widespread appeal: stocks, bonds, and real estate.

ALWAYS Invest in Quality

All savings related to retirement, whether made prior to or after quitting work, should be invested only in quality securities: stocks or bonds of quality corporations or governments where your money will be safe. Speculative holdings should never be in any pension plan! In the stock market, quality is judged by the record of the corporation in terms of Investment Acceptance, Financial Strength, Profitability and Growth.

Common Stocks

In my experience, the most profitable companies almost always are the most profitable investments. At an annual 15% profit rate, everything will double in about five years: earnings, dividends and the underlying value of the company. Eventually, these gains will be reflected in the price of the common stock.

For quick reference, check the ratings of corporations in Standard & Poor's Stock Guide (available from your broker, or, at year's end, from many newspapers). This statistical firm assesses companies whose shares are publicly traded with letters indicating their quality: A+, highest; A, high; A−, above average; B+, average; B, below average; B−, lower than average; C, lowest. NEVER INVEST IN ANY COMPANY RATED BELOW B+.

Wright Investors' Service, a successful international firm managing over $5 billion in pension, profit-sharing and personal portfolios (on whose board of directors I serve) only invests in companies that meet these quality standards:

Investment Acceptance: listing on a major stock exchange or, for a few companies, traded over-the-counter through **NASDAQ (National Association of Securities Dealers Automated Quotations).** Unless a stock attracts the support of major investors—mutual funds, pension plans and insurance companies), it is not likely to move up in market value. A quality stock should be owned by a minimum of 20 institutional investors (also listed in the S&P Stock Guide).

Financial Strength: (1) a sound, uncomplicated capital structure, primarily straight bonds and common stock; (2) long-term debt, as a percentage of total capital, no more than 40% or, for utilities, 60%; for financial firms, 70%. When a company has a high debt ratio, a small stumble in profits can mean a serious drop in earnings and, after paying off interest and amortization on its debt, probably leaving nothing for stockholders; (3) working capital (the money the company has to conduct and expand its business) as shown by the ratio of current assets to current liabilities. Generally, this should be around 2:1, so that, if all bills are paid, the shareholders will own half of the current assets. This ratio varies with the type of business—high for firms dealing in large, expensive products, low for retailers whose inventories turn over rapidly; (4) the percentage of earnings distributed as dividends to stockholders: for most corporations, a maximum of 50%; for utilities, up to 70%. The greater the payout, the less the money available for future growth.

Profitability. This is shown by the Return on Equity (ROE): how much money management earned, as a rate of return on shareholders' investment at book value of each share of common stock. For a quality rating, most institutions look for an average ROE, over 10 years, of at least 11%. This figure is flexible and may be reduced for utilities, financial firms and insurance companies, but not below 8%.

Growth. To be a worthwhile investment, the company should keep boosting its revenues, earnings and dividends (and thus its equity) steadily year after year, fairly consistently, by a minimum of 4% and, preferably, at a higher rate in periods of economic prosperity.

Over the long-term of an investment portfolio, the emphasis should be on quality growth stocks. These days, with stock buy-backs, corporate restructuring, and acquisitions, growth may not always be easy to calculate accurately. Just be sure that it is solid and not based on trick accounting or insider manipulation.

TABLE 4-8   Quality Rating: Minimum Criteria for Investments

INVESTMENT ACCEPTANCE

Market Value	*Trading Volume*	*Institutional Investors*	*Shareholders*
$100 million	$50 million	20	1,000

FINANCIAL STRENGTH

Capital/Surplus	*Long-Term Debt as % Capital*	*Current Ratio Working Capital*
$50 million	Maximum: 40%	2:1 (Utilities: 50%)

PROFITABILITY STABILITY

10-year Average	*Return on Equity*	*Stability vs Market*	*Dividend Payout*	*Revenues Income*
11%	60%	10% to 75%	No significant decline in one year	

GROWTH

Annual Rate 10 years	*Book Value per share*	*Sales/Revenues per share*
+ 4% annually: minimum	+4% annually	+4% annually

Standard & Poor's: A+ = Highest; A = High; A− = Above Average; B+ = Average
DO NOT INVEST IN ANY COMPANY RATED BELOW B+

SOURCE: Wright Investors' Service

Value: How to Judge and Compare

Value indicates whether or not, and to what extent, a stock is likely to advance or decline from its present price. The projections should be limited to three years and reviewed periodically. All you need are annual reports and analyses available from your broker or a statistical service such as Value Line.

For a stock to be regarded as an attractive value, the anticipated returns (appreciation plus income) should be +35% to +50% within 24 months in a normal market; 12 to 18 months in bull periods. This applies to industrials, service companies and financial institutions. With utilities, growth will be slower so reduce those figures, but not the time, by one half.

The simplest-to-use and, generally, most accurate measure of value is the price/earnings ratio: the current price of the stock divided by the earnings per share, usually for the past 12 months. As you become more experienced, you can use a projected ratio based on the profits estimated for the current fiscal year.

This reflects the attitude of investors and shows how many dollars they are willing to pay for each dollar of profits. In depression periods, the average P/E for NYSE-listed stocks was under 10; in normal markets, it ranges from 12 to 16; in bull markets, it's higher.

These multiples vary according to industry groups because investors are willing to pay more for stocks in highly profitable and fast-growing enterprises.

Generally, *be slow* to invest in any stock with a multiple below 8 because investors are pessimistic; *buy* when it's in the 12-16 range; *be cautious* in the 16-25 area and *never invest* when the P/E ratio is over 30. At such a high price, a stock is almost always a speculation.

"Follow the Money"

"Deep Throat's" advice to reporter Bob Woodward during Watergate is applicable to stock investors. Some investors have done very well keeping an eye on a company's cash flow (net income plus depreciation expense). Among other reasons to keep an eye on cash flow: cash flow per share is a good guess for how much takeover artists would pay for a stock. Why? Because that's about how much they can borrow to buy the company. If you can find a quality stock with a stock price significantly below the value of their cash flow, strongly consider studying that stock further for a possible buy. What's the level of cash flow that should attract your interest? Here's how to figure it out.

(1) Divide 1 by the prime rate.
(2) Multiply the result from step 1 by the cash flow per share.
(3) If the stock price is less than the result from step 2, investigate it further.

For example if the prime rate is 9%, 1 divided by .09 equals 11. If the cash flow per share is $5, 11 times $5 equals $55. If the stock is trading for much less (say, $40), and other signs indicate that it is a quality stock, study purchasing the stock for investment.

At all times, consider the future: will the company continue to make more money at the same high rate? One of the major mistakes of amateur investors (and many brokers) is to be overly optimistic and to buy a stock when it is popular and, by definition, overpriced. When the inevitable readjustment sets in, the fall can be fast and far, particularly when earnings slow. Once a stock becomes unpopular, it can take years for its price to come back to the range at which it was bought.

Conversely, it is just as foolish to hold a stock when its price has declined solely in hopes of "breaking even": to stick with Polaroid bought at 150 (which eventually fell to 15).

Use your common sense. If a stock does not do what you bought it for, find out the reasons why and, unless there are likely to be significant changes soon, SELL.

Example: Let's say that you run across a quality company whose stock is selling at 24. Its annual per share profits are $2.00 so the P/E ratio is 12. Over the past decade, the company has boosted its earnings at an average annual rate of 12%. To be conservative, you assume that future growth will be at a 10% annual rate. Thus, the profits per share will rise from $2.00 to $2.20 in the second year to $2.93 in the fifth year.

If the P/E ratio stays the same, the stock price will be about 35. Add dividends of 4% and the total return will be almost $16 which, on the 24 base price, will be +66%. If the multiple rises, the stock could sell at 41: a 17-point gain which, with dividends, would total +121%. And if the market and stock takes off with a P/E ratio of 16, the total return could be +170%.

Timing

Heed these rules in timing selling:

- *When you make a mistake*, either because of misinformation, unanticipated developments or poor judgment: If there are valid reasons to believe the stock will not fulfill the original reasons for purchase, get out. The first loss is almost always the smallest.

- *When the price of the stock has doubled:* Or, if prospects are still favorable, set a stop-loss order at about 10% below the recent high. For instance, when Toonerville shares soar from 30 to 60, give your broker a sell order at 54$\frac{1}{4}$. Use a fraction above a round number so the sale should be made before the price hits a round number and triggers computer-programmed sales by institutional investors. Raise that stop-loss figure as the stock continues to rise: to 59$\frac{1}{2}$ when it hits 65. If you are confident of the long-term prospects for the company, sell half your shares to get back your original capital.

- *When the P/E ratio moves well above the high multiple of the past decade:* to 25 when the previous top was 20.

- *When the industry, or company, becomes unpopular* and stock prices start dropping day after day: The best way to check this situation is by a chart.

- *With income stocks, when the dividend yield falls below 4%.*

- *When you feel uncomfortable about the future of the stock market:* This is the time to consider moving from equity to debt: from stocks to bonds, or, for temporary situations, to money market funds.

Conversely, sell some bonds when the interest rate drops, so that the yield is close to that of quality utilities. Since the prices of bonds move opposite to the cost of money (DOWN when interest rates rise and UP when they fall), such a sale should prove profitable.

- Do not look back. You cannot reverse the effects of your judgment and worrying about a mistake won't make the price of the stock go up.

- Be yourself. Do not try to be a financial genius. You are a tiny amateur competing in a professional's market. You can win only when you stick to selected areas which you understand and can afford.

Caveat: Be wary of contractual plans promoted by some mutual funds. The salesmen will stress the necessity for a mandated program but will skip over the costs. In one 15-year, $50-per-month plan, 53% of the first year's investment will be deducted for expenses! It's a bit better after two years but, of the $1,200 savings, only $830.76 goes to work. The $369.24 pays for "creation and sales charges."

A less expensive solution: discipline yourself to save a fixed sum each month and send in your own check.

Stock Market Mistakes and How to Minimize Them

Here are the most frequent investment mistakes:

Lack of well-defined objectives. With retirement funds, the goals should be to preserve capital, to provide income and to increase wealth . . . in that order. With a 25% decline in the value of a security, you need a 33% gain to break even and a 66% rise to achieve an original goal of a +25% profit!

Greed: If profits come fast and easy, chances are that so will the losses. Learn how to keep your losses low and let your profits run.

Overcaution: not making effective use of your savings by: (1) investing solely for income and thus losing the opportunity for capital appreciation which is the only way to beat the erosion of inflation; (2) delaying purchase too long so that ultimate gains are reduced; (3) being unwilling to admit a mistake by refusing to sell when the price of a stock declines and future prospects dim.

Poor Selection: buying securities or deals on the basis of fads, rumors, tips or unsubstantiated recommendations. Understand how your savings will be used. In successful investing, there is no substitute for knowledge.

Poor Timing: buying a stock when it becomes popular and is, or soon will be, over-valued; selling at the bottom, usually on the basis of fear, not facts.

Lack of Patience: (1) failing to recognize that most significant gains take 24 to 30 months (except in strong bull markets); (2) selling winners and holding losers. *Result*—the only securities left in your portfolio will be those worth less than when purchased.

Falling for "Special Opportunities" such as buying options, futures, commodities, new issues, limited partnerships, etc. Almost all of these are speculations, areas dominated by professionals who have more skill, knowledge and money than most individuals. For the amateur, the possible rewards seldom justify the sure risks.

What to Do

To minimize losses, concentrate on quality and value and rely on strategies and tactics that have proven profitable over a long period of time.

Buy the Company, Not the Stock. Think of every investment as if you were acquiring the whole company. Concentrate on securities of corporations whose products you use or whose executives you know and admire. Conversely, do not buy securities of any organization that you do not trust. Peace of mind is more important than profits.

Set Targets: with growth stocks, a future price to provide total returns of 25% to 50% fairly soon. With income stocks, look for a yield that is a bit better than that of money market funds, about 6% in normal markets; 8% with inflation. When the yield drops too far because of the higher stock price, shift to another company or a fixed income holding.

When the stock tops the target, sell unless you are convinced that the upswing will continue and you can look for a similar percentage gain in the same time frame. *Example:* Rip bought Whistlestop at 30 with a target price of 50. In less than a year, WS soared to 52: a total return, with dividends, of about +80%. To achieve that same profit, WS would have to move to over 90. As this was much higher than Rip could logically project for the next two years, he sold and put the proceeds into another undervalued situation.

It is always better to sell too soon than to hold on in hope. WS did hit 60 but, soon, was down to 48.

Upgrade Your Holdings Periodically. Check every security every month to determine if it is, or soon will be, fulfilling your objective. Every quarter, consider selling your weakest holding. On the average, plan to change about 20% of your portfolio every year.

Following basic rules and relying on fundamentals in investing may not be exciting but there's no better way to avoid mistakes that limit profits and, at some point, assure losses. With savings for retirement, stick to the basics of quality and value.

Bonds: For Income and Preservation of Capital

Bonds are debt: loans which pay interest, usually semi-annually, and are repaid at par ($1,000 or $5,000) at a future date up to 40 years from issue. Their prices move with opposite to the cost of money: DOWN when interest rates rise; UP when they fall. They should be bought for preservation of capital and income. Do not try to trade them for capital gains because you will be dealing with professionals who customarily trade in bond quantities totaling $100,000 face value. Prices are quoted as a percentage of par: 80 means a price of $800.

With taxable bonds, there are two markets: (a) the New York Stock Exchange, where a relatively small number of debt issues of major corporations are traded with daily quotations; (b) the Over-the-Counter market, dominated by dealers and brokers, who handle U.S. Government securities, debt of smaller firms and special offerings via bid and asked prices. The spreads range from $10 to $50. Generally, it's wiser and cheaper to buy shares of bond mutual funds. You will have diversification by type of issuers and maturities and all interest will be reinvested promptly.

Bond Mutual Funds

For most individuals, these pooled investments are the best choice for both personal and fiduciary portfolios. Their shares are relatively inexpensive ($1,000 original cost with the right to add or withdraw smaller sums), provide diversification, reinvest income for compounding, permit switching to other funds under the same management and submit detailed reports for tax purposes.

There are two major types:

Unit Trusts, where the proceeds of the sales of shares are invested in a basket of bonds with no changes until, as the result of calls, redemptions and, occasionally, default, the assets drop to about 20% of the initial offering. At this point, the fund is closed out and assets distributed to shareholders. The original yield is maintained; there's only one sales charge; management fees are small; and, usually, there's no fee for early redemption. Best when yields are high.

Managed Funds, where the professionals trade in anticipation of shifts in the cost of money. If they guess right, the fund will outperform the bond market. If they make a mistake, you can lose money. Not for conservatives (and if you're saving for retirement income, you should be conservative).

Guidelines for All Types of Bonds and Bond Funds

- *Insist on quality:* a minimum A rating, by Moody's or Standard & Poor's (strong capacity to pay interest and repay principal). Lower quality debt yields more but an extra 1% means only $10 a year on a $1,000 investment.

- *Deal with a knowledgeable broker/dealer* whose firm makes markets (stands ready to buy or sell), maintains inventories, and knows where specific types of bonds can be traded.

- *Work backwards:* buy bonds that will mature about the time you will need money or plan to retire. Then, you, or your pension fund, will get a check for face value plus six months' interest in about 30 days.

- *Give preference to intermediate term maturities:* 10 to 15 years hence. Their market values will be relatively stable. Long-term debt will pay more but will be twice as volatile; short-term issues may have to be reinvested at lower rates of return.

- *Buy from your broker's inventory.* Often, the firm will have odd lots (9, 11, 15 bonds) left over and will be glad to sell them at a smaller-than-usual spread.

- *Do not be alarmed* when the values of your bonds decline. You made the investment for income and, when the bonds mature, you will be sure of getting back the full face value. Losses can be annoying but unless you paid a premium, you will always achieve your goal of ample income. This can be a hard lesson for amateurs to accept but that's the way it must be unless you are willing, and smart enough, to protect your assets by trading, selling short and dealing with options.

- *With funds:* get full information on all costs: sales commissions, management fees, extra charges for reinvestment interest, for redemption, etc. When these are deducted, the true yield will be less than advertised.

Beware of super-high yields. The managers probably hold junk bonds or high-coupon issues bought above par. With the latter, those premiums are not amortized, nor losses deducted, until sale or redemption so you will lose money.

• Never buy shares in any fund that uses options. The theory is that such trading can increase income; the fact is that even professionals can be caught by sudden shifts in interest rates.

Tax-Exempt Bonds and Funds

Tax-exempt (municipal) bonds are debts of states, local governments and some public authorities. Their interest is free of federal income taxes and, often, state/local levies. Investment in tax-exempt bonds should be based on tax savings rather than on total investment returns. While working, the best tax saver is a pension plan; after retirement, tax-exemption may not be significant except in states/cities where there are income taxes.

Tax-exempt bonds usually offer lower interest payments than taxable bonds. Buying them makes sense only if the tax savings are greater than the difference between what similar taxable bonds offer, and that depends on your personal tax picture. As a result of the Catastrophic Health Care Bill, which imposes higher taxes on

TABLE 4-9   Tax-Exempt vs. Taxable Bonds: Comparative Yields

If Your Marginal Tax Rate is	*You'll need this taxable yield when taxable bonds offer:*			
	6.5%	7%	7.5%	8%
15%	7.64	8.23	8.82	9.41
28	9.02	9.72	10.41	11.11
33	9.70	10.45	11.19	11.94

20 Year Maturities, Aa Rating; Joint Return

		AFTER-TAX YIELD		
Taxable Income	*Average Tax Rate*	*Municipals 7% rate*	*Corporates 9% rate*	*Governments 7.6% rate*
$ 30,000	15.1%	7.00%	7.18%	6.45%
40,000	18.3	7.00	6.91	6.20
50,000	20.3	7.00	6.80	6.05
80,000	23.6	7.00	6.47	5.80
100,000	25.5	7.00	6.30	5.66
150,000	28.0	7.00	6.09	5.47

The after-tax yield is based on the appropriate federal tax rate and an assumed 7% state tax rate applicable for corporate bonds; government bonds are not subject to state taxes. These figures are approximate because of varying state tax rates.

SOURCE: Internal Revenue Service; Research Institute of America.

affluent retirees, the tax-free income feature has become more attractive. (See Chapter 7). When breaking out whether you can benefit from investing in tax-exempts, see if the new tax surcharge will affect this decision. On the other hand, the cut in tax rates in 1986 made tax-exempt bonds less attractive.

When you live in a state with income taxes, the benefits will be greatest when you buy bonds issued in that state or by Puerto Rico or the Virgin Islands. Thus, a resident of New York City who receives $8,000 interest from bonds of Denver, Colo., will have to pay total income taxes of $1,040 but if he receives the same sum from debt of Buffalo, N.Y. School District, he keeps the full $8,000. (Not in Illinois, Iowa, Kansas, Oklahoma and Wisconsin.)

Tax-exempt bonds should be bought for income when their yield is higher than the net return of taxable debt as can be calculated with the formula of Table 4-10. They are still worthwhile for personal investments of those in the highest tax bracket, may be OK for working folks trying to stay at the 28% tax rate, but are seldom the best choice for retirees because, for federal income tax purposes, their interest must be included when total income is over $25,000 for a single and $32,000 for joint filers. (See Social Security).

TABLE 4-10   How to Calculate Comparative Yields: Tax-Exempt vs. Taxable

ESTR	=	Effective State Tax Rate
NSTR	=	Nominal State Tax Rate: 11%
FTR	=	Federal Tax Rate: 33%
TTR	=	Total Tax Rate
CBY	=	Corporate Bond Yield: 8.8%
SMBY	=	State Municipal Bond Yield: 6.5%
TEY	=	Taxable Equivalent Yield

In a state with an income tax:

$ESTR = NSTR \times (1-FTR) = 11 \times (1-0.33, \text{ or } 0.67) = 7.37\%$
$TTR = ESTR + FTR: 7.37 + 33 = 40.37\%$
$SMBY$ (6.5) divided by $(1-TTR)$ or $(1-40.37\%) = 59.63\%$
$TEY = 6.5$ divided by $.5963 = 10.9\%$

The municipal bond in that state provides a taxable equivalent of 10.9% which is 2.1% more than the return on the taxable bond.

In a state where there's no income tax:

SMBY = State Municipal Bond Yield: 7.0%
FTR = Federal Tax Rate: 28%
TBY: Treasury Bond Yield: 7.5%

The formula is: SMBY (7%) divided by $(1-FTR)$ or $(1-0.28) = 0.72$
Divide 7% by $0.72 = 9.7\%$

The state tax-exempt bond yields an equivalent of 2.2% more than the taxable bond.

TABLE 4-11   Duration Years of Bonds: AAA-rated Municipals

Maturity in Years	Yield	Duration in Years
1	4.55%	1.0
3	5.15	2.7
5	5.65	4.3
7	6.05	5.6
10	6.60	7.2
20	7.55	10.2
30	7.65	11.7

SOURCE: Hugh R. Lamle, M. D. Sass Investors Services, Inc.

- *Calculate the duration:* the time it takes to recoup, from the interest, your investment. This also shows the approximate percentage rise or fall of the bond price when the cost of money changes. (Table 4-11).

Example: With a 10-years-to-maturity bond with a yield of 6.6%, the duration is 7.2 years; the price swing, for each 1% shift in the interest rate, will be 7.2%: UP when the prime rate drops; DOWN when it rises.

- Concentrate on intermediate term maturities: 10 to 15 years. As with taxable bonds, their prices will remain reasonably stable.

Mutual Funds: Convenient but You Lose Control

Mutual funds are pooled investment in stocks, bonds, mortgages, liquid assets, real estate and so forth. The management firm sells shares to the public, invests the proceeds for a fee (and, often, with extra charges for some services) and distributes the income and realized appreciation to the shareholders, directly or by reinvestment for compounding. The majority of established funds invest for specific goals of income, growth or balance, but new offerings are often packaged for marketing rather than superior investment returns.

Types of Funds

Funds are classified according to the method of selling:

Load Funds that are sold through brokers and dealers for commissions from 8.5% for small purchases down to 4% for large, contractual commitments. This fee is deducted off the top, so that less of your investment goes to work: with a 8.5% load, $91.50 of every $100. The salesperson handles all details.

No-Load Funds are bought directly from the sponsoring firm without commission. All of your money is invested but you must handle the setting up of the account, mailing in your checks, arranging for the income to be reinvested or paid to you.

By and large, the performance of both types of funds as been about the same over the years, so you have to decide whether you are willing to pay for convenience.

Added Costs

With all investment companies, there may be additional charges that can affect the net returns:

- A standard management fee of from 0.5% to 2% of net assets. Take a second look at any fund that has administration costs of more than 1.85%.

- Back-end load: a deduction made from the proceeds of cashing in shares: typically, 4% in the first year, 3% in the second year, down to zero in the fifth year after purchase.

- Reinvestment levy where the load fund charges for reinvesting income to buy new shares: to a maximum of 7.5%.

- Marketing fee (12b-1): a special levy that permits fund assets to be used to pay for promotional expenses to attract new investors. Even though the fee is "only 1%," it can bring in millions of dollars to the management company and reduce total investment returns. Over 15 years, at an annual rate of return of 8%, each $10,000 investment will compound to $31,772. With a marketing fee of 1%, this will be reduced by from $2,716 to $4,132 depending on how the cost is allocated!

Good news: the SEC now mandates that funds list all fees, show total expenses, use uniform terminology and spell out performance records for one, three, five and ten years.

Bank/Thrift Mutual Funds (sold through these financial institutions). Legally, banks are prohibited from distributing or promoting mutual funds but they get around this by serving as shareholder agent for funds managed by outside firms.

Few of these have been around long enough to have viable records of performance but they are convenient and, usually, not expensive: an annual distribution fee of $1/2$ of 1% of assets plus a management fee of up to 1%.

Choosing Funds

Concentrate on your goals, the character and reputation of the management company and the proven ability of those professionals to make more money over time. Forget about the temporary, one or two year, records of superior performance so heavily promoted by brokers and some financial publications. Check their portfolios and buy those that hold shares in companies whose names you recognize and which are rated B+ or better. Avoid funds that deal in special situations, new issues and shares of firms traded over-the-counter.

Find out whether the gains were from a handful of high flyers or a number of quality corporations. You are investing, not speculating.

Beware of funds that use leverage, borrow to trade or sell short, deal in options or speculate with options, futures and indexes.

Look for low turnover, under 50% over a two- or three-year period. Higher activity indicates that the fund managers either made mistakes or were more interested in trading than investing.

Insist on integrity, especially in promotional claims. This caveat applies especially to fixed income funds. In calculating the yield, some managers try to present the best possible results by neglecting to mention the expenses normally deducted from income or by enhancing the return by trick calculations.

Beware of "100% government guarantees" for funds of mortgage pass-throughs such as Ginnie Maes and Fannie Maes. The implication is that Uncle Sam will guarantee the current yield (say, 10.5%) and the market value of the shares. The truth is that Federal agencies insure only the interest and principal of the underlying loans. The market value will fluctuate. When the cost of money drops, some homeowners will prepay their high coupon mortgages and the fund will replace them with new, lower-yielding debt so the rate of return will drop to, say, 9.5% and the market value will be lower.

Other Points to Consider

- Choose an investment company that offers money market funds. Then, you can switch all or part of your holdings to the liquid assets funds when the market starts to drop.

- Open a special account with a discount broker who maintains a computerized link with your fund. All you have to do is to call your broker to switch to a fixed income fund from an equity fund or vice versa.

Timing Buying

Before you buy shares of any fund, check the ex-distribution date: the day on which the investor must own shares to be eligible for the payout. On the next day, the price of the shares will drop to reflect the distribution. If you buy shares just before the payout, you will pay more and the payout will be taxable.

Example: Dr. Busy buys 1,000 shares of Zinger Fund at 16: $16,000. The next week, he is startled to see that his shares are quoted at 13. The pain is eased when he receives a check from the fund for $3,000: a per share dividend of $1 and a capital gain of $2. At a 33% tax rate, he nets $2,000 so, in effect, has lost $1,000 on his investment.

What Dr. Busy should have done is to check Standard & Poor's Stock Guide for the last ex-dividend date. By adding three months to that date, he can get the approximate date of the next payout. Thus, if Zinger Fund went ex-dividend on October 8, the next distribution would be about January 8 (if not a Saturday or Sunday).

Performance Is the Key

The most important consideration is the long-term performance, over at least ten years. One of the best guides is the late summer edition of *Forbes* magazine (Table 4-12) that categorizes performance by the total returns in both UP and DOWN markets.

TABLE 4-12   Best-Performing Mutual Funds

10 Top-performing Balanced Funds (ranked by 10-year total return)	*10 Top-performing Aggressive Growth Funds* (ranked by 10-year total return)
1. Vanguard Windsor	1. Quasar Associates
2. Fidelity Equity Income	2. United Vanguard
3. FPA Paramount	3. American Capital Pace
4. Fund of America	4. Evergreen Fund
5. Washington Mutual	5. Stein Roe Special Fund
6. Merrill Capital	6. New York Venture
7. Oppenheimer Equity Income	7. Constellation Growth
8. American Fund	8. Oppenheimer Time Fund
9. Putnam Growth & Income	9. Tudor Fund
10. Neuberger Guardian	10. Neuberger Partners

SOURCE: FundWise Pro, Financial Sciences, Inc., Palo Alto, CA.

How to Figure Your Return with Mutual Funds

The published reports of mutual funds (available at your library) tell you how well they performed annually but they don't tell you how your investments scored over the period of your ownership. Since most folks invest different sums at different times and at different per share prices, individuals have to make their own calculations. Here's how to do this with shares held two years or less:

1. The number of months being measured	13
2. Original investment	$5,407
3. Current value of shares	$9,221
4. Income (from dividends and capital gains) in cash	$115
5. Net redemptions during period	$2,000
6. Gain or loss:	
A. Add line 2 ($5,407) and 50% line 5 ($1,000)	6,407
B. Add lines 3 and 4 ($9,336); subtract 50% line 5 ($1,000)	8,336
C. Divide A by B ($6,407 by $8,226)	1.30
D. Subtract numeral 1 from C (1.30 − 1)	.30%
7. To get the annualized return, divide line 1 (13) into 12; then multiply by line D (30%)	27.7%

Over 11 years, the "winners" reported average annual total returns of from 33.8% to 22.9%. Roughly, an original investment of $1,000 ballooned to over $63,000—before the Great Crash of 1987. What a contrast to the average fund! From 1981 through 1986, only 25% of the professionals beat the S&P 500.

Warning: Never use the rosy projections of brokers or fund managers to calculate your retirement income. Be conservative: for fixed income, annual average returns of 8% to 10%; for stock funds, 12% to 15%.

Money Market Funds and CDs. These should be reserves for emergencies and while waiting for investment opportunities. Usually, this portion should be tied in with your brokerage account so that all income can be swept into a money market fund quickly and keep earning modest interest. If you prefer to hold assets in a bank or thrift, shop around for the best deal: high yield and low cost.

Be wary of any fund or institution whose interest rates are unusually attractive (such as S&Ls in Texas). An extra 1% return is not worth the risk because these institutions will probably be buying low-rated commercial paper and foreign debt.

Be slow to lock in your savings for a long period of time—over three years—because interest rates can change significantly over that period. And remember that early withdrawals are subject to penalties: loss of one to three months' interest or more with some institutions. That penalty is determined by the difference between the rate of your CD and the current market rate of a similar CD.

Example: If you invest $10,000 in a 10-year, 10% CD and want to withdraw in $3^{1}/_{2}$ years when 10-year CDs are yielding 13%, your penalty is figured as follows: the difference between your rate and the current rate (3%) is multiplied by the number of years to maturity (6.5) to determine the percentage penalty on the amount withdrawn (19.5%). You would receive $8,050. The $1,950 penalty is fully deductible as an adjustment to gross income. One solace: no penalty when your CD is in an IRA and you are over age $59^{1}/_{2}$.

For all age groups, 5% in these liquid assets is usually adequate and should be increased only when the stock market is erratic and you are puzzled as to future trends. Try to keep your money working for the best, and safest, returns.

Speculations. At every age, there are some people who will want to take risks with junk bonds, shares of untested companies or hot stocks in the news. When you are young, you have time to recoup losses but, even then, the limit should be 15% of your savings. Reduce this to 10% before quitting work and to 5% in retirement. Never speculate with pension and profit-sharing funds.

For Extra Income: Write Options on Stocks You Own

When investments are not yielding enough income, especially in retirement, consider writing calls on stocks you own or buy. With wise selections, it should be possible to achieve average annual net rates of return of 16% to 18%, double the yields of bonds and almost triple the dividends of utility stocks. There will seldom be substantial appreciation and there may be modest capital losses but, in most cases, these options can be conservative, income-enhancing investments. This technique can also be used with stocks in pension plans.

An option is the right to control 100 shares of a stock at a specified price at or before a specified expiration date: a *call* is the right to buy; a *put,* to sell. Options on some 600 listed (and a few over-the-counter) stocks are traded on major exchanges.

Expiration Date: usually the third Friday of the month in which the option must be exercised or expire: here, September, December and March. These dates are quarterly to a maximum of nine months: January, April, July; February, May, August and so forth. Popular options may be quoted monthly.

Rules for Writing Calls

1. Sell calls on at least 300 shares of stock. Otherwise, the commissions will reduce the returns too much. Roughly, this will require a monthly investment of $7,500 to $12,000 for stocks trading at between 25 and 40.

2. Write calls on a scheduled basis: new options every month to provide a steady flow of extra income. Assuming six-month calls, this requires a portfolio of about $60,000 to achieve monthly returns, from the premiums, of $750 to $1,000. Usually, the dividends will pay most of the commissions.

3. Make a list of half a dozen quality companies with publicly traded options whose stocks are priced under 50. If you don't have enough money to buy 300 shares, settle for 200 or borrow from your broker. The interest on this loan will be tax-deductible and partially offset by the lower commissions.

4. Find the percentage of premium by dividing the stock price by the last quotation for the call. When RR stock was at 40, in September, the March 40 call premium was $3^{1}/_{2}$ or 8.75%. Look for calls with six-month returns of no less than 7%.

5. Paper-test your program with several selections for one month before you commit any money. If this is done during an erratic market, you will soon understand why you must concentrate on the sure income rather than the potential appreciation.

6. Buy stocks on their own merits, not because of high premiums. The prices of options on non-quality companies can go down even faster than they have risen.

7. Look for stocks of corporations that pay reasonable dividends, say 4% or more. As long as you own the shares, you will get that extra income. If you are able to stretch the expiration to seven months, look for companies that pay three dividends. For instance, buy American Home Products in early May and write January calls. The dividends will be paid in May, August and January.

8. Be persistent. Once you start writing calls, keep going regardless of what the stock market does. You may not make as much when there's a strong rally but you are investing for extra income over a fairly long period of time.

9. Keep a bookkeeping system separate from that of your regular investments. This will make it easier for your accountant to prepare your income tax return.

10. Never buy calls. They can be profitable speculations but they are not suitable investments before or after retirement.

Real Estate Investments

The best real estate investment, at any age, is your home. While you live there, it provides tax breaks for payments of property taxes and mortgage interest. After you retire, it can yield steady income from renting or it can be sold, probably at a large profit, with little or no taxes.

Profitable investments in commercial or residential real estate usually require substantial capital, large loans, skilled management and patience. Luck helps, too.

Today, and for the immediate future, such profits will be the exception. In many areas, there will be losses with both residential and commercial property. This does not mean that real estate should not be considered in retirement planning or living but it does emphasize the necessity for the investor, with personal or fiduciary savings, to consider these facts:

- Almost all real estate investments are easy to get into and hard to get out of.

- The secret of success with most property is leverage: to buy with a small cash down payment and a long, large mortgage. For seniors with fixed income and limited life expectancy, this can be an unnecessary worry.

- The real estate market is cumbersome, inefficient, seldom has accurate information and no central exchange—as with securities. You have to do your own research; check future plans for highways, zoning and development.

- The business is not noted for the integrity of its promoters, operators or financiers. It is essential to revise all projections realistically: reducing anticipated profits by 25%, increasing estimated expenses by 20%.

- Property values can change quickly if the land, home, or building is not well located and maintained or there are outside-your-control economic or political problems.

- The tax benefits are dwindling under new legislation.

There are scores of good books, seminars and college courses on real estate but do not waste your time or money with promotions of self-styled experts who reveal "How to Make a Million Dollars in Real Estate in 15 Minutes." All of these wunderkinder have made more money from fees, lectures and royalties than from real estate. Recently, the author of one of the most widely read books filed for personal bankruptcy!

Making Money with Real Estate

In broad terms, real estate profits are made in two ways, with

(1) small properties where you use your own savings or team with friends, become personally involved in management and, if you are handy with tools, make or supervise repairs or renovations. These should be local and when you have spare time, can be an excellent hobby in retirement.

If you're venturesome, you can use leverage: using the net-after-mortgage value of one property as collateral for a loan to buy another. If you're smart and lucky, you can build assets by such pyramiding. But if one unit falters, you can lose them all . . . not a pleasant prospect for those on fixed income.

(2) larger holdings where you buy shares/units in a group such as a syndicate, limited partnership or REIT and leave the financing and management to professionals. The same standards of quality and value as with securities apply.

Pooled Real Estate Investment Opportunities

With these, you supply the money and leave the buying, financing, management and selling to others—hopefully professional enough to be successful. Always check and double check the integrity and performance of these packaged deals because you are relying on statements that, at best, are subject to interpretation and unfamiliar accounting and, at worst, can be manipulated and involve questionable practices.

There are these basic types (with many variations):

Limited Partnerships. These are group investments whose shares cost as little as $5,000 each ($2,000 when the money comes from an IRA). They are formed by local real estate agents or, more likely, by specialists associated with brokerage, mortgage or insurance firms. They use the investors' money to buy existing properties and, at times, for development and construction.

Small private partnerships are excellent when you are working with local people whom you know and respect. But it's important to plan ahead and set up provisions for selling out to the other participants. Otherwise, your heirs can be unwilling partners.

Public partnerships are those with more than 35 investors. The deal must be registered with the Securities and Exchange Commission, which helps protect against fraud. Typically, they require that the investor has a net worth of $75,000 excluding home or $30,000 gross income and net worth of $30,000. Most important, there's usually a secondary market where you may be able to sell shares (albeit at a loss).

With these limited partnerships, you have a wide choice: in type of property (residential or commercial); financing (high or modest leverage); objective (income or growth); or combinations. The best deals are those whose buildings you can see and monitor; the worst deals are blind pools where the managers make all the decisions and you never know where your money is going.

Real Estate Investment Trusts (REITs). These are closed-end mutual funds that invest in real estate. Their shares are traded like regular stocks, a few on exchanges, but most over-the-counter. Their prices reflect demand and supply and tend to move as a group rather than in recognition of any one trust's management skill or ineptitude.

Like regular mutual funds, REITs pay out 95% of their annual operating profits in dividends, so the shareholders pay their own taxes. They are not as attractive a tax shelter as limited partnerships since investors are not permitted to use the losses to offset other income.

REITs can be excellent holdings at any age: *while working,* equity trusts for growth; *after retirement,* mortgage trusts for high income. Because of the specialized nature of the operations, REITs are more difficult to analyze than straight mutual funds. That's why it is so important to look for quality as shown by the long-term ability of management to achieve its stated goals of income or growth.

Before you commit any money in shares of REITs, study the prospectus, learn the types and locations of properties, look for appraisals by independent advisers, review the past records of successes and failures and concentrate on REITs with strong records of success and sensible-to-you management philosophies. Stay flexible; be willing to move out when shares become overvalued and to delay buying, even at bargain prices, until shares of REITs start to become popular.

Checkpoints for All Real Estate Investment

With personal holdings and private partnerships:

- Is the property located to take advantage of growing population, wealthier neighbors, greater demand?

- Is the price below replacement cost?

- Is the value certified by an independent appraiser?

- Are the projected returns based on valid assumptions? income alone? a combination of income plus capital gains at sale or refinancing?

- Will the property reach a break-even point (positive cash flow) by the 12th month?

- Is the financing: (a) equal to or below the market rate? (b) high enough to permit future refinancing?

- Are the fees/commissions/expenses reasonable: 85% of the money for purchase; 15% for commissions, front-end fees and organizational expenses? Will there be extras?

> *Trick Deals*. As with all types of packaged real estate, there are "special opportunities" created by imaginative money managers. Some are no-loads (but hefty management fees); others are partnerships which invest your full payment and recoup through commissions/fees via a bank loan at an interest rate slightly above prime. By deferring these upfront fees, profits compound faster and the interest on the loan may be tax deductible. These packages are sales tools, not investment. You can buy enough trouble with straight real estate!

When you're considering investing in an apartment:

- Are the sales figures accurate? See Table 4-13.

- Do all of the tenants have leases? for how long?

- Is the building competitive with similar ones in the area? in rents, maintenance, asking price?

- Will there be a need for major maintenance/repairs, repaving the parking lot, etc.?

Why You Need to Check All Property Data

Never take the salesman's word for the income and expenses associated with real estate. Have the books independently audited. Table 4-13 shows how minor errors in individual statements concerning annual gross income and annual operating expenses can turn a purported money maker into a substantial money loser.

TABLE 4-13   How Sales Representations Can Vary Significantly
              from Actual Situation

	What the Salesman Said	*What the Audit Showed*
Annual gross income	$120,000	$100,000
Operating expenses		
Real estate taxes	$ 20,000	$ 24,000
Insurance	4,800	7,500
Electricity/gas/heat/water	11,650	12,500
Rubbish removal	1,000	1,200
Repairs/maintenance	2,100	9,000
Supplies	800	1,600
Legal/accounting/advertising	2,100	2,400
Management	8,300	15,400
Total	$ 50,750	$ 73,600
Gross profit	69,250	26,400
Mortgage amortization	43,619	43,619
Net cash flow	25,631	(17,219)
Depreciation: 4%	20,000	20,000
Net income	5,631	(37,219)

With Public Partnerships
- Are the sales/syndication/management fees out of line with those of similar offerings? Have the salesperson get you prospectuses from three different sponsors. According to the National Association of Securities Dealers, the sales/organization/acquisition costs should not exceed 33%.

- How will the revenues be allocated after the limited partners get back 90% to 100% of their investment? Look for 80% to 85% for the investors.

With All Deals
- What percentage of income will be sheltered by depreciation and expenses?

- Is the tax position valid—as stated in an independent law/accounting firm?

- Can you handle the risks inherent in real estate? a down economy, delays/inconvenience in rental or sale, or new competition?

- Can you afford to tie up your savings for at least three, probably five, and possibly, 10 years?

CHAPTER 5

Estate Planning: Balancing Your Needs With Those of Your Heirs

Although it's associated with death, estate planning actually concerns how you manage your assets while you are alive. The goal of successful estate planning is to use your assets in such a manner that your income needs are met, loved ones are protected, your assets are distributed according to your wishes after you die, and your estate is assessed as little tax as possible.

Look for ways to minimize your estate: reducing your estate cuts estate taxes and reduces the bite lawyers take for handling an estate. A retired couple with a net worth over $600,000 can experience tax problems upon the death of the second spouse, unless proper preparations are made.

Saving Money on Lawyer Fees

Lawyers needn't be overwhelmingly expensive. Avoid percentage deals where the lawyer gets a flat percentage of the estate (such as in probate). Having a will drafted is relatively inexpensive: about $200 for simple wills, more for more complex ones. When you compare this to computer programs that claim you can write your own will (but sell for $50 or more), having a professional draft your will (and stand behind it with his or her professional reputation) is a real bargain. Having a lawyer set up a trust may cost as much as $1,000 to $3,000; not chicken feed, but generally a fraction of what it would cost to probate a similar amount.

Based on the average estate, legal fees can be from $7,500 to over $12,000. Cut the estate that has to be probated in half, and you stand to save $3,000 to $6,000 in legal fees. If you think your lawyer's trying to create future fees, instead of helping you save on your estate, ask him or her to explain how what he or she is doing benefits you. If you're not happy with the answer, get another lawyer!

PLANNING YOUR ESTATES

Planning the estate of you and your spouse should be done with a lawyer and, when necessary, with a tax specialist (to project the federal and state consequences at the death of *each* spouse). It should take into consideration that there is no way to know which person will die first. Too many people assume that the husband will be the first to go.

Prepare a list of important documents and their location with the original inventory attached to your will and copies to your attorney, spouse and executor. Revise this list annually. See Table 5-1.

TABLE 5-1   Documents Needed for Estate Planning

Proof of Assets
Employer retirement/profit-sharing plan
Vested assets
Terms of distribution
Annuity contracts
Single premium life insurance policies
Securities: stocks/bonds/mutual funds
With employer: stock option or purchase plans

Tax Returns/Receipts—for last two years
Federal
State
Local

Real Estate
Title/deeds/mortgage agreements with Home(s)
Investment properties

Certificates of Ownership of Automobiles

Valuables: Appraised or estimated values
Jewelry/furs/furniture/equipment/appliances
Collectibles: coins/stamps/art

Membership Certificates of Clubs

Personal Records
Birth certificates
Citizenship papers
Adoption papers
Marriage certificate
Military discharge papers

TABLE 5-1   Documents Needed for Estate Planning (*cont.*)

Children's birth certificates
Divorce/separation records

Personal Data
Names/addresses of:
Family/relatives
Close friends
Business contacts: stockbroker, insurance agent, friends at office and on job
Professional and fraternal organizations

Legal Documents
Wills
Power of attorney
Burial instructions
Trust agreements

Insurance Policies
Life: group and personal
Property & casualty
Homeowners
Automobile
Health

Business/Financial
Agreements such as partnerships
Bank accounts and statements
Credit cards
Brokerage account records
Charge accounts

When you see your adviser, take your income projection and your list of assets from Chapter 2, and your net worth estimate from Chapter 4. Take into account lower Social Security benefits after the death of the partner, as well as higher income resulting from the investment of the proceeds of any life insurance policies. Make a list of the people that you want to leave assets to, as well as those relatives that you DON'T want to leave anything to.

WHY YOU NEED A VALID, CURRENT WILL

A will is a legal document that directs the disposition of your assets by a personal representative (executor) or by transfer to a trust. If you die without a will, a court-appointed administrator will distribute your property—home, pension, investments, etc.—according to state laws which are impersonal and inflexible. If you do not have a will now or have not had this last testament reviewed in the past two years, see a lawyer immediately. Have your will reviewed every two years, as well as after major changes in your life, such as a move to a new state, death or birth within the family, sale/purchase of major assets and so forth.

Choosing Your Executor

The executor is the person or institution who manages and distributes an estate after death. He/she should be readily available, generally familiar with your financial affairs and family, and have the time and skill to take charge of your assets and carry out your wishes. Ideally, an executor should have the humanity of a clergyman and the business sense of a successful executive.

Look for someone who is: (a) at least five years younger than you; (b) respected by your family; (c) experienced in management but not necessarily business. In most cases, the logical (and easiest to make) choice will be a family member who lives close by: a son, daughter-in-law or cousin. Don't overlook your spouse! But anyone that you choose should meet these three conditions.

Always name a successor executor to cover the possibility of illness or unavailability. You can make a change while you live but, after death, such action must be approved by the court and can be costly and irritating.

An institution, such as a local bank or trust company with which you have been doing business, may be selected as an administrator, but the administration will probably be relatively impersonal and expensive: typically, 5% on the first $100,000; 4% on the next $200,000; 3% on the next $700,000 and so forth. Before you name any institution, discuss their philosophy, methods of operation and total fees (some trust companies sneak in extras for services that may not be needed).

Caveat: Appointing a lawyer as executor can be expensive unless you pre-arrange the fees; generally it is unnecessary. Usually, the work requires little legal knowledge and a lot of common sense. An intelligent layman can do the job, retaining an attorney for specific problems.

What Your Will Requires

Your will should be drawn by a lawyer in the state of your residence and should cover these areas:

- *Identification of the individual:* full name, principal residence to avoid problems when he/she owns property in more than one state.

- *Appointment of an executor:* If the executor isn't named in the will, the appointment will be made by the probate court and may be based on political preference rather than on competency.

- *Provision for adequate income for heirs: immediately,* cash and bank accounts for the surviving spouse; *soon,* proceeds from life insurance, pension plans or investments to provide support for the survivors and, if dependent, for the children until the estate can be settled. This liquidity is essential for the surviving spouse who may have little direct income to pay for essential items such as mortgage payment, health care costs, taxes, funeral and legal expenses.

   Consult with your attorney concerning the best way to distribute your assets to your heirs. Also, make sure that provisions are made in case an heir cannot or will not accept a bequest.

- *Specific instructions for bequests:* to your college, Scouts, United Way and to your heirs. Make monetary gifts in percentages, not dollars: ''10% of my net estates to Yale University and 5% to St. Mary's Hospital,'' not ''$20,000 and $10,000'' respectively. Check to see that all of your assets are named in the will.

   With charitable bequests, make sure: (a) you list the proper name and address in case there may be organizations with similar names and purposes; (b) that you do not leave anything to any organization headquartered abroad. There can be unbelievable confusion with taxes and transfer.

Although writing your own will is probably better than having no will at all, you're best off spending the extra money to have an attorney review it. A holographic will (in your own handwriting) is valid in only about half of the states and, then, will probably be questioned in court when a complaint is brought by a qualified relative. No do-it-yourself will can guarantee that YOUR will will be valid (that is, recognized by the court) in your state.

In an accompanying letter of instructions, indicate how the executor is to be compensated, whether a state-mandated bond can be waived and add a clause that exonerates the individual (but not an institution) from liability for official acts except in the case of gross negligence or willful misconduct.

If you do not have confidence in the ability of your beneficiary to manage your assets, set up a trust. Under recent law, the person writing the will can designate who is to receive the trust principal on death of the surviving spouse as long as he/she gets income from the estate. (For more on trusts, see page 107.)

Codicils

Codicils are statements that modify or add to a will. They can be valuable for minor revisions such as:

• To revalidate an original will after changes such as the death of a beneficiary or the birth of a new family member or an addition of an in-law.

• To permit heirs to modify or change some or all of your bequests.

• To cancel a family debt, such as a loan to your daughter-in law used as a down payment for a new house.

Areas for Review

Depending on the size of your estate and number of heirs, it's important to determine the exact distribution of assets. With grandchildren, for example, spell out the details and make revisions when there are new arrivals.
Example: Widower Will has two children: Mike, with four youngsters; Dorothy with one. If Will makes a per capita distribution, each of the grandchildren gets 1/5. But that's not fair to Dorothy because, presumably, she would be entitled to half of the estate. At her death, her child would get 50% of Will's bequest but Mike's kids would get only 1/8 each!

Payment of estate taxes. Instead of letting each beneficiary pay his/her share of the taxes, arrange for them to be paid directly from the residuary estate.

Gifts of specific items such as:

(1) securities to relatives: "To Daughter Donna, 100 shares of IBM as of December 1, 1987 with adjustments for future stock splits/dividends." Otherwise, if there was a 3-1 split, Donna would get only one third of what was intended;

(2) heirlooms: not "my grandmother's necklace" but "the 24 inch cultured pearl necklace with the diamond clasp that once belonged to my grandmother Gladys."

Special Situations

Single folks living together without benefit of marriage (as more seniors are doing) are usually eligible for employee benefits and Social Security, but such common-law liaisons are seldom recognized by courts. Usually, the judge favors the blood relative if not directed otherwise.

Divorce. When this occurs, check with your attorney. Formal separation or remarriage can automatically revoke the terms of a will or trust that names a former spouse as beneficiary. As a result, the property may end up in the hands of a relative of that former spouse.

You'll want to revoke provisions of your will when:

- *a beneficiary dies.* To update, eliminate that section with a new statement such as ''The gift of $10,000 which I left to my Aunt Susan Single in paragraph five of my will is hereby revoked and that gift shall become part of my residuary estate.''

- *there's a new birth.* Add a statement: ''In addition to any other gifts . . . I hereby give, devise and bequeath the sum of $ . . . . to each of my grandchildren who shall be living at the date of my death.''

Protecting the Will

To be sure that the latest version of a will is readily available after death, make at least four copies and file: (1) with your attorney; (2) in a safe, fireproof file at home; (3) with a trusted friend or relative; (4) in your safe deposit box. Never leave the only copy in the bank because, in some states, the lock box will be sealed by the state tax department so there can be no action until there's been official approval.

N.B. If you feel that the deceased had a safe deposit box but you cannot find its location, send $75 to American Safe Deposit Association, 330 West Main Street, Greenwood, Ind. 46142. They will contact their members for such a listing . . . under the correct name or, if available, an alias.

LIFE INSURANCE PRODUCTS

Life insurance has received a lot of criticism recently. Many people say it's a poor investment. But although life insurance has an investment aspect, its primary value is the income protection that it offers in the event of the death of an income earner.

Nevertheless, as with any purchase, you should be sure to buy just as much life insurance as you need, at the lowest possible cost. How much insurance do you need? Using Worksheet 5-1, determine how much you contribute to the costs for your family (that is, you and anyone who depends on you for support) to live. Now subtract the additional costs for you to live. For example, if you were no longer alive, the mortgage payment wouldn't drop, because your family needs a place to live. But the food, clothing, and transportation bills would go down. Next, subtract your take-home pay (or other after-tax income). Then, calculate what your family already would collect if you passed, such as employee benefits and Social Security survivor benefits. The difference is what your family would miss from your contribution to the family budget. To make up this gap, your life insurance should pay a benefit that, if invested, would support withdrawals that would replace that amount until the people that depend on your income would no longer require your support.

WORKSHEET 5-1   Estimating Your Insurance Needs

---

1. How much, after taxes, do you add to the family income? (You can use take-home pay as an estimate.) _____
2. If you passed away, how much would your family save (for instance, food, clothing, and transportation bills you personally incur)? _____
3. Subtract line 2 from line 1. _____
4. If you passed, what income benefits, such as employee benefits and Social Security survivor benefits, would your family receive? _____
5. Subtract line 4 from line 3. This is what your family would miss from your contribution to the family budget. _____

Example: June is married to Al. Both work (she earns $30,000 a year, he earns $27,000); they support two children, 7 and 10. Of their $57,000 in annual income, they pay $12,000 in taxes, and save $3,000 each year towards their retirement, and $3,000 each year for the college education of their children. The family devotes $39,000 to living expenses.

June estimates that living costs strictly attributable to her (entertainment, food, clothing, etc.) amount to $5,000 each year. Let's assume that taxes attributable to her income alone are $8,000, so that taxes on Joe's income alone would be $4,000. Let's also assume that half of the family's retirement savings, $1,500, are attributable to her retirement. If June died, Al would have $24,000 after taxes to pay for $34,000 in living expenses, save $1,500 each year towards his retirement, and $3,000 each year for the college education of their children. That's a gap of $14,500, or $1,208 each month. Based on Table 1-8, a life insurance benefit of $138,993 invested at 8% interest, would support monthly payments of $1,208 for 18 years—until the youngest child turned 25.

This rough example outlines what you should consider when determining how much life insurance you need. However, there are some fine points that you should consider that could cut the amount of life insurance you need, and thus cut your premium cost. For example, if the kids aren't going to go to graduate school, they may only need support through to age 21. That cuts the period of support from 18 years to 14, reducing the amount of life insurance needed to $122,672. And while the younger child may still require support through age 25, the older child will be over 25 and presumably will be self-supporting. That cuts the amount of support that the family will have to provide.

There basically are two types of insurance—term insurance, which has no investment component, and whole life, which builds up a cash value that keeps premiums down. Many studies say that you're better off buying term insurance and investing the savings. That may or may not be practical for you. Keep in mind that, the longer the period you'll need protection, the more sense whole life makes: you don't have to worry about renewal, and you're protected against higher premiums in the future.

What to Do with Your Life Insurance When You Retire

At retirement, limit death benefits to the amount needed to cover the costs of the insured's death: funeral costs, legal fees, estate taxes, major debts, and tide-over money. Keep old policies only when they pay dividends at a competitive rate and can be used to pay premiums to buy additional protection or when you want to leave a large sum to heirs.

Before retirement, find out if your employer will continue to pay the premiums on your company policy. Determine whether the policy is whole life, which keeps on building cash value and can be converted into an annuity, or term, where your heirs receive a lump-sum but there is no cash-value build-up. Personal policies should be cashed in, dropped, or switched. Here are your immediate choices:

Cash In: usually a good idea when the insured has more coverage than will be needed by the spouse.

Drop: reduce coverage for annual savings in premiums. When two policies have the same face value, cancel the newest one since it probably carries the higher premium. If the choice is between two similar policies, one of a mutual firm and the other a stock company, drop the stock policy. Usually, its premium will be lower but since the mutual pays dividends, the costs will even out in less than 10 years. From that point on, the mutual will be cheaper.

Switch: With people living longer and investment yields higher, the cost of life insurance has dropped from what it was when you started buying protection. Switching coverage after you quit work may save money.

Delay switching a universal life policy (part insurance, part investment) until surrender charges are no longer imposed, typically after 10 years.

Always compare the benefits and cost. The death payout may be the same but, with an old policy, there may be penalties for surrender; with the new one, hefty up-front charges.

Stop Paying by using the cash value of the present policy: (a) as collateral for a loan with the proceeds invested and used to pay future premiums; (b) to buy reduced, paid-up insurance; (c) to pay for extended term insurance which will provide the original coverage for as long or longer than your actuarial life expectancy.

TABLE 5-2   How to Determine Whether to Switch Life Insurance Policy

1. Face value of present policy _____
2. Current cash value of policy _____
3. New insurance needed if old policy cashed in (Line 1 minus line 2) _____
4. Annual income if cash value of old policy invested at 8% a year _____
5. Annual premium of old policy _____
6. Annual premium of new policy _____
7. Net payment on new policy (Line 6 minus line 4) _____
8. Premium savings (line 5 minus line 7) _____
9. Cash value of policies at age 65
   Old policy if continued _____
   New policy: current cash value of old
      policy (line 2) minus future
      cash value of new policy _____
10. Dividends
    Old policy _____
    New policy _____

Source: C. Colburn Hardy, *Your Money & Your Life*, American Management Association, New York, NY, 1982.

Beware of Highly Promoted Policies

New life insurance policies are seldom worthwhile for retirees despite the aggressive promotion by show business personalities. The glib claims are dubious at best, false at worst:

(a) the cost of their "guaranteed acceptance" can be ten times that for a similar policy issued by a mainstream firm;

(b) there's often a two-year waiting period between the date of purchase and start of coverage;

(c) the benefits may be reduced with age.

ANNUITIES

In planning retirement, annuities can be valuable in reducing taxes, increasing after-work income and making it possible for you to leave a larger estate. They involve substantial sums, so they should be reviewed with experienced advisers.

Annuities are the equivalent of pension plan agreements with a life insurance company. For an investment of $5,000 to a million or more, the insurer guarantees to pay you and/or beneficiary a fixed monthly sum, usually for life, starting at a preset age, typically 65.

The policy can be purchased, at any age, with a single sum or by periodic savings. These dollars are not deductible on your federal income tax return but their interest, dividends, and appreciation are tax-deferred. Annuities are supplements to, not substitutes for, personal pension plans. Acquisition costs and maintenance and severance fees are high so these investments are worthwhile only when the policies are to be held for 10 years or more.

Methods of payouts of annuities:

Straight: a regular monthly benefit for the life of the individual. The longer you live, the greater the return on your investment.

Refund: not quite as much monthly income, but at the death of the policyholder, the remaining principal goes to a named beneficiary until the original commitment is paid out.

Period certain: medium income with payments guaranteed for a set number of years, typically 10 or 20.

Joint and Last Survivorship: less income but payable to the annuitant and spouse as long as either lives.

Investments

The insurance company invests the premium, as you designate, in one or a combination of portfolios:

Fixed income: Guaranteed preservation of capital but, except in periods of high interest, earn only modest returns of 6% to 8%.

Variable income payouts depend on how well the investment managers perform. If they do well, the assets and returns will increase; if the results are poor, the payouts will decline.

Note: Annuities are not insured and the insurance company can go bankrupt. Most states have guarantee funds to reimburse policyholders if the underwriter is unable to do so.

Tax Consequences

At withdrawal, the portion of the annuity that is considered a return of capital is paid tax-free.

Example: Mrs. Hoppe, age 75, with a life expectancy of about 12 years (144 months), buys a non-refund annuity for $10,000. This pays her $100.62 per month. She can deduct $69.44 from each monthly payment as a tax-free return of capital.

Expected return from contract:	
144 × $100.62 =	$14,489.28
Cost	10,000.00
Interest portion	4,489.28
Monthly payment	100.62
Interest portion:	
$4,489.28 divided by 144 months =	31.18
Return of principal:	
$10,000 divided by 144 months =	$69.44

At death, the annuity dollars will be free of income taxes and do not have to go through probate.

In comparison shopping, ask these questions:

- Is there a bail-out privilege if the yields falls below a specified figure: the right to cash in, without penalty, when the rate of return drops 1.5% below the original rate.

- Is the advertised return gross or net after fees? Is it guaranteed for at least three years? Is is realistic? With one firm, which invested heavily in junk bonds, the guaranteed rate, for 10 years, was 9.25% when U.S. Treasuries were paying 8.5%. That's risky.

- Are there state laws that apply at the place of purchase or where you plan to retire? In Texas and California, there are taxes on premiums.

- What is the true tax benefit? At a 33% rate, a contract may be worthwhile; at 28%, maybe not.

For detailed comparisons of annuities of some 200 insurance firms, write Comparative Annuity Reports, 5127 Toyene Avenue, Albuquerque, NM 87110.

Checkpoints for All Types of Life Insurance Policies and Annuities

- Deal only with quality firms, those with an A in their rating from Best Insurance Reports (available at many libraries) and licensed to do business in high standard states such as Massachusetts and New York. Policies with secondary firms will cost less or pay more but there can be risks of delays in payments or default.

- Work with an experienced insurance agent with an established firm that will be in business 20 years from now when you will be drawing benefits or your heirs will need counsel.

- Make sure that there are switching privileges with the investments: the opportunity to move assets from variable securities to fixed income holdings or vice versa.

TRUSTS: CREATIVE ESTATE PLANNING

When there are substantial assets, trusts can be an important tool to make meaningful gifts, to provide financial protection for heirs and to avoid or minimize taxes.

Federal taxes are a major consideration for most people; most people face income tax rates of 15% to 33%, but federal estate tax rates can range from 37% to 55%.

With a trust, you turn assets over to someone else to hold and manage for the benefit of a third party. Since you no longer control the assets, you and your estate can usually avoid paying taxes. With all trusts, the most important consideration should be the purpose, not the tax benefits. You should know exactly what you want to accomplish, be certain that the trustee understands your wishes and that the terms of the agreement provide the benefits you want.

Trusts have several advantages. They don't go through probate, saving fees imposed by lawyers and courts, as well as estate taxes. They're harder for the disgruntled to challenge, and they're faster than going through probate.

Generally, the same rules apply to all types of trusts but, because their terms are subject to state laws, they should be drawn by a lawyer in your state of legal residence.

Types of Trusts

Trusts are available in a variety of formats but these are the ones that are most widely used.

Gifts to Minors: Children/Grandchildren. Recent legislation imposes new rules on gifts to children under 14: until the child reaches age 14, all income over $1,000 is taxed at the donor's top rate. After age 14, the trust/child pays the tax at his/her own rate, typically, 15%. As these are gifts, each donor can give $10,000 a year ($20,000 for a married couple) to any one individual/trust.

Uniform Gift to Minors Act (UGMA). This is established for the benefit of a minor with a trustee, of your choice, to administer the assets according to your wishes.

To reap the benefits of income splitting, you want the gift to be taxable to the minor and removed from your estate. To accomplish these goals, the trust must:

(a) be irrevocable so that you retain no rights and the property cannot revert to you;

(b) provide that the property and income be expended by or for the child before age 18;

(c) mandate that property remaining in the trust at the 18th birthday passes to the child or, earlier, if he/she dies earlier.

A new format, Uniform Transfer to Minors Act (UTMA) is similar but permits the distribution of the assets to be deferred until age 21 (25 in California) and permits a wider range of gifts such as real estate, royalties, patents and paintings.

If you plan the trust to pay for college costs, estimate today's college costs. Use Table 1-6, using 2% as your rate of return. (Historically, interest rates exceed inflation by 2%-6%; 2% is a conservative estimate of your rate of return after inflation.) The figure that corresponds to the years until the child reaches college age is the gift that you need to make.

Revocable Trust. This can be terminated at any time during the life of the creator. It can hold property that will revert to the donor when the trust is terminated and thus becomes subject to taxes on the income earned by the trustee and, at death, on the full assets. It is useful to permit the owner to look at how his estate plan will operate. If anything is unsatisfactory, the trust can be amended, altered or dissolved.

Irrevocable Trust. This is a trust that cannot be changed or revoked. The only control the donor has is the imposition of conditions on the use of the funds. These have to be carefully limited to avoid trouble with IRS. The property involved is considered a gift so not subject to estate taxes. The beneficiary pays the taxes on distributed income.

Living Trust. This continues as long as the beneficiary lives or for a set period of time. When the trust ends, the principal goes back to the original owner.

One currently popular version is the revocable living trust. Subject of several lengthy books, the principle can be explained in a few sentences. You turn over all your assets to a trust. The trust's revocable, so you can change it whenever you like. Acting as your own trustee, you can determine how the assets of the trust will be managed and distributed. You avoid probate, and escape having to have a will (at least for assets in the trust). However, you still have to worry about estate taxes.

Testamentary Trust. This is created by will and takes effect when the grantor dies. It is valuable in keeping holdings together so that they can be disposed of as you want and without losses that might result if a quick settlement has to be made and the executor has to liquidate the estate.

Q-Tip Trust (Qualified Terminable Interest Property Trust). This allows you to leave your spouse a lifetime income interest in property in your will. Upon his/her death, the property will pass outright to another person whom you designate, usually a child. This format enables the donor to get around the general rule that a property interest will terminate upon some event (such as the death of your spouse) and thus will not qualify for the marital estate and gift tax exclusion. *Excellent for two-marriage families in which the husband wants to guarantee that children from the first marriage receive assets after the death of the second wife.* Wills are often challenged under these circumstances.

Crummey Trust. This is designed to keep the beneficiary from outright possession of the property. The beneficiary has the right to withdraw the lesser of (a) the annual gift tax exclusion ($10,000 single; $20,000 joint) or (b) the entire amount for a limited period.

Life Insurance Trust. When the assets of a trust consists of a life insurance policy or policies and the trust is established three years before death, the proceeds are kept out of your estate and that of your spouse. To keep the tax exemption through to a child, the insurance trust can be combined with a generation-skipping provision.

Generation-Skipping Trust (GST). This is a way to have your money last beyond your child's lifetime. The income can be used for the benefit of your child during his/her lifetime and the principal passed on to the grandchildren free of federal estate tax.

The law does levy a special estate tax on assets when transferred to the third generation, but there are exemptions: each person is entitled to make tax-exempt generation-skipping transfers up to $1 million. The dollar amount of the exemption is fixed at the time of the transfer and continues no matter how large the transferred property grows. So $200,000 in a GST could grow to $1 million or more when it's turned over to the third generation—tax-exempt. This exemption applies to gifts under the annual exclusion ($10,000 or $20,000) so relatively small sums can swell to large inheritances without federal estate taxes.

Foundation Trust. This is a convenient way to maintain charitable contributions in the future and take a tax deduction now. A private trust is funded with cash or marketable securities, from $10,000 to millions. The foundation must make charitable gifts annually. To qualify, the maximum cash must be 30% of Adjusted Gross Income (AGI). For example, with an AGI of $150,000, the maximum deductible contribution is $45,000.

When you give securities, you can deduct their market value up to 20% of your AGI. If the Alternative Minimum Tax applies, you can deduct only the original cost of the shares.

You can be the trustee or choose someone else. Since 5% of the assets must go to charity each year, it's important to maintain liquidity. If not, there's a penalty tax of 15% of the shortfall.

The foundation pays no federal income tax but must file an annual accounting. To defray monitoring costs, IRS collects 2% of the foundation's net investment income.

Exemption-equivalent Trust. This is best for the surviving spouse, providing for his or her needs and also reducing or eliminating taxes on estate assets and subsequent beneficiaries.

The surviving spouse gets all income and can draw on the principal when resources are not sufficient to maintain an accustomed standard of living. At death, the assets pass, free of estate tax, to the beneficiaries of the trust, usually the deceased couple's children.

TABLE 5-3   Comparison of No Trust and Exemption-equivalent Trust

Estate Tax	
Gross estate of husband	$400,000
Marital deduction	(400,000)
Taxable estate	0
Estate tax	0
Gross estate of wife at his death	$400,000
Received from husband	400,000
Taxable estate	800,000
Estate tax	266,800
Unified credit	(192,800)
Estate tax due	$ 74,000
No Estate Tax	
Gross estate of husband	$800,000
Marital deduction	(200,000)
Taxable estate (in exemption-equivalent trust at husband's death)	600,000
Estate tax	192,800
Unified credit	(192,800)
Estate tax due	0
Gross estate of wife	$400,000
Received from husband	200,000
Taxable estate at wife's death	600,000
Estate tax	192,800
Unified credit	(192,800)
Estate tax due	0

Trusts can be especially useful to make provisions for the care of a disabled partner or parent when the caregiver becomes ill or dies and there will be no family member to help. Such decisions are never easy but they should not be delayed after there are signs of mental of physical regression.

These documents must be carefully structured to:

(1) Assure there will always be a responsible party designated to manage the assets and monitor the care.

(2) Make certain that the trust income will not boost the income of the beneficiary above the level that makes the disabled individual eligible for governmental assistance.

A variation of this type of trust permits the family to spell out wishes for future care: residential alternatives, rehabilitation and support services, etc. This relieves the executor of the costly, time-consuming task of making those decisions.

Prenuptial Agreement

These days, more older people are marrying again. Often, so that each partner may retain his/her own assets and leave them to his/her children, many new couples set up a prenuptial agreement.

However, there can be two problems with prenuptial agreements. First, no will or agreement will shut a spouse out of an estate. In New York, the survivor is guaranteed 50% of the estate; when there's more than one child, it's 33%. Second, if one spouse tries to hide some assets, a court can nullify the agreement. *Best solution:* set up a trust to accomplish what each wants.

Charitable Gifts/Trusts

How to handle charitable contributions is one of the most difficult decisions for many retirees. There are ways to contribute to familiar institutions (as well as new worthy projects) without depleting capital so severely that they can be placed in jeopardy by inflation and the probability of major health care expenditures.

Under a Pooled Income Plan, the donor receives income for life, with the principal reverting to the institution at the death of the donor and spouse, or beneficiary. There are also tax benefits: (a) you can deduct the IRS-calculated value of the gift on your income tax return in the year of the contribution; (b) your estate will be smaller, reducing your estate administration costs; and (c) no tax on the higher-than-cost value when you give appreciated property.

There are several variations on this idea; if you're contemplating such a gift, your intended donee can supply you with information on them. IRS requires that all charitable trusts be irrevocable and the donor may not retain any control. Other IRS requirements may apply.

The timing of gifts depends on resources and the age of both partners. ALWAYS CONSIDER HOW LONG EITHER OF YOU MAY LIVE: at 75, about 10 years; at 80, 8 years more.

COMMUNITY PROPERTY AND OTHER FORMS OF OWNERSHIP

Many people think that community property, joint ownership, and other forms of common ownership with a spouse obviate the need for estate planning. Actually, you need to plan just to be sure to take the greatest advantage of these forms of ownership.

Community Property

Generally, property acquired and income earned by either spouse during marriage is considered community property in which each spouse has a half interest. Under federal law, only half of community property is subject to estate tax. When this is willed to the survivor, its value is offset by the marital deduction and thus, not taxed.

Eight states (Arizona, California, Idaho, Louisiana, Nevada, New Mexico, Texas and Washington) have community property laws that apply to income and property of married couples. When you live in a community property state, you should identify all property as separate or community. This classification determines how these assets will pass and how federal estate and gift taxes will apply. Property acquired before the marriage remains separate. If it becomes community property, there's no gift tax. Keep accurate records of cost and date of acquisition.

Find out the rules in your resident state. In some states, property held in the wife's name is presumed to be her separate property; the property held in the husband's name is considered community property.

The assets of a retirement plan are considered community property, so that each spouse has a 50% interest in the benefits.

Community property ownership exists only during the marriage. At divorce, all community property becomes separate and there's no gift tax providing each spouse retains a half interest.

Life insurance proceeds are subject to tax under federal estate tax laws. If the payments are taxable and the insurance is considered community property, half of the proceeds are included in the insured's gross estate. But there may be a gift tax if the beneficiary is someone other than the spouse. To avoid the tax, assign the ownership interest in the policy to a trust.

N.B. If community property funds are used to pay the premiums, the proceeds are usually considered community property.

When you move from a community property state to a common-law state, the property is usually treated as community property. At death, or sale, half goes to the surviving spouse. When the title is held in one name, unless there is a written agreement, the court usually assumes that the property is owned separately by the individual having title.

When you move from a common law state to a community property state, the original ownership is retained. Property held jointly is treated as separate property; property accumulated by a married couple after the move is considered as community property. There are exceptions: in California, with real estate, either spouse who holds title to what is considered community property may lease or mortgage it without the knowledge or consent of the partner.

When you move to, or from, a community property state, consult a lawyer so that you will understand the laws. Ignorance is no excuse when it comes to tax consequences.

Joint Ownership of Property

This is a concept that should be understood at any age, reviewed with an attorney at retirement and, if used, re-reviewed when one partner's mind or health starts to fail. The legal term is joint tenancy: that all property is owned by two or more persons, usually a husband and wife but also a parent and child or two unrelated individuals. There are three major types:

1. *Joint tenancy with the right of survivorship.* Each owner has an equal share of the property. While alive, co-owners can sell or give away their interests without permission of the others. At death, each survivor owns an equal portion of the assets. This format is used primarily with real estate.

2. *Tenancy in common.* This permits two or more people to own individual shares of real or personal property. It carries the right of survivorship in that when a co-owner dies, his/her share goes to his/her heirs, not to the partner.

3. *Joint tenancy.* This is the most widely used form. It usually involves married couples. Each owns an equal share. At the first death, the property automatically passes to the survivor. This may be a good idea for a modest checking

account and for a home whose value has not increased sharply but it can be dangerous and expensive when used with all assets.

The pluses:

- Convenience is that there can be one central account for both partners and assets can be liquidated quickly.

- Builds a sense of family unity and trust.

- Can avoid the publicity and delay and some property from creditors' claims.

The minuses:

- Can inhibit decisions if one partner balks at some action or becomes ill and unable to sign documents.

- Will create problems when there's a divorce or separation.

- At death, can introduce legal uncertainties, complications and extra taxes.

Example: A couple buys a house for $50,000 and registers ownership in both names. At the death of the husband, the property is worth $200,000. Taxwise, the cost bases are: $25,000 for the widow's half; $100,000 for the inherited share. If the house is sold for $225,000, the widow might have to pay a tax on the capital gain of $100,000.

But if the property had been in one name, the tax bite would be less. The cost basis would be $200,000 and the property would pass to the widow tax-free if the total estate was under $600,000.

Check your tax adviser before placing major assets in joint ownership. This is not a substitute for a will and can create unnecessary problems.

Joint Purchase

This is a variation of joint tenancy that can be used when both the parent and child have substantial assets. The senior and junior family members (but not limited to relatives) acquire property together with each paying the value of his/her interest based on IRS tables. It's a good idea when there is only one parent.

The older person pays the larger sum and receives all income while living; the younger one pays the balance and gets the entire property after the parent's death. To qualify, the assets usually must be income-producing.

Estate Taxes

If you have a net worth of less than $600,000, you won't have a problem with federal estate taxes. There's a unified tax credit of $192,800 that offsets the tax applicable to estates up to $600,000.

Property passing to a spouse is generally free from estate or gift tax because of an unlimited marital deduction. For most people, this means no tax on the estate of the first to die. But there's no such exemption with the estate of the surviving spouse.

You can reduce the size of your estate by making gifts to your intended heirs while you are living, either directly or to a trust to benefit someone. You can exclude yearly gifts per person up to $10,000 ($20,000 for a couple) from gift tax.

TABLE 5-4   Unified Gift and Estate Tax Rates

| If taxable amount is | | The tax is | | |
Over	But not over	This	Plus	Over
$0	$10,000	$0	18%	$0
$10,000	$20,000	$1,800	20%	$10,000
$20,000	$40,000	$3,800	22%	$20,000
$40,000	$60,000	$8,200	24%	$40,000
$60,000	$80,000	$13,000	26%	$60,000
$80,000	$100,000	$18,200	28%	$80,000
$100,000	$150,000	$23,800	30%	$100,000
$150,000	$250,000	$38,800	32%	$150,000
$250,000	$500,000	$70,800	34%	$250,000
$500,000	$750,000	$155,800	37%	$500,000
$750,000	$1,000,000	$248,300	39%	$750,000
$1,000,000	$1,250,000	$345,800	41%	$1,000,000
$1,250,000	$1,500,000	$448,300	43%	$1,250,000
$1,500,000	$2,000,000	$555,800	45%	$1,500,000
$2,000,000	$2,500,000	$780,800	49%	$2,000,000
$2,500,000	$3,000,000	$1,025,800	53%	$2,500,000
$3,000,000		$1,290,800	55%	$3,000,000

If you have a net worth in excess of $600,000 that you cannot reduce below $600,000 through annual gifts before you die, or such gifts are impractical, you should see a tax accountant or lawyer. You should also see a professional if a substantial part of your estate is a closely held business, or real estate used in farming. If you own a closely held business, your idea of the business' value, and that of the IRS, may vary greatly.

State Taxes. These are levied on the estate of every individual who was a legal resident at the time of death. They vary from minimal in Florida—one reason why so many seniors retire there—to hefty in New York. (For a table containing state estate tax rates, see pages 194–199.)

Warning: If the deceased owns properties in several states—such as the Georgia retiree who holds on to his old home on Long Island—both states may want to get into the act. Consult your lawyer for advice on how to avoid double taxation: selling property to one of your children, deeding it to a trust or using some other legitimate type of exclusion.

How to Save (and Not Save) on Estate Taxes

To give you an idea of what can, or cannot, be done, here are some examples of how to reduce or avoid federal and state levies.

- *With group life insurance,* assign ownership rights (but not the privilege of converting to an individual policy at retirement) to someone else: son, daughter-in-law. There will be no tax because your interest has no ascertainable value at the time of transfer and the employer can stop paying the premiums.

  Be careful how you do this. When the employer pays the premium, the assignment is subject to the $10,000 annual gift exclusion so the process should be spread over five years. When the benefit of the policy is over $50,000, an IRS table must be used.

- *Joint tenancy* may save estate taxes but may also cause higher income taxes for the surviving spouse. In the estate of the first to die, one half of jointly held property is included regardless of who paid for the property. These assets, up to $600,000, will be offset by the marital deduction.

  But, for income tax purposes, the half included in the estate will be valued at fair market worth at the date of death. Thus, when the property is sold, any profit will be fully taxed.

State taxes are a different story. The deductions vary widely, the rates keep rising and the valuations are subject to different interpretations. Only one thing is sure: if there is an estate tax in the state of your legal residence, it's probably going to be increased in the future. Again, see your lawyer! You may find that a trust can be very worthwhile.

MANAGING THE DEATH OF YOUR SPOUSE

With financial decisions, deal only with people and institutions that had long and close relations with your spouse. Never sign any papers on the advice of someone you do not know or who is not recommended by someone you trust. Confidence men/women are charming, plausible and skilled in flattery.

Retain competent advisers to fill out your income tax, to appraise and, possibly, sell property, and to make investments. Do not go overboard and pay for help you do not need: notifying Social Security, changing the name on credit cards, etc.

Have your lawyer list the essential steps in probating the will, carrying out its provisions and paying taxes plus an estimate of the probable cost.

Review your own will; it probably needs to be revised.

If you are the executor, go over the will with your attorney and close relatives and set a timetable for implementation.

If the executor is an institution or a relative, follow the same procedure.

Ask your life insurance agent for details of your choices as to the use of the proceeds: a lump sum in cash, periodic payments, rollover into an annuity (with tax savings).

Review your lifestyle and do not hesitate to make drastic changes: selling the house, resigning from clubs used primarily for your spouse's business entertainment. You are a different person so choose those services/amenities that meet your needs rather than try to retain no-longer meaningful contacts. You can't eat prestige.

Checklist at Death

Generally, we avoid contemplating death. However, when death comes to a loved one, you can't escape the reality that life goes on, and you must, too. The minor tasks that are occasioned by the death of someone close can help with the grieving process; they keep you busy, so you have less occasion to dwell on your loss while you are still feeling the shock. Here's a list of things to do that people sometimes overlook:

- Make at least six copies of death certificate.

- Change Social Security at local office. If you have been receiving benefits, this can be done by phone; if benefits will be new or changed, take death certificate and your birth certificate to local Social Security office.

- If spouse was veteran, notify Veterans Administration to learn if any benefits are due.

- Notify insurance companies and discuss payments with insurance agent.

- Check with lawyer for will, filing for probate, etc.

- Transfer all securities, bank accounts, real estate, credit cards and other property to your name.

- Check all health insurance policies to be sure you have protection.

Where to Get Information

Financial Planning

- International Board of Standards and Practices for Certified Financial Planning, 2 Denver Highlands, 10065 East Harvard Avenue, Denver, CO 80231.

- International Association for Financial Planning, 2 Concourse Parkway, Atlanta, GA 30328.

- American Society of Chartered Financial Consultants, American College, 270 Bryn Mawr Avenue, Bryn Mawr, PA 19010.

- National Association of Personal Financial Advisers, P.O. Box 2026, Arlington Heights, IL 60006.

- International Society of Pre-Retirement Planners, 11312 Old Club Road, Rockville, MD 20852.

Estate Planning Information: Wills, Trusts, Death, Divorce

Guide Book for Widows and for Those Called Upon to Aid Widows, Connecticut Life, 170 Sigourney Street, Hartford, CT 06105.

Family Wealth Transactions: Trusts, Future Interests and Estate Planning, Jesse Dukeminier and Stanley Johnson, Little Brown.

The Widow's Guide: How to Adjust, Ida Fisher and Byron Lane, Prentice-Hall.

Living with Death and Dying, Elizabeth Kubler-Ross, Macmillan.

What a Widow Needs to Know: A Guide for Widows and Helpers, Eleanor Kurtz, R&E Research Associates, Palo Alto, CA 94303.

Everything Your Heirs Need to Know, David S. Magee, Caroline House.

Life After Divorce, Dorothy Payne, Pilgrim Press.

Thinking Clearly About Death, Jay F. Rosenberg, Prentice-Hall.

Essential Guide to Wills, Estate, Trusts and Death Taxes, Alex J. Soled, Chancery Publishers.

A Personal Guide for Living with Loss, Elaine Vail, John Wiley & Sons.

CHAPTER 6

Your Health—How To Keep It Up

Health care costs have risen rapidly lately—at a rate triple that of inflation. And, as the population ages, technology advances, AIDS continues to take an increasing portion of American health care resources, and senile dementia becomes more prevalent, you can expect increases of as much as 15% a year in the future. What does this mean for you? In planning your retirement, expect that your anticipated health care costs will double within 10 years of retirement.

Worse yet, financing health care bills is a mess and growing more confused. In future years, retirees will pay more for Medicare, working people will get lower benefits or have to supplement employer contributions, and every taxpayer will have to pay more to subsidize health care for the indigent. Without proper protection and planning, some 10% of the elderly will be forced to seek governmental assistance and another 20% will have to reduce their standard of living. The impact will be modest in the early years of retirement but can be devastating for the Old-Olds—those over age 80.

It is clear that, as a nation, we are not effectively using the billions we spend on health care. And with a tremendous federal deficit, political posturing, and vested interests, enactment of national health insurance is unlikely for the foreseeable future.

The one sure way to control your health costs as much as possible is to make health care protection a major factor in your pre- and post-retirement planning. Although health care, in retirement, may be the most expensive and difficult-to-handle area, pre-planning, common sense and adherence to proven rules of diet, exercise and moderation can make a big difference. You can also save through wise selection of health insurance.

EFFECT OF AGE ON HEALTH

As you grow older, doctors and hospitals will become an ever-greater reality of life. Your need for, and dependence on, both of these services generally rises with age. To a surprising degree, you can minimize your need for expensive health care services. About 80% of the diseases, illnesses, and injuries suffered by retirees could have been prevented or postponed if the individual in question had eaten less, drunk less, given up smoking, exercised more, or simply used common sense. Your body's tolerance for careless habits declines when the body falters.

Consider these facts:

- Retirement increases the chances of a heart attack by 80% because of financial worries, loneliness or boredom.

- 50% of retirees have not sought dental care in the last five years compared to 11% for those under age 35.

- 30% of retirees have no health insurance because this benefit was tied to a job while they were active, and was paid for by the employer.

- Despite the fact that employers pay $4.6 billion for health insurance for retirees, most present policies do not cover long-term care and most plans are not adequately funded.

But don't become too alarmed. You can take encouragement from these facts:

- 80% of all retirees are mentally alert and physically competent. Even the Old-Olds (those over 80) do pretty well: 75% can walk without help and 80% can bathe and dress themselves.

- Cancer deaths, for seniors, are only 10% higher than for those under age 65.

- Heart disease affects only half as many men over age 65 as those in the 34-65 age group.

- 90% of all major operations of seniors turn out OK.

- Good health of retirees is closely related to income. For those over age 65, with incomes over $25,000, only 15% had major health problems but, for those with incomes under $10,000 a year, 35% suffered illness and injury severe enough to require hospital care.

- Of those over 65: 56% do not complain of arthritis; 63% can hear well; 80% do not have cardiac problems.

- Financially, the costs of health care may be irritating but they are not overwhelming. According to figures released by the National Health Forum of George Washington University, the retiree currently pays 25% of the total health care bills—an average annual cost of $1,059. Medicare picks up 49%, Medicaid and other governmental programs pay 19% and private insurance, 7%.

MAINTAINING YOUR HEALTH

You can improve your chances for a longer, healthier life through good nutrition, exercise, plenty of sleep, living a lifestyle that involves minimal stress, and avoiding health-endangering habits such as smoking, alcohol and drug abuse. This probably isn't news to you. But the fact is, the sooner you start down the path towards good health, the better your chances of avoiding painful and debilitating illnesses.

Too many people wait until their first heart attack or stroke to change their ways. At that point, it can be too late. I know of a woman who smoked two packs a day of unfiltered cigarettes, worked 18 hours a day, and ate a high-fat, high-sugar diet. She developed diabetes, and had a major heart attack at just 39 years of age. The heart attack frightened her into giving up smoking, moderating her work schedule and her diet, but the damage had already been done. Within three months of the first heart attack, she had a second one that killed her.

Everyone knows someone who seems to be able to ''break all the rules'' on diet and exercise. But you have to keep in mind that heredity is the major factor in longevity, and, along with environment, a major factor in your susceptibility to disease. However long a person who smokes a pack a day and drinks to excess may live, that person would probably live even longer if he or she followed good health habits.

Taking care of yourself is even more important if diseases such as cancer, heart disease, diabetes, and high cholesterol levels run in your family. If you're genetically predisposed to disease, you need to do everything you can to shift the odds in your favor.

Alcohol Abuse among the Elderly

Alcohol abuse is an all-too-frequent situation among elderly who are lonesome and confused. This is an illness that requires treatment. The first step to a solution is for the individual to recognize that there is a problem. For information in this area, and to learn successful techniques to help yourself, write to Al-Anon National Information Center, 1 Park Avenue, New York, NY, 10016.

Younger people often think, ''It (cancer, a heart attack, or stroke) can't happen to me.'' Well, yes it can. If you've escaped a serious illness so far, remember that the odds are just that much greater that your ''number will come up'' soon. Consider yourself blessed; enhance that blessing by following good health habits. If you've suffered a serious illness, you should know the benefits of avoiding further illness through following good health habits.

In recent years, more people have become health-conscious: walking, jogging or working out at a fitness center; dieting and eating nutritious foods; limiting the intake of drugs and liquor; not smoking and making a conscious effort to get plenty of sleep. In retirement, all of these ''good habits'' should be continued or initiated. You have plenty of time, can set your own schedule and can find partners—your spouse, old friends or new acquaintances at your club or senior center. In most cases, these activities should be conducted under the supervision of a qualified instructor.

Preventing Sickness

Disease prevention is more effective, less expensive, and less inconvenient that disease cures. Here are some basic rules you should keep in mind as you grow older:

- Every older woman should have a mammogram annually to catch the onset of breast cancer. Such care will cut in half the possibility of an operation. Besides, for those over age 65, the bill may be paid by Medicare.

- Diabetes has little to do with blood sugar. A better control is a daily regimen of 30 minutes of brisk calisthenics, walking or swimming.

- One aspirin a day may lessen the chance of a second (not first) heart attack; ask your doctor if this regimen is for you.

- Loss of memory should not be a problem and can be eased. Primarily, this is due to the fact that, as retirees, we no longer need to keep things organized and classified. Since the brain responds to instruction, memorize a poem and declaim it daily or write down what you had for breakfast or what your grandchild told you over the phone.

- Limit your consumption of alcohol to three drinks a day with the amount of mixer double that of the liquor.

- The five things that go wrong with the human body as we age are:

  Wear and tear: those arms, legs, arteries, eyes and ears have been working hard for over 60 years. They can become tired, too.

Loss of reserves: the body can handle a certain amount of abuse but there comes a time when the repairs and comebacks slow and, eventually, fail.

Build-up of debris: (a) the floating objects in the eye which, often, presage glaucoma, can often be eliminated by proper care and nutrition; (b) accumulations of fats in arteries can be reduced by lowering the cholesterol level with better diet and medical help.

Automatic destruction. Since the body was not designed for eternal life, the ability of some systems to make repairs tends to weaken.

Internal police departments become inept or corrupt. Immunizing systems attack elements in the belief that they are invaders, not aiders, or they falter and are no longer able to battle intrusions and infections. For instance, everyone has cancer cells; the problem arises when the body is no longer able to keep them under control.

The prevention: regular meals with grains, fruit and vegetables, lots of fish and chicken and fewer fast food snacks because of the beef fat and french fries.

Keeping Informed

Many hospitals are wooing seniors with special services that are available free, or, more frequently, for a membership fee of $20 a year. Those who are eligible (typically, those drawing Social Security) get free health screening, assistance with Medicare claims, a monthly newsletter, registered-with-name key ring and admission to periodic health care lectures, plus preferred service at hospital admission, with physician referrals, travel and tour planning and counsel on prescriptions.

Pills, Drugs, and Elixirs

Many older people take too many drugs and, with the new Medicare legislation that subsidizes the cost of prescriptions, the situation will get worse. Each year, retirees receive 400 million prescriptions for over 20,000 different types of pills, tablets, powders and liquids.

Many of these do provide temporary relief and some strengthen and lengthen life. However, years of reliance on medication can lead to drug abuse. With seniors, the dangers increase with age because of body changes and the inability of internal systems to clear out drugs promptly and fully.

Here are caveats for all medicines:

- Magical cures, for anything from baldness to cancer, are usually quack nostrums which, at best, are merely expensive wastes of money. At worst, they can be dangerous and debilitating. Miracle drugs and major scientific breakthroughs take years to develop, test, and be approved.

- Keep a list of all medicines you are taking (or have taken) and have this available for your physician and pharmacist.

- With all new prescriptions, ask your physician about possible adverse reactions when taken with alcohol, caffeine, or other drugs.

- Never use any medicine until your physician has approved it.

- Follow the directions on the label, or those given by your physician. Make sure you take the right dose at the right time, under the right conditions. If there are ill effects (such as rash, nausea, or headache), or no improvement, consult your physician immediately.

- Continue taking medicines only as long as prescribed.

- Store medicines in their original container in a cool, dry place.

Guides for Drug Side Effects

There are three new books that explain potential side effects of prescription medications:

50+: The Graedon's People's Pharmacy for Older Adults (Joe and Theresa Graedon, Bantam, $13.95) is a guide to possible reactions to hundreds of medications.

Worst Pills, Best Pills (Dr. Sidney M. Wolfe, Public Citizen Health Research Group, 2000 P St., NW, Suite 700, Washington, DC, 20036, $12) lists 104 pills older adults should not use and safer alternatives.

The Sexual Pharmacy (M. Lawrence Lieberman, New American Library, $18.95) lists drug and food supplements that have general and sexual side effects.

Before you buy over-the-counter medication, try natural alternatives. For example, a brisk walk and a glass of warm milk may be as effective as a tranquilizer or sleeping pill.

- Throw away all old medicines once a year. Most lose potency; some may become harmful.

- On trips, carry an adequate supply. Do not try to have prescriptions refilled while travelling, especially in foreign countries.

Dietary Supplements

One of the most recent food fads is calcium, the element that is so important in building strong bones. Nowadays, calcium is being added to fruit juices, canned foods, and even soft drinks.

Calcium is critical to diet as you grow older. Without sufficient quantities, the body secretes a hormone that causes the available calcium to be taken from the bones. This demineralization results in osteoporosis, a condition where the bones are so porous that they cannot fulfill normal functions, and the individual's head and shoulders round and sag.

The recommended daily minimum intake of calcium is 800 milligrams. Women may require a higher intake. You can obtain this amount of calcium from $2^1/_2$ cups of dairy product, such as milk, yogurt, or cottage cheese. If you're sensitive to dairy products, look for calcium from green leafy vegetables, and dried peas and beans.

CHOOSING A PHYSICIAN

When you move to a new location, one of the first things to do is to find a doctor in whom you have confidence. You should not embark on a new exercise or dietary routine without consulting your physician. A physician will be able to let you know if you suffer from some silent ailment that could be exacerbated by the new routine.

TABLE 6-1   Calcium Content in Various Foods

Food and Serving	Calcium (Mg)
Skim milk, 8 oz.	300
Yogurt, skim milk, 8 oz.	452
Swiss cheese, 2 oz.*	548
Cheddar cheese, 2 oz.*	412
Sardines, 4 oz.	494
Salmon, 4 oz.	365
Blackstrap molasses, 1 tbsp.	137
Spinach, 8 oz., cooked	167
Collards, 8 oz., cooked	220
Figs, 5 dried	126
Raisins, 8 oz.	102
Beet greens, 8 oz., cooked	144
Kale, 8 oz., cooked	206
Almonds, raw, 8 oz.	332
Chick peas, dry, 8 oz.	300
Tofu (soy bean curds), 3½ oz.	128
Mustard greens, 8 oz., cooked	284

* Both of these cheeses are high in fat and cholesterol and are not recommended as sources of dietary calcium.

SOURCE: *LifeSpan Plus,* Miller, Miller, and Miller, Macmillan Publishing Co.

Having a primary care physician can save money. Primary care physicians are cheaper than specialists. When you need a specialist, your physician can refer you to the right specialist for you. Your physician will also maintain your complete medical history; this can avoid expensive tests down the road.

When you move, ask your current physician for a referral. You can also get names from the local medical society, friends, medical schools, and hospitals. Look for someone who is familiar with senior citizens and is on the staff of at least one nearby hospital.

Once you have put together a list of potential physicians, start with the physician whose office is conveniently located, preferably along a bus line (you may not always be able to drive). Establish contact by phone. Give the nurse an idea of your needs, and ask whether you are the type of patient this physician treats. Look for doctors who will accept payments from Medicare (or, if you are a recipient, Medicaid).

If there's interest on both sides, ask for the doctor to call you so you can explain your special ailments and needs. At this time, discuss the details of fees, methods of payments, and availability of specialists. These days, with so many group practices, you may be referred to another partner. The competent, concerned physician will be honest and try to do what's best for you.

If you make a choice, arrange an appointment and go early so you can check the office for cleanliness, attitude of the staff, and types of patients in the waiting room. Then, judge the physician. If he or she is disorganized, or speaks in a language which you find hard to understand, say thanks, pay the bill, and move on.

Once you settle on a physician, avoid changing physicians for at least six months unless you are very unhappy. If you decide to switch physicians, explain the reasons for your dissatisfaction and ask for the names of colleagues who may be better able to provide the care you seek. Remember that you have responsibilities as a patient to be on time for your appointments, to follow instructions, to keep your physician informed of any significant changes, and to pay your bills.

Health Maintenance Organizations

Health Maintenance Organizations (HMOs) are the fastest growing medical care providers. If you join this type of health care service, you will automatically have a physician, either by assignment or by choice.

With an HMO, the individual (alone or in a group) pays a monthly or annual premium in return for almost total health care service, including visits to the physician, hospital stays, operations and, in some cases, drugs, eyeglasses, foot care, etc. To receive such benefits, the enrollee must go to designated health centers and, usually, deal only with HMO-paid physicians and staff.

Enrollment is usually through a group, but it is also possible for an individual to sign up at an annual cost of about $900 per individual and $2,500 for a family of four.

The HMO concept started on the West Coast some years ago. There were many failures in the early years. Increasingly, HMOs today are managed in cooperation with insurance companies. In some areas, the insurance carrier also handles Medicare so payments are coordinated.

For information on selecting an HMO, see page 178.

EXERCISE

There's a saying that ''you won't lose it if you use it.'' That saying applies to exercising your body. If you exercise your heart and lungs, you'll keep them (and yourself) young.

Exercise offers you these benefits:

Aid digestion and elimination, improve circulation

Strengthen and tone muscles of the abdomen, back, legs and feet

Repair and improve aging body, increase flexibility

Reduce risk of cardiovascular disease

Reverse slowing of reflexes

Lower blood fats and blood pressure

Burn calories to help control weight

Strengthen heart and lungs and increase oxygen intake

Increase energy and resistance to fatigue

Enhance ability to dissolve blood clots

Help to cope with anxiety, depression and stress

Help to relax and to sleep better

SOURCE: *The Senior Citizen Handbook*. Marjorie Stokell and Bonnie Kennedy, Prentice-Hall, Englewood, N.J.

TABLE 6-2   How Exercise Burns Up Calories

Activity	Per Hour
Walking outdoors	366
Jogging	1020
Swimming	725
Golf (if you walk)	330
Bicycling	480
Bowling	485
Tennis	420
Dancing	240
Ping-Pong	290
Household Chores	120

SOURCE: *The Lighter Side of Life*, Milton M. Lieberthal.

The right kind of continued exercise can help you to be a more enjoyable companion, to feel better and to live longer. But there must be common sense and moderation! Let's take physical exercise as an example. Your goal should be total body fitness within the limits of your strength and desire. Establish a program that is regular and maintained, and that will give you a feeling of challenge and satisfaction. Be flexible: for example, you should plan relatively more stressful activity, such as tennis singles, in your early retirement years. Plan on doubles when your agility and endurance lessens. Walking or swimming are good exercises that allow you to be in control. So are aerobic or stretching exercises, but these are enjoyed better with a group.

When exercising, remember that your body's ability to recover from injuries declines as you age. Listen to your body: give aching muscles and joints the rest they need.

It's difficult to get started in an exercise routine. But it's your body, and your life. Schedule time in your day for exercise. Do what you can. Don't set too-high standards for yourself. In a few weeks, it will become enjoyable, and you'll find yourself looking forward to your activity periods.

DIET

Your life can be lengthened by a proper diet. You should consult with your physician to determine what sort of diet is right for you. Most Americans consume a diet

TABLE 6-3   Calculating Fat in Foods

According to Surgeon General Everett C. Koop, Americans should reduce the fat in their diets to 30% of the calories consumed. To estimate your intake, use this formula:

X = Grams of fat × 9
Y = X divided by total calories of serving
P = Y × 100

P equals the percentage of fat in the food consumed. For example, if a single serving contains 300 calories and 10 grams of fat,

10 grams × 9 = 90
90 divided by 300 = 0.3
0.3 times 100 = 30

30% of the calories is fat. Most package foods list calories and fat content on the label or container.

that is too high in animal and saturated fats. You probably consume too much red meat, as well. The fact is, the dairy, beef, and pork lobbies have brainwashed the national health establishment into recommending inclusion of healthy portions of their products into the recommended daily diet of Americans, when the health benefits of these products can be debated.

Easy Ways to Cut Out Fat

Studies indicate that you can lose weight effectively without calorie counting (and without feeling hungry) if you switch to a low-fat diet.

- Snack on popcorn. It's tasty, high in fiber, good for your gums and your digestion, and low in calories and fat. Pop it in a hot-air popper, and avoid using oils, butter, or margarine.
- Switch from regular milk. If you drink two glasses of milk a day, and switch to skim or low-fat milk, you could lose 10 pounds a year.
- Substitute fruit, sorbet, angel food cake, low-fat frozen yogurt or fruit ices for cake, ice cream, and cookies.
- Avoid cheese, potato and macaroni salads, bacon bits, diced ham, croutons, and creamy dressings when at the salad bar.

When Americans think of their diet, usually they think in terms of caloric intake. A few may worry about the level of fat in their diet. Too many don't think at all; they just eat what they like. And diets have gotten a bad name: most people, when they think of a diet, think of it as something to get off. Diets, to them, represent denial of foods they like in amounts they want.

With all of that in mind, I reiterate: see your doctor. Consult with him or her about what you should eat, and in what amounts. If he or she can't tell you what diet to follow, you can be referred to a specialist who will.

You need an expert to formulate a diet because:

- your health and medical history is critical. For example, if you are lactose-intolerant, dairy products aren't a good source of calcium and protein for you. You'll need substitute foods. If you have an existing medical condition (such as high blood pressure or diabetes), that must be taken into account when determining what foods are right for you.

- you can't formulate a diet that takes into account all your health requirements. Almost everyone knows that you need a certain amount of protein,
vitamins, carbohydrates, and that you want to avoid excessive levels of fat,
calories, and sodium (to name three categories). But it may not be as simple
as "taking one from each of the four major food groups"—the standard
advice for generations. As no food is perfect, each can have drawbacks. It
takes an expert to determine which ones are right for you, and to determine
the proper balance.

- the only good diet for you is one you can follow. Let's face it—a book might
be able to recommend a perfectly healthy diet. But if that diet consists of
foods you dislike, or foods that are difficult for you to prepare, you won't
keep that diet. And then what good will it do you? A physician or dietitian can
take into account your circumstances and your favorite foods, and produce a
diet that is enjoyable, convenient, and healthy.

Are Your Eating Habits Changing?

Although you should be careful not to overeat, for many older Americans, losing interest in food is a problem. This can be a product of
decreased senses of smell and taste, medication, digestive problems,
or even the quality of food that you can afford. But the result is the
same: a decreased interest in food.

If this is a problem, try

- planning meals that include your favorite foods
- using herbs or lemon to bring out flavors, especially if on a low-
sodium diet
- new recipes that use your favorite foods
- inviting others to meals; make it an event!

You can liven up foods by adding fruits, cheeses (if your diet allows), fruit juices or wine, nuts, and ketchup, mustard, and other
condiments.

Having said all this, there are some basic rules you should follow. First, avoid
fad diets. Specifically, use liquid protein diets ONLY under a doctor's supervision,
and only as a last resort. Second, avoid overconsumption of "in" foods. These days,

oat bran is the "in" food. But if you eat too much oat bran in addition to your regular diet, you'll consume too many calories and grow fat. And if you give up other foods to eat more oat bran, you may be sacrificing other nutritional benefits.

Be reasonable when consuming vitamins. It's not always true that "if some are good, more are better." Excessive dosages of vitamins can be hazardous, even fatal. The fact is that your body simply will expel vitamins that it doesn't need (provided, of course, that you're not taking them at a level high enough to be dangerous). That makes excessive vitamin taking a waste of money. You may wish try varying levels of different types of vitamins (as long as you stay below toxic levels), and if you feel better, so much the better. But basically, you'll be best off if you stay within the official guidelines.

TABLE 6-4   Recommended Daily Dietary Allowances for Retirees

	Men	*Women*	*Dangerous level*
Calories	2400	1700	na
Protein	65g	55g	na
Vitamin A	5000 I.U.	5000 I.U.	50,000 I.U.
Vitamin E	30 I.U.	25 I.U.	na
Vitamin B6	2.0mg	2.0mg	na
Calcium	0.8g	0.8g	2000mg
Iron	10mg	18mg	100mg
Magnesium	350mg	300mg	3000mg
Niacin	1.7mg	1.5mg	100mg
Riboflavin	1.2mg	1.6mg	na

na = not applicable or none

Source: *LifeSpan Plus*, Miller, Miller, and Miller, Macmillan Publishing Co.

You always want to make sure that you're not consuming too many calories. Again, your doctor or dietitian can help you determine what calorie level is right for you. If you follow an active lifestyle, limiting your calorie intake to the level of someone who stays inside all day could be harmful. If you're feeling hungry, you can avoid this without consuming more calories each day by eating more meals, with smaller portions each meal. Another way that works for many is to engage in exercise precisely when you feel like "raiding the refrigerator"; many times, hunger is just a sign that you're bored.

Whether you are dealing with exercise or lifestyle or food, get as much information and counsel as you can from your library, local meetings and authoritative

TABLE 6-5   Ideal Weights for Older Adults

| Height | Women | | | Men | | |
Ft. In.	Small	Medium	Large	Small	Medium	Large
5 0	104-115	113-126	122-137			
5 2	108-121	118-132	128-143	128-134	131-141	138-150
5 4	114-127	124-138	134-151	132-138	135-145	142-156
5 6	120-133	130-144	140-159	136-142	139-151	146-164
5 8	126-139	136-150	146-167	140-148	145-157	152-172
5 10	132-145	142-156	152-173	144-154	151-163	158-180
6 0	138-151	148-162	158-179	149-160	157-170	164-188
6 2				155-168	164-178	172-197

Source: Metropolitan Life Insurance Co.

publications. Giant Food Inc., in conjunction with the National Cancer Institute, publishes a guide called "Eat for Health" that lists fiber, fat/cholesterol, calories, sodium, and fat ratio for various foods by brand name. It's sold for a modest fee; write Giant Foods, Consumer Affairs Dept., Box 1804, Washington, DC, 20013.

- Be skeptical of articles in newspapers and magazines with headlines that promise instant cures and health improvement. There are few worthwhile pills, tonics, or foods that are not prescribed by your doctor.

- Get educated: read authoritative books recommended by your physician, not the highly promoted How To's of Rasputin-eyed healers and glib pitchpersons turned medical experts. Attend lectures and seminars sponsored by local hospitals, aging groups and medical associations.

MAINTAINING YOUR SEXUAL HEALTH

People are physically capable of sexual activity up until death, no matter how old you are. What MAY occur is that having sex may become more difficult as you become more infirm. The solution? Keep your health (including your sexual health) up!

Sex (as you've probably figured out by now) is good, and good for you. As Mae West said, "When it's bad it's good, and when it's good, its even better!" And there's no reason why it can't get better as you grow older—you have more time, you don't have to worry about pregnancy, you can be more uninhibited (the kids aren't likely to interrupt), men are able to last longer, and women are often more able to reach orgasm.

If you're having problems participating in, or enjoying, sex, a physical illness or a psychological ailment is probably to blame. See your doctor for help. If you're just recovering from an ailment, take it slow—but don't feel that your sexual life has ended. For example, if you're recovering from heart trouble, use positions where your partner does most of the moving. NEVER be embarrassed to discuss your capacity for sexual activity with your physician.

Common ailments associated with aging need not interfere with sexual activity. Many women have difficulty with lubrication after menopause, but your gynecologist can probably recommend estrogen therapy, creams, and other lubricants. Similarly, men with prostate conditions may be able to obtain relief through prescriptions and other forms of treatment. (But never let a prostate condition go unattended; in extreme cases, castration is the treatment for prostate cancer.)

Once you and your partner have retired, you may find that little things that didn't create a problem when you were apart for most of the day can be major obstacles to intimacy now that you're together so much. These can be manifested in sexual dysfunction. Follow these sexual do's and don'ts:

DO engage in different positions to find those that are both comfortable and mutually satisfying.

DON'T be afraid to discuss sex with your partner. If you're not enjoying it, say so. If you'd like your partner to do something that would heighten your enjoyment, say so.

Apart from your faith's views on the subject, DON'T frown on masturbation, if one partner is unable (or uninterested) in engaging in sex. But if you shun your mate sexually, a deeper problem exists that requires counseling and discussion.

DON'T set sexual goals; sex is not goal-oriented. If you or your partner don't reach orgasm, that's OK as long as sex is enjoyable to the both of you.

Apart from the physical enjoyment in sex, it can have important psychological benefits, by enabling you to feel more alive, more vital. In many ways, it's true that you're "as young as you feel." People with healthy appetites for sex, and healthy sex lives, usually don't go around feeling sorry for themselves.

STRESS

If you remember nothing else, remember this: STRESS KILLS. When you're older, however, stress is a bigger threat than ever. Your number one goal in retirement should be to avoid stress wherever possible, and when stress is unavoidable, to minimize it to the utmost.

What is stress? Simply, it's your body's reaction—physically, psychologically, and chemically—to stimuli that make you excited, afraid, depressed, or confused. It's been documented that the death rate rises sharply among people who have experienced a stressful activity during the past two years. For example, one study reveals that the death rate for widowers in the first year after the death of the spouse is ten times that of similar nonwidowers.

What causes stress? Usually, some event that causes your psychological (and physical) status to change significantly. Here are some common events that cause stress:

separation and divorce

moving

being placed in a nursing home

illness or death of a spouse, life partner, child, or other person close to you

having to care for a spouse, life partner, child, or other person close to you

financial difficulty

loss of employment

incapacitating illness

loneliness and boredom

conflicts, particularly conflicts within families

being approached for financial assistance (especially if your first instinct is to decline to extend assistance)

incarceration

any change in your everyday routine

retirement itself

By anticipating stressful situations, you can take steps to avoid the situation or minimize the harm that the stress can cause you. However, these events are only typical stress-causing events. If there are other events that you know cause you stress, plan to deal with those situations and the stress that they create.

WORKSHEET 6-1   Checking Your Stress Level

	Often	*Occasionally*
Do You		
worry about the future?	_____	_____
have trouble falling asleep and getting a real rest?	_____	_____
try to relieve tension with a cigarette, drink, or tranquilizer?	_____	_____
become irritated over little things?	_____	_____
feel tired and lacking in energy?	_____	_____
suffer from headaches or stomach trouble?	_____	_____
feel overwhelmed with too many things to do?	_____	_____
worry that you're under too much stress?	_____	_____
Are You:		
overly concerned about your status in the community, at your club, or with friends?	_____	_____
dissatisfied with your life, or your relationship with your spouse or your family?	_____	_____

Give yourself 2 points for every YES answer you have under ''often'' and 1 point for every YES answer you have under ''occasionally.'' Any YES answer to any item is a warning sign of stress. However, if you have 4 points or more, there is a good chance you are under too much stress. Seek help from your physician or a trained counselor. They may help you change your lifestyle to a less stressful existence.

Minimizing Stress

The key to minimizing stress is to keep your life on as even a keel as possible. Try to become as organized as you can—the more easily you can live your everyday life, the greater the degree to which you can avoid the little things that can ''drive you crazy.'' If you establish a routine, you establish a normalcy to life that you can cling to when stressful events occur.

It's sad to say, but the family may be the source of more stress than any other factor in our lives. Family members can cause stress in any number of ways—when they come to live with you, when they go away, when they're born, when they die, when they need help, and when they won't provide help. Obviously, the answer isn't to divorce yourself from your family. However, if your family relationships are causing problems, maybe you're too close to them (or they're too close to you). If that's the situation, a greater physical separation may be the answer.

Don't be afraid to discuss problems within the family. Everyone must retain respect for other people's lifestyles and property. It's easy to take people for granted; if you feel you're being taken for granted, or taken advantage of, say so.

How to Cope With Stress

Although solving a stressful situation may not be easy to do, the general solution to coping with stress is easy to understand. Stress is caused by something external that has disrupted the desired equilibrium in your life. Therefore, to cope with stress, you want to try to either remove the external circumstance, or else compensate for it as much as possible.

What does all this mean? Simply put, it means don't worry—be happy. If you're worrying about something, recognize first that you are worrying about a problem. (If you're worrying about more than one problem, attack one problem at a time.) Next, plan on how you're going to solve the problem. Isolate what the difficulty is. Focus on different ways to solve the problem. Discuss it with trusted friends and, if appropriate, trained professionals. If you need further information to solve the problem, get the information—from experts, or from people familiar with the situation.

Some problems can't be solved. This doesn't mean they can't be dealt with in a logical, systematic manner. Suppose you've lost your spouse, either through death or divorce. You're filled with sorrow. Your life is in disarray—the things that your spouse used to do for you, you must now do for yourself. The activities you once shared now go unshared; perhaps you've even withdrawn from participating in them altogether.

What to do? First, recognize that what you're feeling is normal, and is itself simply a means with coping with the change in your life that your spouse's departure represents. Next, try to make a list (that's right, write it down) of everything your spouse meant to you, did for you, and shared with you. Then, try to figure out substitutes for what your spouse provided. Mind you, these aren't replacements—individuals are unique, and no one can be replaced by anyone, especially a loved one—but by coping, you can minimize the disruption to your life to the greatest possible degree.

For example, if you and your spouse enjoyed bridge games, try to get another partner. If playing bridge conjures up painful memories, or if your new partner just can't measure up, try taking up another engrossing game, such as chess. If your spouse kept the house straight, and you can't (or won't), get a housekeeper. If your mate kept you from being lonely, become involved in other activities. Perhaps you could help coach a Little League team, or volunteer to counsel pregnant teens. If you enjoyed an active sex life, don't be ashamed to seek outlets for sexual release, includ-

The Ten Amendments for Widows

Virginia Graham's delightful book, *Life After Harry: My Adventures in Widowhood* (Simon and Schuster), contains sound advice on coping with widowhood by a woman who has gone through it. Miss Graham's ten amendments for widows are sound advice on living for widowers too:

1. Yes, there is life after what's-his-name. You don't have to jump into the grave after your husband, You can be a full person on your own.

2. Never settle for a man simply because he's still breathing. You can demand the best in all of your relationships.

3. Don't let the world take advantage of you because you're alone. Beware of scams. If it sounds too good to be true, it's too good to be true.

4. Your children are separate people. Don't make them your life and don't let them make yours.

5. You can be beautiful . . . the face you wake up with in the morning is not necessarily the one you're stuck with for the rest of the day.

6. You can find out again just how much fun life can be as a "merry widow" in the world.

7. When one door closes, another one opens . . . and new opportunities are knocking all the time.

8. You can love living alone . . . and discover the delicious pleasures of a single life.

9. Your senior years can be golden, not brass. You're getting older, but you're also getting better.

10. You never have to feel ashamed to be alone in the world. A table for one can be a grand adventure.

ing masturbation or other partners. Be sure to consult with trained counselors, however, whenever coping with stressful events with a significant emotional component.

Whenever we extend ourselves emotionally, we risk rejection. In the course of everyday life, we're usually prepared for that eventuality, and can deal with it. When people experience rejection in the course with coping with emotional stress, however, they will often misinterpret that rejection as an indication that there is no solace for the grief they feel. You must be prepared for false steps without feeling that these false steps are signs that going on with life is hopeless, and that you can never get over your loss. Suppose you find another bridge partner, and you have a dispute. The answer isn't that your spouse was the only bridge partner for you. Either (a) you were the only bridge partner for your spouse, or (b) your new bridge partner isn't right together with you. The answer isn't to relapse into depression; either get a new partner, or give up bridge and take up a new pastime.

If the stressful event has caused you to feel guilty, your strategy should be to either expiate yourself of the guilt, or to get over it. Marlon Brando once said that guilt is a useless feeling, and he's right. What good does it do to feel guilty? If you know you've done wrong, feeling guilty does nothing to help the injured person feel better. Make it up to that person, and then you can replace your guilty feelings with the satisfaction that you had the integrity to see your faults and correct the harm you had done to another. If you know you've done right, you've done nothing to feel guilty about. So stop it.

The best way to cope with stress is to avoid it wherever possible. It's a fact that others are often the cause of stress, and that stressful situations can occur over and over. If a personality conflict is the cause of stress, discuss it calmly with the other person (no matter who it is). If you cannot discuss it calmly, wait until you can. If the problem is a matter that cannot be discussed calmly, or is incapable of resolution, avoid the other party; if appropriate, seek an attorney to obtain legal relief. Although litigation isn't pleasant and too many Americans are all too willing to sue their neighbors, the fact is that courts exist to resolve disputes. If a neighbor won't return a rake, and insists that the rake isn't yours, take your neighbor to court. Don't just go into his or her garage and try to take it back.

One typical example of stress caused you by another is when someone else wants something from you that you either cannot provide, feel unwilling to provide, or feel uncomfortable providing. Nip the problem in the bud. Explain, politely, that theirs is a request that you cannot satisfy. Express understanding of their circumstances; express sympathy and regret if you feel it (but don't lie). Suggest alternatives that are possible given the other person's circumstances (if a child wants to borrow money, and you know they have a bad credit rating, don't tell them to go to a bank). Make it clear that, failing a radical change in a given circumstance, your decision is final, and that you will not consider a future request. DO NOT justify your decision; this will just lead to arguments over the validity of your justification. If your reasons are valid to you, they are valid for you.

Whenever you have doubts about your course of action, remember this thought—if this stress continues, I could soon be dead, and then I will be unable to help anyone or do anything. But if I alleviate this stress, it is much more likely that I will live to help others at a later time.

Physical activity is one way to alleviate tension resulting from stress. Another is to engage in an engrossing activity. For example, I once owned a miniature slot car set. For relaxation, I would set one car at the highest constant speed possible, and race against that car. It's amazing how much you must focus on that car, to the extent that you block anything else on your mind. A thorough body massage, and a warm bath can also be relaxing. But avoid eating, drinking, or drug abuse, as these can become harmful habits that you use as a crutch to cope with crisis.

If you're a chronic worrier, a recent study indicates that you'll feel better if you plan to worry every day, at the same place and time, for just 30 minutes a day.

See your physician for stress or depression that you cannot adequately alleviate. You may be a candidate for prescription or therapy to alleviate the effects of stress on your health.

MANAGING HEALTH CARE PROBLEMS

For retirees, health problems are different than those of younger people. In general terms, they fall into two categories: *Diseases* that can eventually be fatal such as heart attacks, cancer, diabetes, and Alzheimer's disease; and *recurring problems* such as arthritis, hypertension, hearing or visual impairment—almost all of which can be eased or controlled with proper treatment or lifestyle.

With age, the three things that go wrong with the human body are:

- Wear and tear: the eyes, ears, arms, legs and arteries have been working hard for over 60 years. They can become tired, too.

- Loss of reserves: the body can handle a certain amount of abuse but there comes a time when the repairs slow and, often, fail.

- Build-up of debris such as: (a) the floating objects in the eye—they may presage glaucoma but can usually be eliminated by proper care and better nutrition; (b) accumulation of fats in arteries—these can be reduced by lowering the cholesterol level with better diet and medical help.

Use Home Tests Wisely

Do-it-yourself medical tests should not be used to make self-care medical judgments. They aren't intended to form the basis of a diagnosis. Use them as a warning only; if a test comes up positive, see your doctor for confirmation, and follow the expert advice. And if you're already exhibiting symptoms, don't let a test dissuade you from seeing your doctor.

For almost all afflictions, the best method of prevention and control is proper food: regular meals with grains, fruits, vegetables, lots of fish and chicken and fewer high-cholesterol snacks.

Diseases Faced by the Elderly

Cancer, heart disease, and high blood pressure (also called hypertension), together kill over one million Americans each year. Their impact is disproportionately felt by the elderly. Knowing the warning signs of each, and what to do in a medical emergency might save your life, or that of a loved one.

Cancer. Each year, 400,000 Americans die of cancer. Many need not have died. It's a fact that many of us, faced with a fear that we may have something that will cause our death, will avoid facing the problem. Ironically, though, this inaction only hastens our death. Many cancers have high cure rates when detected in time to allow for effective treatment.

To stay alive longer, you must pay attention to changes in your body. And if you detect changes that could be a sign of something bad, don't hide from that fact. Face it; get medical help immediately. This is especially true for people who have had relatives who have suffered from cancer, as cancer often runs in families.

These symptoms, says the American Cancer Society, are early danger signals that might indicate cancer:

- Unusual bleeding or discharge

- Lump or thickening in the breast or elsewhere

- Sore that refuses to heal

- Change in bowel or bladder habits

- Cough or hoarseness

- Indigestion or difficulty in swallowing

- Change in a wart or mole

Cancer is treated through surgery, radiation therapy and chemotherapy. Don't kid yourself; cancer treatment isn't pleasant. But great strides have been made to reduce the discomfort of radiation therapy and chemotherapy. Furthermore, it beats dying from cancer, which is much more uncomfortable than treatment.

Too many of us don't take the threat of cancer seriously until it occurs. If you doubt this, just think: what if smoking caused AIDS? How many people would still smoke? Fact is, both AIDS and cancer will kill you. The only difference between the two is that there are effective treatments for many forms of cancer. Yet, relative to the number of people who actually contract AIDS, many more Americans have adopted safe sex practices than have adopted cancer-safe lifestyles. Just like seeing one AIDS victim is enough to get anyone to practice safe sex, visiting a few victims of cancer in its advanced stages should be enough to get any intelligent adult to avoid living lifestyles that are at risk for cancer.

Here are steps you can take to reduce your risk of cancer:

- Reduce and eliminate cigarette smoking

- Perform breast self-exams monthly and have a mammograph annually

- Have a pap test yearly

- Avoid excessive exposure to the sun

- Have a proctoscopic exam every few years

- Have a regular physical exam.

There are many cancer-causing agents in our environment. Avoiding them may involve moving to another table or moving to another state, but inaction could make you just another victim. Here are cancer trouble spots to avoid:

- cigarette smoke

- asbestos dust

- emissions and discharges from chemical plants, factories, plastics manufacturers, gasoline stations, and automobiles

- nitrates and nitrites in food preservatives (particularly in pork products such as ham, cold cuts, and bacon)

What Are the Chances That Smoking Will Kill You?

According to the Surgeon General, every year, smoking causes

- 115,000 people to die from heart disease

- 106,000 people to die from lung cancer

- 57,000 people to die from chronic lung disease

- 31,600 people to die from other cancers

- 26,500 people to die from stroke

If you smoke, you're about 20 times more likely to die from lung cancer, and about 4 to 5 times more likely to die of stroke, than non-smokers.

- tap water that you suspect may be contaminated with dioxin, polychlorinated biphenyls (PCBs), ethylene dichloride (EDC)

Heart Disease. Heart disease is still the number one cause of death among Americans. A heart attack has been described by victims as having a "refrigerator drop on your chest." Apart from the pain that a heart attack causes, the panic is fearsome: debilitating diseases allow you time to adjust to the prospect of death, but a heart attack can kill you before you know you're going to die.

Common signs of a heart attack include:

- Severe chest pain

- Shortness of breath

- Pain radiating from your chest, to your arm, back, or jaw.

- Unusual or irregular heartbeat

- Loss of consciousness

If you (or someone you know) exhibits one of these signs, seek medical help immediately. You may not be suffering from a heart attack; you may be suffering from an anxiety attack, or another ailment. Many ailments mock the symptoms of heart disease. Better to be mocked as a hypochondriac than mourned as a victim.

If someone you know may be suffering a heart attack, get the person to lie down. Try to keep them calm: extreme fear can make the effects of the heart attack even worse. If you know CPR, apply it. Get the victim to cough in a regular pattern until help arrives. Call for emergency aid as soon as possible. People suffering heart attacks should NOT be driven to a hospital emergency room unless specifically instructed to do so by medical authorities, and should never drive themselves.

Get help even if the signs "go away." A heart attack will often repeat itself. And don't listen to suspected victims who insist that "everything's okay." When you see your doctor, be sure to tell him or her everything that could be relevant, including stressful events that have occurred over the past year, such as death, divorce, or economic hardship.

The incidence of heart disease among middle-aged Americans is declining. Heart disease is a disease that you can beat, if you only commit yourself to a rational lifestyle.

- Minimize your intake of salt

- Keep your weight down

- Keep your cholesterol level down by avoiding saturated fats such as butter and lard, and minimizing your consumption of beef, pork, eggs, shellfish, milk, and cheese

- Don't smoke

- Engage in exercise (after consultation with your physician), preferably extended aerobic exercise that exercises your heart and lungs

- Make sure your blood pressure is controlled

- Try to avoid smoke and car exhaust

Managing a High Cholesterol Level

Nowadays, almost every kind of food is available in a low-cholesterol or no-cholesterol variety (even chocolate-chip cookies and potato chips). When reading the labels, though, avoid oils high in saturated fats (such as coconut and palm oils) that increase blood cholesterol. Look for (and use in frying) unsaturated oils such as corn and canola oil. Olive oil is 100 percent fat, but can lower the level of harmful cholesterol in your diet, so if you can afford the fat and calories, it's an alternative.

TABLE 6-6   Cholesterol, Saturated Fat, and Calories In Different Foods

Food	CSI	CAL
Fish, poultry, red meats (3.5 oz)		
Whitefish (snapper, perch, sole, cod, halibut), shellfish (clams, oysters, scallops) water-packed tuna	4	91
Salmon	5	149
Shellfish (shrimp, crab, lobster)	6	104
Poultry, no skin	6	171
Beef, pork, and lamb:		
10% fat (ground sirloin, flank steak)	9	214
15% fat (ground round)	10	258
20% fat (ground chuck, pot roasts)	13	286
30% fat (ground beef, pork, and lamb-steaks, ribs, pork and lamb chops, roasts)	18	381
Cheeses (3.5 oz)		
2% fat cheeses (low-fat cottage cheese, pot cheese), tofu (bean curd)	1	98
5-10% fat cheeses (cottage cheese, low-fat cheese slices)	6	139
25-30% fat cheeses*	6	317
11-20% fat cheeses (part skimmed milk)	12	256
32-38% fat cheeses (gruyere, cheddar, cream cheese)	26	386
Eggs		
Whites (3)		51
Egg substitute (equivalent to 2 eggs)	1	91
Whole (2)	29	163
Fats (¹/₄ cup, 4 tablespoons)		
Peanut butter	5	353
Most vegetable oils	8	530
Mayonnaise	10	431
Soft vegetable margarines	10	432
Hard stick margarines	15	432
Soft shortenings	16	530
Bacon grease	23	541
Very hydrogenated shortenings	27	530
Butter	37	530
Coconut oil, palm oil, cocoa butter (chocolate)	47	530
Frozen desserts (1 cup)		
Water ices, sorbet	0	245
Frozen yogurt, low fat	2	144
Sherbert	2	218

TABLE 6-6   Cholesterol, Saturated Fat, and Calories In Different Foods (*cont.*)

Food	CSI	CAL
Frozen yogurt‡	4	155
Ice milk	6	214
Ice cream	13	272
Rich ice cream	18	349
Specialty ice cream, 22% fat	34	684
Milk products (1 cup)		
Skimmed milk (0-1% fat) or skimmed milk yogurt	‹1	88
1% milk, buttermilk	2	115
2% milk or plain low-fat yogurt	4	144
Whole milk (3-5% fat) or whole milk yogurt	7	159
Sour cream	37	468
Imitation sour cream	43	499

*Cheeses made with skimmed milk and vegetable oils.

‡Made with added cream.

Note: The CSI (cholesterol/saturated fat index) was designed to help assess the potential for elevated blood cholesterol levels and atherosclerosis in foods. A low CSI is desirable.

Table reprinted with permission from The Lancet Ltd., May 31, 1986. *The Cholesterol/Saturated Fat Index: An Indication of the Hypercholesterolaemic and Atherogenic Potential of Food.* Connor, Sonja I. et al. Oregon Health Sciences University.

What are the chances that moderating your lifestyle will help you avoid heart disease? High cholesterol levels double your risk of heart disease. Other heart no-no's (that is, too much salt, excessive weight, smoking) can double, triple, or quadruple your risk. In fact, breaking three of the rules on page 146 makes you an ODDS-ON candidate for a heart attack.

Stroke, Embolism, and High Blood Pressure. A stroke is when a blood vessel to your brain is blocked or ruptures. Brain cells fed by that blood vessel die, causing anything from slurred speech to paralysis to death.

These are signs of the onset of a stroke:

- severe headaches, especially above the eyebrow, or in the base of the skull

- vision disorders

- paralysis

- vomiting

- disorientation

- coma

If you suspect that you (or someone around you) may be suffering a stroke, get emergency medical aid immediately.

As strokes are caused by blood vessel blockages and breakages, to avoid a stroke you want to keep your blood vessels as uncongested as possible (to avoid blockages) and your blood pressure under control (to reduce stress that could cause ruptures). The regimen you use to avoid heart disease (outlined above) will also help you avoid stroke. Other things you can do to lower your blood pressure are:

- avoid caffeine

- avoid loud noises and stressful situations

- eat onions and garlic, which contain hormones called prostaglandins. Prostaglandins are effective in treating high blood pressure (HBP), as well as asthma, peptic ulcers, heart attacks, and glaucoma.

TABLE 6-7   Caffeine Level In Different Foods and Beverages

Food or Product	Caffeine (in Milligrams)
Coffee, drip or percolator, 8 oz.	85-150 + (depending on strength)
Coffee, instant, 8 oz.	60-100 (depending on strength)
Tea, regular, 8 oz.	28-60 (depending on strength)
Coca-Cola, 12-oz. can	64
Tab, 8 oz.	49
Pepsi, 8 oz.	43
Cocoa/hot chocolate, 8 oz.	10
ANACIN, 1 pill	32
EMPIRIN, 1 pill	32
EXCEDRIN, 1 pill	65 (Excedrin PM has none)
MIDOL, 1 pill	32.4
Cold remedies, 1 pill	Most have caffeine as one of the ingredients

SOURCE: *LifeSpan Plus*, Miller, Miller, and Miller, Macmillan Publishing Co.

TABLE 6-8   High Fat/Low Fat Menus

HIGH FAT MENU
1800 Calories
20% protein, 27% Carbohydrate, 53% Fat
(CSI* = 90)

	Cal	*Chol (mg)*	*Total Fat (gm)*	*Sat Fat (gm)*
Breakfast				
1 orange	80	0	0	0
cheese omelet:				
1 egg	80	250	6	2
1 oz cheddar cheese	100	30	8	6
2 strips bacon	90	10	10	5
1 white toast	70	0	0	0
2 tsp butter	70	25	8	4
Lunch				
hamburger:				
3 oz patty	240	80	20	9
1 bun	140	0	0	0
mustard	0	0	0	0
lettuce/tomato	10	0	0	0
20 french fries	220	10	10	2
1/2 cup coleslaw	60	4	4	0
1 chocolate chip cookie	70	6	5	1
Supper				
4 oz sirloin steak, fat-trimmed	280	100	16	15
1 sm baked potato	70	0	0	0
+ 1 Tbsp butter	100	35	12	6
+ 1 Tbsp sour cream	30	5	3	3
1/2 cup broccoli	25	0	0	0
+ 2 Tbsp cheese sauce	65	65	5	5
Totals	1800	620	107	58

LOW FAT MENU
1800 Calories
25% protein, 57% Carbohydrate, 18% Fat
(CSI* = 17)

	Cal	Chol (mg)	Total Fat (gm)	Sat Fat (gm)
Breakfast				
8 oz orange juice	80	0	0	0
1 banana	80	0	0	0
1 cup bran flakes	140	0	0	0
1 cup skim milk	80	0	0	0
2 wholewheat toast	140	5	0	0
1 oz part-skim ricotta cheese	60	10	3	2
Lunch				
tuna sandwich:				
1/2 cup tuna in water	120	50	1	0
1 Tbsp diet mayonnaise	50	5	5	1
2 wholewheat bread	140	0	0	0
lettuce/tomato	10	0	0	0
carrot/celery sticks	25	0	0	0
1 large apple	100	0	0	0
1 pc angel food cake	110	0	0	0
1 cup skim milk	80	5	0	0
Supper				
4 oz chicken breast (baked w/o skin)	200	80	6	2
1 lg baked potato	140	0	0	0
+ 1 Tbsp diet margarine	50	0	6	0
+ 1 Tbsp parmesan cheese	25	8	2	2
+ 2 Tbsp non-fat yogurt	10	0	0	0
+ chives	0	0	0	0
1/2 cup broccoli	25	0	0	0
tossed salad	25	0	0	0
+ 1 Tbsp ranch dressing	30	0	5	2
1 cup fruit salad	80	0	0	0
Totals	1800	163	28	9

*CSI adapted with permission from Oregon Health Sciences University Portland, Or. 1985

CAL = calories; mg = milligrams; CHOL = cholesterol; gm = grams; SAT = saturated

SOURCE: Georgia Kostas, MPH, RD, ''Cholesterol,'' *Nutrition Tips* series, Cooper Clinic Nutrition Program, Dallas, TX. © 1986. Printed by permission.

An embolism occurs when a blood clot lodges in the pulmonary artery in the lung. An embolism can kill quickly, so summoning emergency aid when one is suspected is vital.

Signs of an embolism include:

- shortness of breath

- coughing up blood

- pain in the leg

- fever

- irregular pulse

Twenty percent of all Americans suffer from high blood pressure. HBP can cause death from heart attack, stroke, and kidney failure. Women and blacks are particularly at risk.

Nearly half of those who suffer from HBP are unaware of their condition. It's essential that you monitor your blood pressure regularly. If your blood pressure is greater than 140 (systolic) over 85 (diastolic), you should be concerned about your blood pressure level. Make sure that your doctor knows about any family history of high blood pressure.

If you suffer from HBP, follow your doctor's advice. That includes cutting your intake of sodium (to 1,000-2,000mg per day), and taking your medication regularly. Blood pressure medication can have side effects: it can affect your mood, your sexual appetite, your ability to maintain an erection, to name just three. But whatever the side effect, let your physician know about it. Often, these side effects can be avoided through changes in dosage, or other medications.

TABLE 6-9   Sodium Content of Different Foods and Beverages

Food, Serving	Sodium (in Milligrams)	Food, Serving	Sodium (in Milligrams)
Alka Seltzer	521	Eggs, 2 poached	122
Apple, 1 raw	2	Fast-food cheeseburger	535-1435
Apple pie, 1 slice	482	Fish	
Bacon, 4 oz. (sliced)	771	Mackerel, fresh, 8 oz.	110-320
Bacon, Canadian, 4 oz.	2145	Salmon, fresh, 8 oz.	108
Bread, commercial		Salmon, canned sockeye, 8 oz.	1148
(white or whole wheat), per		Tuna, canned in oil, 8 oz.	1733
slice	117-177	Frozen TV dinners	680-2500:
Broccoli, 8 oz. (cooked)	16		avg. 1000
Bromo Seltzer	717	Ham, cured, 8 oz.	1700-2500
Canned soups, 8 oz.	814-1808	Milk, whole, 8 oz.	120
Cantaloupe, 1/4	12	skim, 8 oz.	126
Carrots, 8 oz.	50	Peanuts, salted, 8 oz.	600-980
Cheese		Peas, fresh, 8 oz.	2-3
Cheddar, 2 oz.	354-380	canned, 8 oz.	400-700
Cottage, 8 oz.	680-900	Pickle, dill or sour, 1 med-large	900-1400
Natural Gruyère or Swiss,		Pizza, 1 slice with cheese	450
2 oz.	148-180	Pretzel, 1	100-260
Processed American, 2 oz.	480-800	Raisins, 8 oz.	17-25
Processed pasteurized Swiss,		Sal Hepatica	1000
2 oz.	762-776	Salt, 1 tsp. (5.5 gm)	2132
Cherries, raw, 8 oz.	1-2	Sauerkraut, canned, 8 oz.	1700
Chicken breast, 8 oz.	188	Sirloin steak, 8 oz.	125
Corn, 1 ear fresh (cooked)	(trace)	Soy sauce, 1 tbsp.	1319
Corn, canned cream-style, 8 oz.	604-670	Turkey, light meat, 8 oz.	186
Cornflakes, 8 oz.	251	Yogurt, 8 oz.	105

SOURCE: *LifeSpan Plus*, Miller, Miller, and Miller, Macmillan Publishing Co.

Recent studies indicate that up to 40 percent of those who suffer from HBP can be treated through diet modification, not costly drugs. Drugs can cost $300 to $1,000 a year, and have undesired side effects, so ask your doctor if a low-sodium diet is for you.

Recurring Problems

Some ailments are particularly associated with aging. Chief among these are arthritis, diabetes, menopause, and prostate trouble. Menopause and prostate trouble, in particular, occur in a person's fifth and sixth decades. Although not necessarily deadly, knowing about these maladies can make their onset less uncomfortable and avoid the incapacitating effects that can occur if these problems go untreated.

Arthritis. *Arthritis* is an umbrella term used for hundreds of different types of rheumatic disease, including gout, osteoarthritis, and rheumatoid arthritis. The usual symptoms are pain, stiffness and inflation of joints: knees, hands, shoulders and lower back.

If you show signs of arthritis, you should obtain medical help. Some forms of arthritis, left untreated, can cripple. There are no cures but there can be effective treatments such as aspirin, medicinal ointments and heat. There is no scientific evidence that the irritation is eased by special diets, exotic foods or vitamins, but many folks praise the efficacy of such treatments.

Best remedies are rest, relaxation, proper weight and a common-sense diet with few desserts and pastries. The impact of most highly advertised drugs and creams is more mental than physical. Grin and bear it and be glad it's not worse.

Diabetes. *Diabetes* is a disease in which your body fails to make proper use of certain foods. It is caused either by too little insulin or by a defect in the action of insulin (a hormone produced by the pancreas).

Signs of diabetes include:

- excessive thirst

- frequent urination

- fatigue

- slow healing

- skin rashes

- sweating

- impotence in men

- itching around the genitalia in women

Diabetes develops frequently in older individuals who are overweight, so keeping your weight down is a must. The consequences of diabetes are serious; they can include gangrene, blindness, and even coma and death.

There is no total cure but it can be controlled with proper care:

- Diet: Half of all cases of adult-onset diabetes can be controlled through a diet high in fiber (such as fruits, vegetables, and beans) and complex carbohydrates (whole grain and brown rice). The diet should also be low in refined sugars, carbohydrates such as white bread and pastries, fat, and animal protein. The American Diabetes Association (2 Park Avenue, New York, NY, 10016) will send you, upon request, daily menus that conform to these dietary conditions.

TABLE 6-10 Fiber Content of Different Foods and Beverages

Food Serving	Fiber Content (Grams)
White bread, 2 slices	trace
Whole wheat bread, 2 slices	4.8
White rice, cooked 8 oz.	0.4
Brown rice, cooked 8 oz.	2.2
Apple	3.1
Cherries, 15	1.2
Strawberries, 8 oz.	5.2
Banana	1.8
Grapefruit	5.2
Orange	1.8
Lentils, cooked 8 oz.	8.0
Carrots, one large	3.7
Pear	2.8
Meat, cheese, eggs, milk	none

SOURCE: *LifeSpan Plus*, Miller, Miller, and Miller, Macmillan, Inc.

- Medication: Insulin may be taken through injection. However, you may be able to use oral alternatives that are available. And a special high-pressure air gun has been developed that allows insulin injection without breaking the skin. Whatever is taken, be sure to take only the proper amount. Persons taking oral hypoglycemic agents should avoid alcohol and over-the-counter cold and headache remedies unless approved by their physician.

- Exercise: A daily regimen of 30 minutes of brisk calisthenics, walking or swimming will burn up sugar and reduce the amount of insulin that you need. If you are a diabetic, keep sugar or candy on hand in case of an attack of insulin shock.

Menopause. Menopause generally occurs between the ages of 40 and 55. Menopause delayed beyond age 55 may be a sign of an increased risk of cancer. Although menopause sometimes occurs with no symptoms, signs of menopause usually include:

- Hot flushes and sweating

- Tingling sensations in various parts of the body

- Headache

- Fatigue

- Upset stomach

- Nervousness or depression

- Changes in the external genitalia and pubic hair

- Changes in the elasticity of the vagina

Extreme discomfort in menopause can be treated by sedatives, antidepressive medication, and estrogen therapy. Estrogen therapy should be carefully monitored, because it can cause cancer. Women experiencing painful intercourse after menopause can benefit from estrogen therapy. However, lubricants such as K-Y jelly may be an alternative in all but the most severe cases.

Prostate. The prostate gland is a common source of illness in older men. One out of three men over 50, and one out of two men over 60, will suffer from an enlarged prostate.

The three most common prostate ailments are enlarged prostate, prostatitis, and cancer of the prostate. Prostatitis is an inflammation of the prostate. An enlarged prostate is uncomfortable, but not life-threatening. Cancer of the prostate, however, can be fatal if left untreated, and the warning signs for cancer of the prostate are the same as those for an enlarged prostate.

Here are the warning signs of prostate trouble:

- Unsatisfying urination

- Weak or slow urination

- Blood in the urine

- Pain in the bladder area

- Discomfort upon sitting

- Painful ejaculation

- Impotence

- Low back pain

Prostate ailments should be treated immediately. They can develop into even worse ailments. Treatment for prostate cancer, depending on the stage of progression, can include surgical removal of the prostate, surgical removal of the testes, administration of estrogen (female hormone), and radiation treatment. One new non-surgical form of treatment (currently being tested by the West Contra Costa Urological Surgical Group, San Pablo, CA) is balloon dilation, which cuts the 3-12 week recovery period associated with surgery to a few days.

Eye Care. This is an often-neglected area because too many seniors assume that their eyesight declines with age and that treatments and operations are costly and seldom successful. The truth is that almost all eye conditions can be successfully treated if they are diagnosed promptly.

To avoid confusion, let's define the professionals who can help:

- Ophthalmologist: an M.D. qualified to treat and operate on eyes and prescribe lenses.

- Optometrist: examines eyes, sells and fits glasses but cannot treat diseases of the eye.

- Optician: sells and fits glasses, usually by a prescription from an ophthalmologist.

These are the most frequent types of eye problems of the elderly:

Glaucoma: a disease of the eye that damages the optical disk and can lead to loss of vision. In the early stages, there are no symptoms, but the ophthalmologist can detect its onset by measuring the pressure within the eyeball: a quick, painless process. Eyedrops can be helpful but they must be used with care so a single senior should arrange for assistance with, or supervision of, this treatment.

Macular Degeneration: affects that part of the eye that receives and analyzes light from the center of the visual field. Usually, it can be treated with lasers and does not lead to blindness. The victim can read with a high-power magnifying glass and large-type publications.

Cataracts: form slowly when the protein molecules in the lens degenerate causing the lens to become cloudy and, eventually, block the passage of light to the retina. The surgery is quick and 95% successful. A tiny needle is inserted into the eye to clean out degenerated protein and a plastic lens may be inserted to replace the diseased one.

With age, eyes falter, become irritated more easily, and may require more frequent rest. Vision may continue to be good or may need to be supplemented with prescription glasses. If you suffer from occasional periods of blurring, seeing halos or moving black spots, see your doctor. These can be eased with medicine, plenty of rest and good reading habits: read by bright, but not glaring, light.

For special service or check-up, call the National Eye Care Project, sponsored by the 7,000 members of the American Academy of Ophthalmology, at 1-800-222-EYES. These physicians will check anyone over age 65 not currently under the care of a professional or not examined in the past three years. The checkup is free. The costs of glasses, prescriptions and medical or hospital treatments must be paid for, but, in most cases, will be covered by Medicare or Medigap insurance.

For further information: The National Society to Prevent Blindness, 79 Madison Avenue, New York, NY 10016, or The American Foundation for the Blind, 15 West 16th Street, New York, NY 10011.

Mental Health. Without the traditional routines of a job and community involvement, many retirees face few challenges, become upset and, often, depressed. These down periods are hastened by ill health, worry and stress. One way to tackle such situations is to recognize the potential problem and stay ahead of trouble by establishing a different focus. For example, if your day starts out badly, alter your routine to avoid depression. Or seek help from your minister or professional counseling; you'll find a welcomed emotional outlet.

Here are some areas of mental concern and ways to cope:

Problem	**Solution**
Feeling guilty over past actions	Talk with a friend or counselor
Unhappy relationship with relatives	To a friend of both, talk over the misunderstandings and pressures. You'll feel better and, later, may be able to establish a more direct discussion
Feeling lonesome	Force yourself to attend church, AARP meetings, senior center
Nobody loves me	Go to your house of worship, pray for help and buy a pet.
Fearful of the future	Write down specific areas of concern (money, health or family), list the details of each situation. A week later, review each commentary. If you do not feel relieved, consult a counselor
Afraid of robbery or physical harm	Ask the police to check your home and make recommendations on security; then, buy a barking dog.
I'm confused	At night, write down the schedule for tomorrow on an hour-by-hour basis; before going to bed, review the day to see how well you met your commitments.

If the depression or disinterest continues for more than two weeks, seek professional advice. You can get recommendations from your physician, pastor and aging agency.

Alzheimer's Disease. One major affliction for the elderly is Alzheimer's disease (often referred to as senile dementia). Two million suffer from it today; by the year 2000, the number of sufferers is projected to increase to 3.8 million. There's little hope of recovery until some treatment or cure is discovered.

Signs of Alzheimer's disease include:

- Gradual loss of memory

- Disorientation

- Severe mood swings

- Growing malaise

Alzheimer's disease is not the inevitable result of old age. Its causes aren't fully understood (although chromosome loss or genetic damage is a suspect), but a recent study indicates that Alzheimer's disease isn't an inevitability of age. It can also be caused by treatable disorders, or by alcohol or drug abuse, or by an adverse chemical reaction. Therefore, the prospect of treatment isn't hopeless. Often, exercise, vitamins or foods may help the victim's condition.

The physical and emotional strain of providing constant attention to Alzheimer's disease victims make caregivers a secondary victim of the disease. New programs offer support and respite, such as senior centers that are open on weekends with professional staff. Groups of Alzheimer's disease families are joining together for comfort, information and, increasingly, research.

If you fear that a member of your family may become a victim of Alzheimer's disease, find out if there is an Alzheimer's support group in your area. If there is none, talk to your local medical association, hospitals and Area Agency on Aging to learn how to set up a local support group.

Hearing Loss. With age, many people experience difficulty in hearing. This occurs when the complicated relay system of the ear is interrupted by one of two types of deafness: (1) *conduction*, caused by damage to some part of the middle ear; (2) *nerve damage* resulting from problems with the inner ear or auditory nerve.

The loss may be due to wax, disease, a severe fall, excessive noise, illness or abnormalities such as otosclerosis, a bony growth that closes the window to the inner ear. Almost all of these difficulties can be eased or eliminated with proper care. The best results come from early treatment by a physician (otologist).

The solution may be as simple as the removal of an accumulation of wax or a small tumor, or as complex as a surgical implant of an electronic device that stimulates the auditory nerve so that it can send messages to the brain.

Hearing aids can be helpful, especially the new designs that are more effective, convenient, attractive and, often, more expensive. To get the best type for your needs (and individuals vary widely), consult a non-profit hearing clinic where each individual can be fitted. In smaller communities, you may have to rely on local retailers whose recommendations are likely to concentrate on the higher-priced models.

Often, the most difficult problem will be to get the individual to seek help. When increasing deafness causes mumbling, confusion, and a personality change, the individual should be pressured to visit a physician, join a local deafness group or find a lip-reading instructor. The senior will be better able to cope, and friends and relatives will feel a lot better, too.

For information: American Speech-Language-Hearing Association, 1081 Rockville Pike, Rockville, MD 20852; Better Hearing Institute, 1430 K Street, NW, Washington, DC 20005, or write for a free copy of *Hearing Aids,* Consumer Information Center, Dept. 582J, Pueblo, CO 81009.

Backache. One of every three older Americans suffers from some sort of severe back pain at some period. This can be the result of lifting the wrong way, slipping on a wet floor, a sudden twist, an unexpected growth or, more likely, personal factors such as obesity, tension, anxiety or depression. With age, the back's shock-absorbing capacity is lowered by 20%.

To prevent back trouble:

(a) exercise, preferably by swimming and walking, or, for greater effectiveness, special techniques to strengthen the back muscles;

(b) lift heavy objects properly by placing the feet close together, bending knees outward and pushing up with your legs;

(c) keep erect: stand with shoulders back and sit in a straight-back chair or, with a recliner, prop up your legs;

(d) do not sit too long in one position. On a long ride by car or plane, stretch every half hour.

Slight back pains can be alleviated with ointments, aspirin, a heating pad or a muscle relaxant and, as a last resort, an operation. If you know of anyone who has gone through this ordeal, you have probably already started being more careful.

Foot Discomfort. This is one of the most frequent complaints of seniors. It may not be just your feet, because many ailments start at the extremities: diabetes as a foot ulcer, arthritis in swollen joints or heart disease in swelling ankles.

When your feet send you a message, pay attention and find out the why. Start with your shoes: avoid pumps, high heels and tight fits. When you buy new ones, wait until after noon because your feet tend to swell during the day. Select those that extend one-half inch beyond the longest toe. Always buy shoes for comfort, not style.

For extra protection, keep your feet warm and dry and wear an extra pair of woolen socks when it's cold. Bathe with warm water, dry thoroughly, rub with lanolin or oil to loosen the skin, and trim toenails straight across. When discomfort continues, see a podiatrist. Many problems are covered by Medicare.

> ### Back Pain: Whom to See?
>
> If you're suffering from back pain, especially low back pain, there are many "doctors" you can see. The doctor who went to medical school will be an orthopedist. Or you could see a chiropractor (also allowed to be called "doctor"), someone trained in manipulation of spinal vertebrae, or an acupuncturist (many of whom are also medical doctors).
>
> Rely on your family doctor or general practitioner's advice, at least for an initial visit. It's best to try an orthopedist first; low back pain could be a symptom of a disease, such as prostate trouble in men. Insist on acceptable credentials from anyone you allow to treat you.

Be particularly careful about your feet if you are diabetic. Even minor tasks such as trimming your toenails should be handled by a podiatrist.

Skin Protection. Sunshine can be enjoyable but can also be dangerous for older folks. Even small amounts can make the face and arms look leathery, thick and wrinkled and, sometimes, lead to skin cancer. Usually, those spots can be removed surgically but when too frequent, they can lead to severe illness. Cancer is never to be taken lightly.

For protection, stay out of the sun. If you must go out in the sun, wear a hat and sunglasses, and use sunscreen products containing solutions that screen out harmful rays. If you bathe daily, use regular soap; detergents remove natural film and cause skin dryness. Use bath lotion because the production of body oils decreases with age, and use emollient creams around eyes when there are signs of sagging and wrinkles.

EMERGENCIES

There is little in life more terrifying than seeing a loved one fall victim to a medical emergency. The minutes spent waiting for assistance seem like hours, and there is nothing like the helplessness that you feel watching a loved one suffer without assistance.

The odds are that, sooner or later, you or a loved one will face such an emergency. Planning now can mean the difference between a relatively happy outcome and death.

- Know where the closest hospital with *complete* emergency facilities is. Many ''hospitals'' specialize, or lack emergency facilities. Time wasted in going to such a hospital could be the difference between life and death.

- Have the phone numbers for
    police and fire departments
    ambulance service
    paramedics
    your doctor
readily available. Write them down on the inside cover of this book, so you'll be able to find them in a hurry. (Even better, if you have a programmable telephone, assign each number its own pushbutton.)

- Call 911 for an emergency; 911 offers automatic call location. (Use 911 for emergencies only; time devoted to a non-emergency situation could cost someone their life. When in doubt, don't use 911.)
When calling for emergency aid, you'll need to tell the dispatcher on the other end:
    The address of the emergency
    Your phone number
    A brief description of the problem
    Your name
After the dispatcher has hung up (NEVER hang up on the dispatcher; he or she may need more information), call the victim's doctor if there is time. Also get information on your insurance policy. Without proof that you can pay, hospitals may delay acceptance of a patient, or transfer the patient to a public hospital as soon as it can. In many instances, people have died as a result.

These are signs of a medical emergency:

choking	paralysis
severe chest pains	severe abdominal pain
unconsciousness	shortness of breath or
convulsions	difficulty breathing
prolonged vomiting or	severe bleeding
diarrhea	sudden loss of vision
slurred speech	

There are measures you can use until the emergency personnel come. If you've learned cardiopulmonary resuscitation (CPR), you can administer it to persons exhibiting symptoms of a heart attack. The Heimlich maneuver could save the life of someone choking on food lodged in the esophagus. Basic first aid could stop bleeding that would otherwise prove fatal. For instruction on these techniques, contact the local branch of the American Red Cross.

AVOIDING QUACKS AND HEALTH FRAUDS

As advanced as American health care is, many of us are often frustrated by what it cannot do for us. We may read of treatments available abroad that are unavailable here. Or we may read that the "health care establishment" is responsible for suppressing a wonder drug.

In an age where burglaries were conducted on behalf of the President of the United States, arms were sold to terrorists by our own government, and doctors, lawyers, politicians, law officers, and businessmen of every stripe are regularly sentenced for crimes that involve an abuse of the public trust, it would insult your intelligence to assert that beneficial drugs could not be suppressed in order to increase profits for a few at the expense of the suffering. Ultimately, you must make up your own mind concerning the utility of health services offered by those outside the medical profession. But when you make these decisions, keep these facts in mind:

- If it hasn't been approved by the FDA, it's probably dangerous for you. The Food and Drug Administration has stringent procedural requirements (read: paperwork) that can tie up release of a drug for many months, even years. But there are procedures to get around those requirements, and they do work. Likely as not, drugs not approved by the FDA haven't even been submitted for testing; their sponsors know they'll be proven ineffective at best, and dangerous at worst.

- If the cure is simple, it's probably not a cure. Difficult problems rarely have simple solutions. And if the cure is so simple, why isn't it widely known that a cure is available? After all, if the Nazis couldn't keep the Holocaust quiet, and Nixon couldn't hush up Watergate, what makes you think a health establishment so inept that it can't discover a simple cure on its own can cover up this startling news?

- Just because you're probably going to die doesn't mean you will die. Many people subscribe to "quack" cures after being told by conventional medical practice that "there's nothing more we can do." The feeling is, "what have I got to lose?" Well, your money, for one thing. Patronizing quacks means supporting an element of society that preys on the weak and desperate. But even if you think that the purveyor in question isn't a crook, think this: if you (or a loved one) is so far gone, what makes you think ANYTHING is going to help you? Any medicine takes time to work, and if you're considered terminal, you won't be alive long enough to give even the greatest wonder drug time to work. The fact is that doctors are sometimes wrong; lots of folks are alive today, months and years after their doctors told them they'd be dead. But many "unconventional treatments" are downright bad for you. Once, laetrile was the rage as a super cancer cure. In fact, many of the people who took laetrile were poisoned by it, before they would have died of cancer. Balance this against the lives purportedly "saved" by laetrile; how many of the saved lives were remissions that would have occurred anyway? How many of the laetrile poisonings would have gone into remission?

Don't misunderstand: there will always be a place for unconventional medical treatments. Once, vegetarian regimens, herbal treatments, and acupuncture were scoffed at. Today, they have been accepted by the medical establishment in many instances. Every new idea will be mocked until it has gained acceptance, or rejected as unworthy. However, be skeptical in adopting unproven methods. Use your common sense. Be especially wary of proponents who appear to be in the health business not for the good of their fellow man, but for the bucks. And discuss any new form of treatment with your doctor. Before you reject what your doctor has to offer, hear him or her out on the new treatment you're considering shifting to.

For more information:

Health Care

Alzheimer's Disease and Related Disorders Association
360 No. Michigan Avenue
Chicago, IL 60601

American Association of Homes for the Aging
1129 20th Street
Washington, DC 20036

American Health Care Association
1200 15th Street, NW
Washington, DC 20002

American Society for Geriatric Dentistry
1221 West Michigan Street
Indianapolis, IN 46202

Home Health Service and Staffing Association
815 Connecticut Avenue, NW
Washington, DC 20006

National Association for Home Care
519 C Street, NE
Washington, DC 20002

National Council of Health Centers
2600 Virginia Avenue
Washington, DC 20037

National HomeCaring Council
235 Park Avenue South
New York, NY 10003

National Hospice Organization
1901 No. Fort Myers Drive
Arlington, VA 22209

National League for Nursing
10 Columbus Circle
New York, NY 10019

The Society of The Right To Die
250 West 57th Street
New York, NY 10017.

Medical/Nutritional

Medical Tips for the Pre-Retiree and Retiree, Quenton Cramer, Vantage Press

Movement Is Life: A Holistic Approach to Exercise for Older Adults, Eva D. Garnett, Princeton Books

Old Enough to Feel Better: A Medical Guide for Seniors, Michael Gordon, Chilton Books

LifeSpan Plus, Miller, Miller, and Miller, Macmillan, Inc.

CHAPTER 7

How to Pay for the Care You Need

Good health of retirees is closely related to income. For those over age 65, with incomes over $25,000, only 15% had major health problems but, for those with incomes under $10,000 a year, 35% suffered illness or injury severe enough to require hospital care.

Financially, as noted in Chapter 6, the costs of health care may be irritating but they are not overwhelming. According to figures released by the National Health Forum of George Washington University, the retiree pays 25% of the total health care bills—an average annual cost of $1,059. Medicare picks up 49%, Medicaid and other governmental programs pay 19% and private insurance, 7%.

Whether and how these roles will change will be the result of compromises and political pressure. The seniors are now the single largest voting bloc and also the major beneficiaries of federal spending: $170 billion, not counting Social Security. The elderly can look for more benefits but, in most cases, paid largely by the more affluent! In planning retirement, look ahead 10 years and double the anticipated costs of health care.

HEALTH CARE INSURANCE FOR THE ELDERLY

As the result of recent legislation, a larger portion of the medical, hospital, and home health care expenses of retirees will be paid for by government-sponsored programs: Medicare for everyone who is eligible for Social Security, and Medicaid for those with limited incomes and assets. The one major exception is the most costly: long-term nursing home care. Here, there is progress as the insurance industry is developing affordable coverage which can be purchased before, or in the early years of, retirement.

These broad benefits can be supplemented by private insurance policies, some paid for by employers but most by individuals. This Medi-Gap coverage pays all or part of the out-of-pocket expenses.

Medicare: a broad federal program under the Health Care Financing Agency (HCFA) that provides health care benefits to every American over age 65 who is eligible for Social Security plus certain disabled persons. The monthly premiums are deducted from your Social Security check but can be paid directly. Benefits are paid by an insurance company in each state.

A general enrollment period is held January 1 through March 31. If you fail to sign up at age 65, your monthly premium will be 10% higher than the basic premium for each 12-month period and your protection will not start until July 1 of the enrollment year. That means that if you delay enrollment until age 70, you will pay almost 50% more!

If you are entitled to Railroad Retirement benefits, you can also sign up for Medicare but must send your request (and, later, claims) to the Travelers Insurance Company office in your state.

For details of enrollment, premiums, forms and payments, get a copy of *Your Medicare Handbook* at your local Social Security office.

Medicaid: a federal/state-funded program for the indigent. For elderly, this is usually the last resort, primarily because it pays for Medicare premiums, co-payments and deductibles on behalf of those with incomes below 100% of the poverty level ($6,870 for a family, $5,440 for an individual). For seniors, the major benefit is that it pays for the costs of nursing home care.

Under new legislation, there's Spousal Impoverishment Protection whereby Medicare programs must permit the spouse of someone who enters a nursing home for long-term care to avoid being wiped out financially. The well spouse can keep the home, have monthly income of $786 (rising to $1,000 in 1993) and retain liquid assets of $12,000.

Explaining the New Medicare

Medicare is the core health care insurance for the elderly. Table 7-1 summarizes the key provisions but some details may be revised by Congress or administrative rules, so watch the press and check annually with your physician, hospital, or senior center.

There are two types of benefits: Part A, hospital insurance, and Part B, medical insurance, primarily for physician services such as treatment in the office or hospital, diagnostic tests, x-rays when part of the treatment, transfusions, physical therapy, speech pathology, etc. Medicare does not cover routine physical checkups, hearing and eye exams, and similar checkups.

The annual costs keep rising. Including the Catastrophic Health Insurance (CHI), premiums will amount to $346 in 1989, $420 in 1990, and an anticipated $500 in

Table 7-1   Health Care Insurance for the Elderly

Part A	*Medicare Pays*
Hospitalization	Unlimited patient days after annual deduction of $560 (to be increased in future).
Extended Care (Skilled Nursing)	First 8 days, all but $25.50 per day; 9-150 days: 100% of costs. Beyond 150 days, nothing.
Home Health Care	Coverage for daily care (7 days per week) for up to 38 days.
In-home Care for Chronically Dependent	Coverage for homemaker/home health aide, personal care of LPN services for up to 80 hours per year.
Hospice	All approved costs except for a portion of out-patient prescription drugs and 5% of in-patient co-insurance. Maximum: two 90-day and one 30-day benefit periods. After 210 days, extension if recertified as terminally ill.
Mammography Screening	For women over 65 and younger disableds every other year.
Prescription Drugs	Pays for out-patient costs over $550 per year in 1990 (with 50% co-payment); $600 in 1991 (40% co-pay); $652 in 1992 (20% co-pay).
Part B	
Doctor's Fees: Out-of-pocket Limit	In 1989, after $75 deductible, 80% of allowable charges; in 1990, all bills above $1,370 for out-patient hospital care and some ambulatory services, 20% of co-insurance for Medicare-approved costs. To be adjusted annually.
Spousal Impoverishment	State Medicaid must permit spouse of patient in nursing home to keep $768 of monthly income (up to $1,000 in 1993) and $12,000 in liquid assets. Home ownership excluded.

SOURCE: U.S. Congress

1991. Under CHI, there will be a 15% surcharge based on Federal taxes on income. For singles, taxes will kick in above $15,000; for couples, over $20,000. For every $150 of income tax, the new levy starts at $22.50 in 1989 and rises to an anticipated $42 in 1993. There is a cap: in 1989, $800 per individual; in 1993, $1,005. By 2005, the total tax, for joint filers, could rise to $8,000!

Part A

For those who have heavy medical expenses, the payments will be significant. Under Part A, Medicare will pay as follows:

Hospitalization: after a deductible of $560 a year (rising annually), all hospital costs no matter how many stays a year, provided the care is "reasonable and necessary" as determined by a committee of physicians. This includes costs of a semi-private room, board, nursing, special care units, lab tests, X-ray and radiation therapy, casts and surgical dressings, splints and appliances, rehabilitation services and operating and recovery room expenses.

For inpatient care in a participating hospital (not all institutions are eligible) in each benefit period, Medicare pays for all covered services above that $560 for an unlimited number of days.

Keep in mind that the charges made by the hospital may be above those allowed by Medicare, and that there may be extra bills for special medical and laboratory services. In most cases, you will have to pay these costs on your own.

Nursing Home: All but $22.50 a day for the first 8 days; 100% of costs from the 9th to 150th day. No previous hospital stay required; custodial care isn't covered. The need for care must be certified by a physician.

Home Health Care: 38 days (24 hours each) of skilled nursing care per year. In some cases, an extension is possible.

Hospice Care (including home care): all costs without limit, except for a portion of out-patient co-insurance, up to 210 days with possible extension. The patient must be expected to die in less than six months.

Respite Care: up to 80 hours a year for nurses or home health aides to relieve the caregiver(s) for the patient at home. Also pays expenses for doctor's fees or drug deductible that are over the Medicare cap.

Mental Health: the first $1,000 annually. Visits to monitor medication dosage are covered under Part B and do not count towards this limit.

Part B

This is medical insurance, generally, to pay for part of doctor bills: treatment in the office or hospital, diagnostic tests, x-rays when part of a treatment, transfusions, physical therapy, speech pathology and home health care.

Doctors' Fees: after $75 deductible, 80% of fees approved by Health Care Financing Administration (HCFA) charges with the beneficiary paying the balance directly or through private insurance. For out-of-pocket expenses (co-payments and deductibles), there's an annual cap of $1,370, rising to $1,900 by 1993. Medicare pays up to that limit when the individual becomes responsible.

Medicare does NOT cover routine physical check-ups, hearing and eyeglass exams, drugs and medicine you buy, private duty nurses, custodial care, homemaker services and similar related items. On the average, Medicare covers from 40% to 45% of medical bills. Under the new law, this percentage will rise significantly.

Prescription Drugs: in 1990, after a deduction of $550 a year, Medicare will pay 50% of the cost of intravenous drugs used at home; the deductible will increase to $600 in 1991, and almost all prescription drugs will be covered. The portion paid by Medicare will increase to 60% in 1991 and 80% in 1993. Deductibles are subject to change.

Spousal Impoverishment Protection: Medicare programs must permit the spouse of a person entering a nursing home for long-term care to avoid being wiped out financially. The well spouse can keep the home, have monthly income of $786 (rising to $1,000 by 1993) and retain liquid assets of $12,000 (not including home).

Although this can be helpful, to avoid dire straits, consider transferring assets to a child two years before the individual enters the nursing home. Before making a final decision, consult with an attorney and a professional counselor.

Payments of Claims. There are two ways benefits are paid:

(1) By assignment where the physician or supplier submits the claim and receives a check from the Medicare carrier in your home state. The maximum charge, set by HCFA, varies around the country. Most physicians will not accept assignment because of the paperwork and the fact that their fees are usually higher than the mandated limit. However, under pressure from retirees, an increasing number of physicians are relaxing their objections and are willing to deal directly with Medicare for some patients. For a list of cooperating physicians, check your local health department, county or state medical association, senior center, hospital or Area Agency on Aging.

(2) By reimbursement of a patient who personally pays the bill. Here, you do all the work. You must pay the full bill yourself, file a claim with the Medicare carrier in your state and, if you have coverage, with the Medi-Gap carrier. To do this, you must keep accurate records and, at the start, should review procedures with your physician's aide, the hospital service department or an experienced adviser at an Aging agency or your local AARP chapter. Claims must be submitted within 15 months after the service was rendered.

You will have to pay, directly or through supplementary insurance, the initial portions of bills under both Part A (the deductible, currently the first $560) and Part B (currently $75, plus 20% of the difference between what Medicare pays, plus all of the physician fees above those approved by medicare.)

Financing Health Care Costs

The one sure thing about health care costs is that they will continue to rise and that governmental projections will be far too low. With Medicare, Federal outlays for basic services, at $7.5 billion in 1971, skyrocketed to $80 billion by 1987, and are anticipated to be $116 billion in 1991. The new Catastrophic Health Care legislation will add $17 billion to these costs by 1995.

For those who outlive their actuarial life expectancies, these soaring medical fees can be disastrous. A $5,000 medical bill is a typical expenditure for many retirees. Even reduced by $2,000 in Medicare coverage, this can dent the savings account and reduce future income of persons whose incomes are basically fixed.

If you anticipate a need for nursing home care, and don't want to have to exhaust your life's savings before you qualify for Medicare, you may want to transfer assets to the healthy partner or a child. This must be done two years before the individual enters the nursing home. If you decide to take this step, consult with an attorney.

Some states have set more humane standards and Congress is considering allowing the non-institutionalized spouse to keep income equal to 150% of the Federal poverty level: about $925 per month.

Medi-Gap Insurance. This is private insurance that supplements Medicare by bridging part of the gap between total hospital and doctor bills and payments by Medicare: the $560 deductible, part of the 20% difference between what Medicare approves and what is charged, and bills for extra benefits and services. There's no way to buy complete payment for all health care costs but, for $500 to $800 per year, a retiree can own insurance which, with Medicare, can cover 80% to 90% of the bills. In many years, the supplementary insurance will pay back 60% to 90% of the premium. The terms and costs of this insurance will change as a result of the Catastrophic Health Care legislation, but it will continue to be available.

This is the kind of policy that is promoted so vigorously by direct mail, radio and TV, usually by Hollywood personalities. (When watching these advertisements, ask yourself why these paid performers, who have vastly more financial resources than most seniors, should be experts on insurance.) Consider such insurance only after checking the quality of the issuing company and comparing the restrictions, benefits and costs. *Best bet:* Try to continue the policy available at your job, even if you have to pay the annual premium.

When you must buy your own coverage, be careful in choosing a policy. Many companies promise big benefits and low premiums but set limits and keep raising the annual costs.

- Deal only with a reputable company whose financial strength is rated ''A'' by Best's Insurance Reports and whose loss ratio (the amount which the company pays out in benefits for each dollar of premium) is high. Congress mandates a minimum payout of 60%. For non-profit Blue Cross/Blue Shield, the average is 90%. You can probably obtain a copy of Best's Insurance Reports at your library.

- Review your policy carefully. By law, in many states, you have 10 days from the date you receive the policy to return it and get a full refund of the premium.

- Be skeptical of policies that are aggressively promoted. The costs of such advertising can boost premiums and lower benefits.

- Avoid any policy that covers only extended hospital care. On the average, a retiree stays in the hospital 12 days a year and only 3% remain over 90 days.

- Do not duplicate coverage. By law, there can be no double payments. If one company picks up the tab, other policies will be worthless. If you are covered by two policies—one from your employer and the other from your spouse's employer—the payments can be coordinated but not paid twice.

- Be truthful with answers on your insurance application. False, misleading or omitted data can permit the insurance company to deny payment of the claim or cancel the policy.

- Find out how much is paid per day for room and board in a hospital. How much are medicines and other expenses? What is the deductible?

- Does the policy cover only your costs or include other family members?

- What is the maximum amount the policy will pay for each illness or injury? Will the limits apply to future illness or injury?

- Is there a waiting period (the time between purchase and eligibility)? This should be a few weeks and never more than six months.

- What are the definitions of pre-existing conditions? Some companies will pay no claims if they can prove that you knew, or should have known, of an illness when you signed on. Watch out for phrases such as ''bodily injury sustained directly and independently of all other causes.'' The company can deny an accident claim if it can show that the injury was related to something else. A more acceptable term would be ''accidental bodily injury sustained.''

- Check the renewal terms. The policy should be guaranteed for life, not ''renewable at the option of the company.'' With the latter, you can be dumped if your payments have been too large. *Best deal:* a group policy with

---

Trouble Ahead

Most large employers offer retirees continued health insurance benefits but few have put aside funds to pay for them. According to Employee Benefit Research Institute, unfunded liabilities are $85 bil-
lion for those already retired plus up to $1 trillion for future
pensioners!

If you're in your 60s and have cause to be worried about the solvency
of employer health benefit reserves, add another $500 a year to your
after-work budget for extra coverage. By the time younger people
retire, the situation should be improved.

---

a well-established organization. This will be cheaper for the insurance company to administer so you get a lower cost, better benefits, almost certain
renewability, and moderate rate changes.

• Never buy "dread disease" insurance. Typically, this is a policy that pays
only for costs of cancer illness. The premium may be small but there's little
chance of collecting.

• If you are told you are ineligible, do not panic. Your state Blue Cross/Blue
Shield has open enrollment periods during which every applicant will be
accepted. And, in some states, there is special insurance for people with
chronic health problems. In Florida, the State Comprehensive Association
offers policies to state residents who have been turned down twice for major
medical insurance and do not have other coverage: $500,000 lifetime maxi-
mum benefit for each policyholder with deductibles of $1,000, $1,500 or
$2,000 and 80% reimbursement for covered hospital and medical expenses
thereafter. The cost is 50% to 200% more than that of a standard policy with
annual increase in premiums. At age 45, the yearly cost is $1,563 with a
$2,000 deductible. Coverage is available to Medicare recipients at compar-
able cost. Check your State Insurance Department.

For more information, write to: National Insurance Consumer Organization, 344
Commerce Street, Alexandria, VA. 22314; Office of Beneficiary Services, Health
Care Financing Agency, 5325 Security Blvd., Baltimore, MD 20207; Health Associ-
ation of America, 1850 K Street, NW, Washington, DC 20006.

Veterans' Benefits. If you, or a spouse or parent, served in the Armed Forces,
don't overlook veterans' benefits. Veterans' benefits include pensions, disability

compensation, medical services including hospitalization and outpatient care, dental care, aids and services to the blind, prosthetic devices, mental health care, nursing home care, alcohol and drug dependency programs, commissary and exchange privileges, and burial benefits.

You can qualify for veterans' benefits if you are a veteran with an honorable or general discharge and have either a service-connected disability or are disabled by age or disease. You can also qualify if you are the surviving unmarried spouse or disabled child of a veteran who was a member or retired member of the armed forces, and who either died as a result of service-connected disabilities, or had service-connected disabilities, but died from some other cause. For full information, ask for Federal Benefits for Veterans and Dependents, from the General Printing Office, Washington, DC, 20402.

SAVING ON HEALTH CARE AND DRUGS

Home Care for Comfort and Savings

This is just what the name implies: a service that allows elderly to stay in their own homes at reasonable expense and out of costly nursing institutions. When folks can remain in familiar surroundings, they feel more at ease, more in control of their lives and more comfortable, physically and mentally.

Home care is useful for:

(a) those recently hospitalized who still need nursing;

(b) the frail or disabled elderly who have trouble with dressing, bathing and household chores;

(c) those who need respite from caring for a victim of Alzheimer's disease;

(d) the Old-Olds, such as the widow looking for a companion to accompany her to the shopping mall or her house of worship, or the man who has had a stroke so that he has trouble walking and can no longer drive a car.

The caregivers include housekeeper/companions, live-in nurses, therapists and case managers who coordinate medical care, check mail, file insurance claims and collate papers for tax returns.

Costs vary according to the local wage scale but will always be cheaper than nursing home or hospital care.

This home care concept is attracting more interest:

Eye Care Assistance

This is an area often neglected by the elderly but one where there can be welcome professional assistance. Many seniors think that their eyesight declines inevitably with age. If they do worry about their budget, they often ignore the problem and hope for the best.

This is foolish and unnecessary. Almost all eye conditions can be successfully treated if they are diagnosed promptly.

Eye care is available to anyone over age 65 not currently under the care of a professional or not examined in the past three years. The hotline: 1-800-222-EYES.

The exam is free; the costs of eyeglasses, prescriptions and hospital treatment must be paid for, but, in many cases, will be covered by Medicare or Medi-Gap insurance.

- Insurance companies offer policies, for groups and individuals, that pay 100% of many basic procedures.

- Major corporations are taking steps to pay for a portion of the costs for their employees and their families and new retirees.

- Many states offer financial aid based on need. In Florida, the state pays $94 to $358 per month when personal savings are minimal. These dollars can also be used to buy bed pads, special foods and prescription drugs.

For information: check the yellow pages, the Area Agency on Aging and senior center. Once you have located a prospective service, be sure the employees are bonded, insured and closely supervised.

Health Maintenance Organizations (HMOs)

These are the fastest-growing medical care organizations and are, despite failures due to over-enthusiastic, incompetent management, a powerful factor in the health field, especially for the elderly. They will become more important in the future as they are acquired or sponsored by well-financed and experienced insurance companies.

With an HMO, the individual, alone or in a group, pays a monthly or annual premium in return for almost total health care services: visits to the physician, hospital stays, operations and, in some cases, prescription drugs, eyeglasses, foot care, etc. To receive such benefits, the enrollee must go to designated health centers and, usually, deal only with HMO-paid physicians and services. Enrollment is usually through a group but it is also possible for an individual to sign up . . . at an annual cost of about $900 per individual and $2,500 for a family of four.

An HMO can be a viable health care alternative if chosen wisely from a checklist like the one that follows.

Does the HMO provide payments for:

Same services and treatments as Medicare

Additional benefits such as:
 Unlimited days in hospital
 Annual physical exam
 Eye care: routine exam, refractions, prescription glasses, or contact lens
 Prescription drugs: any limits?
 Hearing aids: exam, accessory
 Dental care: routine? If special, what are the limits?
 Foot care
 Chiropractic visits
 Mental health: how many outpatient visits annually?
 Treatment at local center when referred by HMO MD?
 Special programs for victims of depression, senility, and Alzheimer's?

Special situations such as:
 Emergency care from non-HMO provider
 Non-emergency care from outside of HMO geographic area
 Second opinion of HMO MD? Non-HMO MD?

Physicians:

Can I select my own? What help can I expect?

Can I change if not satisfied?

What percentage of physicians, in the specialties I need, are board-certified? (National average: 62%).

Do at least 50% of MDs accept new patients? (This will ensure better choices.)

Will MDs, therapists or nurses make house calls to homebound patients?

What arrangements can be made for outside help from Visiting Nurses, Red Cross and so forth?

What is anticipated average waiting period for non-emergency appointment?

When, where and how fast can I get emergency care?

How many of staff are trained in geriatrics?

Enrollment and Disenrollment

Can I join at any time? If not, what are enrollment periods? (HMOs with Medicare contracts must offer an annual 30-day enrollment period).

Can I drop out at any time? (It can take up to eight weeks for the HMO and Medicare to process severance or reinstatement. Conversely, before you drop Medicare for an HMO, be sure you have written confirmation of your change of status. Otherwise, you will have to pay for what should be standard benefits.)

Information

Are there booklets or tapes that explain premiums and benefits?

Is there a map of the service area showing location of HMO medical centers?

Does the booklet list: (a) participating MDs with names, addresses and phone numbers? (b) hospitals or laboratories, skilled nursing facilities and other entities used by the HMO?

What assistance is available to HMO members to help them understand and properly utilize services? Is there a printed form explaining grievance procedures and how to present and follow up on complaints? Is there a hotline? Ombudsman?

Will there be meetings to help HMO routines, different types of care, special procedures for emergencies?

Will there be special class for HMO enrollees on health and nutrition?

Before you make a final choice, double-check with friends and neighbors to learn answers to such questions as:

Is medical service prompt and competent?

Does staff take time to answer questions, provide assurance and smile?

At the office, are there long waits and, when you are treated, are you rushed through?

Finally, visit one or more medical centers to see how they meet your personal needs:

Is the location convenient? Near bus lines?

Is there plenty of parking in a neat, well-maintained area?

Are the office rooms bright and cheery?

Is special transportation available from a community agency?

Do not expect too much with any HMO. In Florida, I could not find a single one that offered two-thirds of these ''services.''

Hospice for the Terminally Ill

This is one of the most successful new programs for those whose life-spans are limited. It provides a means for the terminally ill to live out their lives with, or near, their family and friends and to die with dignity. When a physician certifies that the patient can be expected to live less than six months, he or she is eligible for hospice care with its fine support services and with many bills paid by Medicare.

Experts help the individual and family to cope, with emphasis on the quality of the remaining time rather than on means to extend life. The care can be in a special institution or in the home. If there is no such service available in your area, start a group with your friends, a local hospital, a community agency and physicians.

Saving on Drugs

Needed prescriptions can be a daunting financial burden for retireds. The rising cost of prescriptions has offset the benefits of increased insurance reimbursement and income tax deductibility. There are, however, steps you can take to cut the cost of prescriptions.

One step you can take to cut the cost of prescriptions is to ask your physician if a generic drug can be prescribed instead. Many doctors prefer to prescribe brand-name drugs, although most experts agree that there is no difference between generic drugs and their brand-name counterparts. Generic drugs can be 25% less than their prescription counterparts.

Living Will

This is a legal document involving the right of a patient to control his or her own medical care and to die with dignity. After numerous battles, the courts have ruled that the individual can maintain reasonable control over the right to a natural death and not be subject to treatment that sustains patients beyond the point where there is any quality of life.

A number of states have enacted laws that:

(1) authorize the appointment of a "health care proxy" to act on the patient's behalf if and when necessary;

(2) expand the coverage to include the permanently unconscious as well as those terminally ill;

(3) permit withholding of life-sustaining treatment which, "when administered to a qualified patient, will serve to prolong the process of dying or to maintain the patient in a condition of permanent unconsciousness."

Such a document eliminates the need for concerned relatives to go to court to obtain decisions about life-supporting systems. To avoid such a tragedy, sign a Living Will. For the proper form, and information, write to The Society of The Right To Die, 250 West 57th Street, New York, NY 10017.

Other steps you can take are common-sense ones:

- Ask your doctor for free samples he or she may have received from drug companies.

- Shop around. Patronize drugstores that advertise discount prices, and compare prices.

- Buy in bulk. The per-pill cost of a 100-pill prescription can be less that the per-pill cost of a 20-pill prescription. Ask your physician if a larger prescription is suitable for you. If your prescription is increased, have your doctor write a new, larger prescription, instead of simply getting refills on the old prescription.

COPING WITH NURSING HOMES

One of the major fears of all elderly is confinement in a nursing home. Traumatic for both the patient and caregiver, nursing homes are always expensive: $1,500 to $3,000 a month. Almost half of those over age 75 who enter a private nursing home will be bankrupt in 12 weeks and more than 70% of such residents will exhaust their savings within one year.

Choosing a Nursing Home

When the time comes when a loved one must go to an institution, it's important to recognize that you have to do the best with what is at hand: to be willing to lower your expectations and accept the fact that most of these ''homes'' are trying to provide the best service they can within the limits of the income they receive, the staff they can afford to pay and the cooperation received from the patients. Here are guidelines to find, choose and monitor a nursing home:

Get a list of homes from an aging agency, United Way, governmental department or the classified pages of the telephone directory. For recommendations and comments, ask friends, neighbors, social workers and the referral desk at your hospital.

From the patient's physician, find out what kinds of nursing care will be needed—skilled, intermediate, custodial—and whether special services may be helpful: physical therapy, remedial treatment, etc.

From literature and phone calls, be sure the home is licensed, certified for participation in governmental programs and relatively free of violations.

- Are there extra services such as special diets, barber or hairdresser, manicurist, podiatrist? What will they cost?

- Is the location convenient to a hospital, the patient's physician, and concerned relatives?

- Does the home accept Medicaid? If the patient should be forced to accept this subsidy, will he or she be able to remain? If not, will you be notified soon enough to alert state authorities and to make other plans?

- Will the rates be guaranteed for a reasonable period of time?

Once you have narrowed the choice:

- Visit the home to see how clean, neat and well-organized it is. Be ready to make allowances and concentrate on how the residents feel or, at least, appear to react. Are they reasonably happy, smiling, relaxed? Does the staff speak respectfully of their charges?

- Is there an odor of urine? This indicates that there is a lack of instruction on incontinence for the staff and patients.

- Are the hallways clear and well lighted? Are the fire exits convenient and marked?

- Do the rooms have space for chairs for visitors, storage space for clothing, mementos, and personal items?

- Is there a locked drawer or a special, controlled, safe box?

- At mealtimes, take a look at the type of food and how it's served. Does the staff help those who cannot feed themselves?

- In off-hours, are there patients slumped over in chairs or cowering in a corner? If some are restrained, is this by doctor's orders or for the convenience of the staff?

As a final check, ask:

- What medical services are offered? By whom and how often?

- How many skilled nurses and aides are on duty at night? Will you be informed promptly when there are health problems?

- Do they keep charts on the patient's health? Are these kept up-to-date and do they cover all essential information: when an injury, sore or illness started, what treatment is recommended by a physician and whether or not there has been progress?

- Are there annual checkups of all patients? By law, the Medicaid nurse must make annual exams but there are no such requirements for private-pay patients.

When the patient is admitted:

- Are the financial terms clear, in writing with spelled-out steps to take when there are questions?

- Is there a posted bill of patient rights?

- Label all belongings, even dentures, and make a complete list with a copy to the administrator. On each visit, check to see if anything important is missing. If so, report this immediately.

- Visit the patient several times a week at different hours of the day. Be friendly with the staff and try to time your visit to when you can be most helpful.

- Form a family council with relatives of other patients to act as liaison between the staff, management and patients.

- When there are problems, especially suspected wrongdoing, file a complaint with the ombudsman council or regulatory authority. These volunteers have the right to visit the home at any time, to investigate complaints and, when justified, to seek corrective action and, when necessary, closure.

Nursing Care Insurance

Until recently, policies to pay for these costs have not been readily available. The concept has been a challenge to insurers to design a product that is both profitable and affordable to the elderly. But the situation is changing rapidly, as the insurance industry recognizes that nursing home care is the largest unmet need that insurance was designed to solve.

Most companies guarantee renewability and all of these policies cover senile dementia, such as Alzheimer's disease. Currently, policies cover three types of nursing home care and one home service:

- *Skilled care:* given by nurses, therapists and other licensed professionals on a daily or continuous basis. This is seldom needed for more than six months after admission to the nursing home.

- *Intermediate care:* includes less intensive ministrations by professionals.

- *Custodial care:* usually provided by non-professionals who help patients with such basic tasks as bathing, dressing and walking, usually for a long period.

- *Home health care:* provided by a professional or trained non-professional, depending on need, in the home.

Note that there are wide variations in coverage, eligibility, and rates for nursing home care. Daily benefits currently range from $50 to $100; home care ranges from $25 to $50. Coverage can be from three years (1,095 days) to five years (1,825 days).

Terms for eligibility and costs relate to the age of the insured: at 55, costs range from $250 to $350 annually; at 79, about $1,500. Few companies offer coverage to those over 80. You can get coverage for Alzheimer's disease if the insured hasn't developed it yet.

Before you sign up for any of these types of policies, keep in mind that only 10% of elderly will ever be in a nursing home and for half of these, the stay will be temporary.

Protecting Assets from Nursing Home Payments

Under the new Medicare laws, there are only two ways to transfer a house to someone else for less than fair market value without having that home subject to confiscation to pay for nursing home costs:

> to a spouse or disabled, dependent child who lives in the house; or

> to a nondisabled child who has lived in the house for a year and had an equity interest in the house.

Transfers made more than 30 months before applying for Medicaid will immunize the house from confiscation, and should be considered if the prospect of eventual nursing home care is inevitable, such as in the case of Alzheimer's disease. And transfers for fair market value will be respected whenever made. If protecting a house, or asset, from being included in nursing home support is a consideration, see a lawyer for advice.

Where to Get More Information

Health Insurance Association of America
1001 Pennsylvania Ave., NW
Washington, DC 20004

Insurance Information Institute
110 William Street
New York, NY 10038

CHAPTER 8

Housing—Meeting Your Lifestyle Needs for the Rest of Your Life

In retirement, housing should be judged by different standards than those while working: not prestige, luxury or personal pleasure, but comfort, security, convenience and reasonable cost. Choose housing where you and your partner will be comfortable, both when you're together and, later, when there is only one survivor.

Emotionally, leaving your established residence can be a difficult decision, but it may be the wisest course. A big house can be a problem when there are only two old folks and a burden when there's one survivor. Few older couples need, or can afford, the extra space. They can no longer climb stairs, clean the bathrooms, and make the small repairs and replacements that can be so annoying.

For most retirees, this will mean planning to plan to move twice: first, to a smaller unit and, when one or both suffer failing health, to an apartment, condominium, or town house where there will be built-in supports, such as neighbors, health services and community centers.

WHERE TO LIVE

Three years before retirement is the time you should make the decision to stay or move. If you stay in the same home, reconsider your decision several years after retirement, when you have had a chance to judge whether this is still the best lifestyle for you.

Usually, these are the choices:

Stay in the Old Home: probably too big, unless there can be company, such as a friend, relative or boarder. The latter type of "guest" may be wise when the house is in (a) a resort area where there will be transients (greater income but more work for you) or (b) a college town where students can swap chores for a lower rent.

When You're Alone

After one partner dies, the survivor is usually faced with a housing decision. The old home may be too large, too expensive or too lonesome and there will probably be a need to create or build support systems. At that point, the move to make depends on financial resources, physical condition, family situation and lifestyle, actual or desired.

No matter what choice is made, do not delay more than three months after the settlement of your spouse's estate. Be realistic: no matter how lost or lonesome you may feel, you still have the rest of your life to live! Do not be afraid to discuss this future with your spouse while you are both living, so that you can plan for the inevitable future that one of you must face alone.

Although location is important, pay more attention to the people and services that you will need. If you plan to live with your children or other relatives, you will have to make compromises between your needs and the environment that you are in. But if you're going to make it on your own, seek housing that fits your new lifestyle. In addition to considering a house, apartment, or condominium where you can still live alone, take a look at the alternatives that can combine the companionship of group living with broader services at lower costs.

Move into an Owned Unit, such as a smaller house or condominium. This choice depends on how active you are, or want to be, and what you can afford in dollars and upkeep work.

Rent an Apartment or Condominium: The big advantage here is convenience. It's easy to be away for days or weeks, and you generally will have fixed housing costs. But space will be limited, you probably won't have a garden to work in, and there's pressure to conform.

Move in with Others, such as children, family, or friends. This can provide security but your happiness will depend on the location, your individual responsibilities, your degree of personal privacy, and the comfort that everyone living together has with each other. Do you want to become a built-in baby-sitter? Will you have to make such an important financial contribution that you cannot leave later? These are the kinds of questions you should ask yourself before making this move.

Sign Up for a Retirement Community. This could be a house, condominium, or apartment where you will have security, service, and companionship. You will have to accept constraints, practice some degree of conformity, and put up with the beliefs and prejudices of your neighbors.

Your decision will largely depend on available resources, your health, and your ability to cope independently. If your income is marginal, start thinking about a job, full or part time (see page 21). If you are going to work, you should know where, and as what, before you decide where to live.

The checklist on page 190 contains some common reasons for staying where you currently live, and for moving after retirement. See how many apply to you. If other criteria are appropriate for you, add them to the checklist. Assign each reason a point value (from 1 to 10) based on that reason's importance to you. Add up all the points for all the reasons for staying, and compare that with the total of the points for all your reasons for moving; the greater point total should determine whether to stay or move. Also, in column 2, see what your answers will be after you, or your spouse, becomes ill or dies.

Review your checklist annually until you and your spouse have both decided to make a firm commitment.

Geographic Choices

If moving seems the best solution for both of you, you first have to decide where to. Choose a location that you can afford now and in the future. Don't over-estimate the financial resources you're likely to have—inflation and rising taxes will probably cut the purchasing power of your fixed income by 30% to 50% before you pass on.

To find the kind of retirement you want and can afford, start with these communities listed as most desirable by Rand McNally:

TABLE 8-1 Top Retirement Communities

Murray-Kentucky Lake, Ky.	Brownsville-Harlingen, Tex.
Clayton-Clarkesville, Ga.	Bloomington-Brown County, Ind.
Hot Springs, Ark.	San Antonio, Tex.
Grand Lake, Okla.	Port Angeles, Wash.
Fayetteville, Ark.	Mountain Home, Ark.
St. George-Zion, Utah	Charleston, S.C.

SOURCE: *Retirement Places Rated*, Bayer and Savageau, 1987.

WORKSHEET 8-1   Where to Live

	Points	
Reasons for Staying	Now	When I'm Alone
Comfortable, familiar, convenient	_____	_____
Mortgage paid	_____	_____
Know, and generally can control, expenses	_____	_____
Property well maintained so anticipate no major expenditures for roof, furnace, air conditioning, etc.	_____	_____
Near family and friends	_____	_____
Both of us are part of the community	_____	_____
Unable or unwilling to get rid of possessions, mementos, or files	_____	_____
Pleased with physician, dentist and hospital	_____	_____
Have trustworthy advisers: lawyer, accountant, banker, insurance agents	_____	_____
Others _____	_____	_____
_____	_____	_____

	Points	
Reasons for Moving	Now	When I'm Alone
Rising expenses for taxes, maintenance	_____	_____
House too large and inconvenient	_____	_____
Too many stairs to climb	_____	_____
Too much maintenance inside and out	_____	_____
Changing neighborhood: more noise, crime, traffic	_____	_____
Inconvenient for shopping and transportation	_____	_____
Hard to take weather: too cold in winter	_____	_____
Too many friends have gone away	_____	_____
Available services limited	_____	_____
Present property not likely to appreciate	_____	_____
Better recreational opportunities elsewhere	_____	_____
To seek new challenges: friends, personal interests	_____	_____
Others _____	_____	_____
_____	_____	_____

TABLE 8-2   How States Rate As Retirement Havens

This survey of 48 states (insufficient data for Alaska and Hawaii) was based on 10 criteria. Seven criteria were given equal weight: availability of housing, property taxes, utility rates, living costs, unemployment rate, employment growth and ratio of retirees to working age population. The other three were assigned variable weights: lower for growth of retired population; higher for weather conditions and availability of typical services/amenities.

State	Points	State	Points
Utah	305	West Virginia	−103
Louisiana	295	Wyoming	−130
South Carolina	280	Nebraska	−138
Nevada	260	Ohio	−160
Texas	230	Wisconsin	−170
New Mexico	200	Delaware	−195
Alabama	185	Indiana	−195
Arizona	175	Illinois	−223
Florida	160	Missouri	−225
Georgia	155	Pennsylvania	−230
Colorado	140	South Dakota	−235
North Carolina	110	Iowa	−240
Tennessee	100	Michigan	−245
Kentucky	86	Montana	−250
Virginia	75	Minnesota	−265
Washington	40	North Dakota	−280
California	35	Connecticut	−285
Oklahoma	30	New Hampshire	−300
Maryland	−5	New York	−355
Idaho	−15	Rhode Island	−373
Oregon	−15	Vermont	−385
Kansas	−20	New Jersey	−390
Arkansas	−63	Maine	−428
Mississippi	−50	Massachusetts	−498

SOURCE: WEFA, Inc. (formerly Chase Econometrics, Inc. and Wharton Econometrics Forecasting Associates, Inc.).

TABLE 8-3   Consumer Price Index:
            Comparative Cities

City	All Items	Median Housing Cost (1988)
Boston, MA	318.0	$181,200
Cincinnati, OH	329.8	69,700
Dallas/Ft. Worth, TX	339.5	84,800
Denver, CO	357.2	81,800
Honolulu, HI	294.1	215,100
Los Angeles, CA	320.2	180,100
Miami, FL	171.7	82,900
Minneapolis/St. Paul, MN	336.2	85,200
New York, NY	314.3	184,800
Philadelphia, PA	314.2	102,400
San Francisco, CA	333.1	206,400
Washington, DC	321.1	132,500
City Average	322.2	(USA) 90,200

SOURCE: U.S. Bureau of Labor Statistics
         Home Sales, National Association of Realtors

The Consumer Price Index measures the cost of a defined ''basket'' of goods in a given community at a given time. Generally, the lower the CPI, the farther your dollar will go. However, if possible, try to find out what it will cost YOU to live in a given location—the goods you consume may not match those that the government uses in measuring the CPI. Here is a comparison of the Consumer Price Index for major U.S. cities, along with 1988 median housing prices.

Be judicious in using these figures, because special factors may affect the CPI for a given locale. The Miami figure, for example, is very low because of a $25,000 homestead exemption and no state income tax. And Floridians can expect that future taxes will be much higher because of the need to pay for roads, bridges, environmental protection and expanded social services. The Dallas/Ft. Worth total, well above the average, is probably an exaggeration of today's circumstances, given a decline in costs attributable to sharply lower oil prices.

For most retirees, the most important expenses are taxes—on income while living and on your estate after death. In communities where there's a local and state income tax (such as New York City), affluent taxpayers may find it smart to establish a domicile in a low income tax/no income tax state, such as Florida or New Hampshire. If you have a large estate, you may face state estate tax rates of up to 30%.

Consider a Nevada domicile, where there are no estate taxes. Always consult an experienced tax attorney to set up the best deal, and review your decision every year or two.

On pages 194–199, you'll find a table of recent income, property, and estate tax rates for all 50 states and the District of Columbia. Use this chart to estimate which states will have the heaviest tax burden for you, and to estimate how much taxes will cost you every year (and after you pass away). Wherever you live, you can reduce these income taxes by investing in municipal bonds in your state of residence.

Choosing a Specific Community

Once you have zeroed in on one or two areas, find out all you can about available services, organizations, types of residents, lifestyle and probable future. Avoid moving into a declining neighborhood. Look for signs of lack of care, such as untrimmed trees, loose shutters or peeling paint, and backyards with trash piles, topless garbage cans and ill-kept trees. If you're not convinced a new neighborhood is for you, don't let price, prestige or pressure from friends, family or the real estate agent change your mind.

Investigate the area personally (preferably at different times during the year). Drive around the back streets and park where you can watch traffic through a busy corner. Does the traffic light stay green long enough for a cane-dependent senior to walk across safely? Are there police around to check speeders? Later, drop by the Chamber of Commerce to get literature on available services, plans for future highways and other major developments, and job opportunities.

If you're hesitant about leaving family, friends and familiar scenes, try renting in the new area for at least one month. While there, try activities that you're likely to engage in after retirement. Visit community centers, art galleries and libraries, eat at restaurants, and drive around to learn how the area may change in the next few years.

If your heart is set on a location that's too expensive for you, look for less expensive housing that may be a few miles away, but has some of the key features that you're looking for.

When you get back home, use Table 8-5 for discussion with your partner. If you can afford to live in the area, and you both feel that this would be a desirable environment for you for the next 10 years, subscribe to the local newspaper for a month. Then, recheck your original comments. Make your own decisions, not those expressed by friends or family. Resolve to make a final decision within two weeks. One final step: use the same checklist with the community where you now live. You may be surprised to find what an attractive place it is!

TABLE 8-4

| | State Income Tax Rates | | | | | State Exemptions | | | | | | |
	up to $5,000	$5,000 to $10,000	$10,000 to $20,000	$20,000 to $40,000	over $40,000	Single	Married	Head of H'hold	Dep'dnt	Blind	Over 65	Sales Tax
Alabama	2%-5%	5%	5%	5%	5%	$1,500	$3,000	$3,000	$300			4.00%
Alaska	no state income tax											none
Arizona	2%-6%	6%-8%	8%	8%	8%	$2,125	$4,250	$4,250	$1,275	$1,063	$2,125	5.00%*
Arkansas	1%-2.5%	2.5%-4.5%	4.5%-6%	6%-7%	7%	$20	$40	$40	$20	$20	$20	4.00%
California	1%	1%-2%	2%-4%	4%-8%	8%-9.3%	$52	$104	$104	$52	$52	$52	4.75%
Colorado	5%	5%	5%	5%	5%	$1,950 per federal exemption						3.00%*
Connecticut	7%**	7%**	7%**	7%**	7%**	$100	$200	$200			$100	7.50%*
Delaware	0-3.2%	5%	6%	6.6%-7.6%	7.7%	$1,250 per federal exemption						none
District of Columbia	6%	6%	8%	9.5%	9.5%	$1,025	$2,050	$2,050	$1,025	$1,025	$1,025	6.00%*
Florida	no state income tax											6.00%*
Georgia	1%-4%	4%-6%	6%	6%	6%	$1,500	$3,000		$1,500			3.00%
Hawaii	2.25%-6.25%	6.25%-7.25%	7.25%-8.25%	8.25%-9.75%	9.75%-10%	$1,040 per federal exemption				$7,000	$1,040	4.00%
Idaho	2%-6.5%	7.5%-7.8%	7.8%	8.2%	8.2%	$1,900 per federal exemption						5.00%
Illinois	2.5%	2.5%	2.5%	2.5%	2.5%	$1,000 per federal exemption						5.00%*
Indiana	3.4%	3.4%	3.4%	3.4%	3.4%	$1,000	$1,000		$1,000	$1,000	$1,000	5.00%*
Iowa	0.4%-5%	5%-6.8%	6.8%-7.2%	7.55%-8.8%	8.8%-9.%	$20	$40	$40	$15	$20	$20	4.00%*

h-husband, w-wife, p-parent, gp-grandparent, d-descendant, c-child
pub-public institutions (including governments)
char-charity
i-spouse of child, s-sibling, a-ancestors
sc-stepchildren, sp-stepparent
n-nieces and nephews
/-of

* Food exempt from sales tax.

** Connecticut only taxes capital gains

| Real Property Tax Rate (per $1,000 of assessed value) | | | | | | Estate Tax Rates | | | | |
Average	Low	High	Class	Class	Description	up to $50,000	$50,000 to $100,000	$100,000 to $200,000	$200,000 to $400,000	Over $400,000
46.85	28.00	70.60		n/a		0%-0.8%	0.8%-1.6%	1.6%-2.4%	2.4%-3.2%	3.2%-16%
9.47	1.25	14.80		n/a						
97.55	70.30	133.67		n/a		0%-0.8%	0.8%-1.6%	1.6%-2.4%	2.4%-3.2%	3.2%-16%
38.86	30.30	53.00		n/a		0%-0.8%	0.8%-1.6%	1.6%-2.4%	2.4%-3.2%	3.2%-16%
11.02	10.00	21.35		n/a		0%-0.8%	0.8%-1.6%	1.6%-2.4%	2.4%-3.2%	3.2%-16%
73.84	49.05	129.28		n/a		equal to Federal estate tax credit; prorated for non-domiciliaries based on proportion of instate property in estate				
33.80	10.00	72.90		AA	h, w	0%	0%	0%	0%	2.86%-4.29%
				A	p,gp,d	0%-4.29%	4.29%	4.29%-5.72%	5.72%-7.15%	8.58%-11.44%
				B	i	5.72%-7.15%	7.15%	7.15%-8.58%	8.58%-10.01%	11.44%-14.30%
				C	others	11.44%-12.87%	12.87%	12.87%-14.30%	14.30%-15.73%	17.16%-20.02%
				D	pub/char	entirely exempt				
17.25	12.05	36.52		A	h, w	2%	2%	2%-3%	3%-4%	4%
				B	p,gp,c,i,d	1%-2%	2%-4%	4%-5%	5%-6%	6%
				C	s,s/d/p	5%-6%	6%-7%	7%-8%	8%-9%	9%
				D	all others	10%-12%	12%-14%	14%-16%	16%	16%
				E	char	entirely exempt				
20.30	20.30	20.30	Realty	A	p, h, w, c, d, a	1%-2%	3%	5%	5%	5%-23%
31.00	31.00	31.00	Pers.	C	all others	1%-2%	3%	5%	5%	5%-23%
				D	publ	entirely exempt				
22.09	15.65	58.80		n/a		0%-0.8%	0.8%-1.6%	1.6%-2.4%	2.4%-3.2%	3.2%-16%
55.22	30.95	90.05		n/a		0%-0.8%	0.8%-1.6%	1.6%-2.4%	2.4%-3.2%	3.2%-16%
7.58	5.25	8.68	bldgs.	n/a		equal to Federal estate tax credit; prorated for nonresidents				
7.90	5.34	9.81	land			based on proportion of instate property in estate				
19.38	12.88	26.81		n/a		for domiciliaries, equal to Federal estate tax credit				
88.97	30.44	161.72		n/a		0%-0.8%	0.8%-1.6%	1.6%-2.4%	2.4%-3.2%	3.2%-16%
117.74	69.76	229.23		A	s, c, d, p	1%-2%	2%-3%	3%	4%-5%	5%-20%
				B	s, d/s, i	7%	7%	10%	10%	10%-15%
				C	all others	10%	10%	15%	15%	15%-20%
30.78	23.05	38.74		A	h, w, p, c, d	1%-4%	5%-6%	7%-8%	8%	8%
				B	s,i,sc	5%-7%	7%-8%	9%-10%	10%	10%
				C	other persons	10%	12%	15%	15%	15%
				D	outstate char	10%	10%	10%	10%	10%
				E	for-profits	15%	15%	15%	15%	15%
				F	instate char	entirely exempt				

TABLE 8-4 *(continued)*

	up to $5,000	State Income Tax Rates $5,000 to $10,000	$10,000 to $20,000	$20,000 to $40,000	over $40,000	Single	State Exemptions Married	Head of H'hold	Dep'dnt	Blind	Over 65	Sales Tax
Kansas	4.05%	4.05%	4.05%	4.05%-5.3%	5.3%	$2,000 per federal exemption					$60	$60 4.00%
Kentucky	2%-4%	5%-6%	6%	6%	6%	$20	$40		$20	$40	$40	5.00%*
Louisiana	2%	2%	4%	4%	4%-6%	$4,500	$9,000	$9,000	$1,000			4.00%*
Maine	2%	2%-4%	6%-8%	8%	8%	$40 per federal exemption						5.00%*
Maryland	2%-5%	5%	5%	5%	5%	$1,100 per federal exemption						5.00%*
Massachusetts	5%-10%†	5%-10%†	5%-10%†	5%-10%†	5%-10%†	$2,200	$4,400		$1,000	$2,200	$700	5.00%*
Michigan	4.6%	4.6%	4.6%	4.6%	4.6%	$1,800 per federal exemption						4.00%*
Minnesota	6%	6%	6%-8%	8%	8%-8.5%	$1,950 per federal exemption						6.00%*
Mississippi	3%	4%	5%	5%	5%	$6,000	$9,500	$9,500	$1,500	$1,500	$1,500	6.00%
Missouri	1.5%-3.%	4%-6%	6%	6%	6%	$1,200	$2,400	$2,000	$400			4.23%
Montana	2%-4%	4%-6%	6%-8%	9%-10%	10%-11%	$1,140	$1,140		$1,140	$1,140	$1,140	none
Nebraska	2%-3.2%	3.2%	3.2%	3.2%-5%	5%-5.9%	$1,130 per Federal exemption						4.00%*
Nevada	no state income tax											5.75%*
New Hampshire	5%	5%	5%	5%	5%	$1,200	$2,400			$1,200	$1,200	none
New Jersey	2%	2%	2%	2.5%	2.5%-3%	$1,000	$2,000		$1,000	$1,000	$1,000	6.00%*
New Mexico	1.8%	1.8%-3%	3%-5.8%	5.8%-7.7%	7.7%-8%	$2,000 per Federal exemption						4.75%
New York	3%-4%	4%-7%	7%-8.375%	8.375%	8.375%	$1,000 per dependent only						4.00%*
N. Carolina	3%-5%	5%-6%	7%	7%	7%	$1,100	$2,200	$2,200	$800	$1,100	$1,100	3.00%

h-husband, w-wite, p-parent, gp-grandparent, d-descendant, c-child, pub-public institutions (including governments)
char-charity, i-spouse of child, s-sibling, a-ancestors, sc-stepchildren, sp-stepparent, n-nieces and nephews, /-of

Note: For Massachusetts, property tax classes are: I, residential; III, commercial; IV, industrial.

* Food exempt from sales tax.

† Interest, dividends, and capital gains are taxed at 10%; other income at 5%.

Real Property Tax Rate (per $1,000 of assessed value)						Estate Tax Rates				
Average	Low	High	Class	Class	Description	up to $50,000	$50,000 to $100,000	$100,000 to $200,000	$200,000 to $400,000	Over $400,000
158.42	120.83	198.97		A	a, d, c, sc, d/c, i, sp	1%-2%	3%	4%	4%	4%-5%
				B	s	3%-5%	7.5%	10%	10%	10%-12.5%
				C	all others	10%	10%	12%	15%	15%
				D	char	entirely exempt				
4.83	2.69	8.66		A	p, s, c, sc	2%-5%	5%-6%	7%	8%	8%-10%
				B	s,n,i,s of p	4%-10%	10%-12%	14%	16%	16%
				C	all others	6%-14%	14%-16%	16%	16%	16%
				D	char	entirely exempt				
92.73	63.84	121.38		A	d, a, h, w, c	2%-3%	3%	3%	3%	3%
				B	other relatives	5%-7%	7%	7%	7%	7%
				C	strangers	5%-10%	10%	10%	10%	10%
				D	char	entirely exempt				
22.87	11.60	32.12		n/a		equal to unused portion of the credit (allocated for nonresident) that Fed Estate Tax allows for state taxes				
14.83	5.50	35.71		n/a		for estates over $100,000, equal to unused portion of the credit that Fed Estate Tax allows for state taxes				
14.19	3.08	23.20	I	n/a		5%	7%	9%	10%	11%-16%
18.89	5.62	33.20	III&IV							
61.02	38.38	84.86		n/a		equal to unused portion of the credit (allocated for nonresidents) that Fed Estate Tax allows for state taxes				
127.28	97.32	232.94		n/a		maximum Federal tax credit allowable for state death taxes				
114.72	65.37	155.56		n/a		1%	1%-1.6%	2.4%	3.2%	4%-16%
41.25	23.90	77.70		n/a		0%-0.8%	0.8%-1.6%	1.6%-2.4%	2.4%-3.2%	3.2%-16%
338.83	196.94	537.55		n/a		equal to unused portion of the credit (allocated for nonresidents) that Fed Estate Tax allows for state taxes				
28.75	23.07	37.93		n/a		equal to unused portion of the credit that Fed Estate Tax allows for state taxes				
22.55	14.96	29.68		n/a						
25.39	27.51	112.60		n/a		equal to unused portion of the credit that Fed Estate Tax allows for state taxes				
50.06	7.60	210.76		AA	h,w	entirely exempt				
				A	p,gp,c,c/c	0%-2%	3%	4%-5%	6%-7%	7%-16%
				B	non-profit orgs	entirely exempt				
				C	s,i	11%	11%	11%	11%	11%-16%
				D	all others	15%	15%	15%	15%	15%-16%
				E	publ	entirely exempt				
27.59	15.78	48.67		n/a		equal to state death tax credit (allocated for nonresidents) allowable under Fed Estate Tax				
206.09	26.81	611.91		n/a		2%	2%-3%	2%-5%	4%-5%	5%-21%
13.64	7.40	17.10		A	d,a,c,sc	1%-3%	4%	5%	6%	6%-12%
				B	s,d of c,s/p	4%-7%	8%	10%	10%-11%	11%-16%
				C	all others	8%-10%	11%	12%	12%-13%	13%-17%
				D	char	entirely exempt				

TABLE 8-4 *(continued)*

| | State Income Tax Rates | | | | | State Exemptions | | | | | | |
	up to $5,000	$5,000 to $10,000	$10,000 to $20,000	$20,000 to $40,000	over $40,000	Single	Married	Head of H'hold	Dep'dnt	Blind	Over 65	Sales Tax
N. Dakota	no state income tax					$1,950 per Federal exemption						5.50%*
Ohio	0.743%	1.486%	2.972%-4.4	4.4575-5.2	5.201%-	$650	$1,300		$650			5.00%*
Oklahoma	0.5%-3%	4%-6%	6%	6%	6%	$1,000 per Federal exemption					$1,000 $1,000	4.00%
Oregon	5%-7%	7%-9%	9%	9%	9%	$89 per Federal exemption						none
Pennsylvania	2.1%	2.1%	2.1%	2.1%	2.1%	None						6.00%*
Rhode Island	22.96%	22.96%	22.96%	22.96%	22.96%	$1,950 per Federal exemption						6.00%*
S. Carolina	3%-4%	4%-7%	7%	7%	7%	$1,950 per Federal exemption						5.00%
S. Dakota	no state income tax											?
Tennessee	6% on income from stocks and bonds (exempt if over 65 and income not over $9000 (if single) or $15,000 (if joint return)					$1,250	$2,500					5.50%
Texas	no state income tax											6.00%*
Utah	2.6%-7.	7.35%	7.35%	7.35%	7.35%	75% of Fed exemption amount						5.09%*
Vermont	25% of					$1,950 per federal exemption						4.00%*
Virginia	2%-3%	3%-5%	5.75%	5.75%	5.75%	$800	$1,600		$800	$800	$800	3.50%
Washington	no state income tax											6.50%*
W. Virginia	3%	3%	4%-6%	6%	6%	$2,000 per federal exemption						5.00%*
Wisconsin	4.9%	4.9%	6.55%-6.93	6.93%	6.93%						$50	$25 5.00%*
Wyoming	no state income tax											3.00%

h-husband, w-wife, p-parent, gp-grandparent, d-descendant, c-child
pub-public institutions (including governments)
char-charity
i-spouse of child, s-sibling, a-ancestors
sc-stepchildren, sp-stepparent
n-nieces and nephews
/-of

* Food exempt from sales tax.

Real Property Tax Rate (per $1,000 of assessed value)						Estate Tax Rates				
Average	Low	High	Class	Class	Description	up to $50,000	$50,000 to $100,000	$100,000 to $200,000	$200,000 to $400,000	Over $400,000
359.90	272.91	476.14		n/a		0%-0.8%	0.8%-1.6%	1.6%-2.4%	2.4%-3.2%	3.2%-16%
64.35	41.00	142.80		n/a		2%-3%	3%	4%	5%-6%	6%-7%
80.68	55.60	123.64		n/a		0.5%-2%	2%-2.5%	3%	3%-6.5%	6.5%-15%
27.71	18.39	40.66		n/a						
133.80	53.82	375.07	City	n/a		equal to unused portion of the credit				
164.64	47.18	568.78	Boro			that Fed Estate Tax allows for state taxes				
29.89	10.87	79.38		n/a		For decedent dying after 12-31-90, estate tax is maximum credit				
						that Fed Estate Tax allows for state taxes				
236.92	156.20	297.00		n/a		6%-7%	7%	8%	8%	8%
38.02	8.42	75.37	A		i,c,c/c	0%-3.75%	6%	7.5%	7.5%	7.5%
			B		a	3%-7.5%	12%	15%	15%	15%
			C		s,d/s,i	4%-10%	16%	20%	20%	20%
			D		s/p,d/s/p	5%-12%	20%	25%	25%	25%
			E		char	6%-15%	24%	24%	24%	24%
			F		all others	6%-15%	24%	24%	24%	24%
			G		h, w	entirely exempt				
48.48	26.00	90.30	A		h, w, c, a, d, s, sc	5.5%-6.5%	6.5%	6.5%	6.5%-7.5%	7.5%-9.5%
			B		all others	6.5%-?%	9.5%	12.5%-13.5%	16%	16%
			C		char	entirely exempt				
15.29	4.98	26.03		n/a		0%-0.8%	0.8%-1.6%	1.6%-2.4%	2.4%-3.2%	3.2%-16%
0.02	0.01	0.12		n/a		0%-0.8%	0.8%-1.6%	1.6%-2.4%	2.4%-3.2%	3.2%-16%
26.53	20.90	31.80		n/a		equal to Fed credit for state death taxes (prorated for nonresidents)				
9.69	2.00	16.90	Realty	n/a		0%-0.8%	0.8%-1.6%	1.6%-2.4%	2.4%-3.2%	3.2%-16%
37.96	6.00	70.70	Person							
31.17	5.00	63.00	Mach.							
14.23	9.50	28.85		n/a						
7.99	6.49	9.57	I	n/a		0%-0.8%	0.8%-1.6%	1.6%-2.4%	2.4%-3.2%	3.2%-16%
15.45	11.25	19.07	II							
30.90	24.54	38.14	IV							
31.60	25.40	39.58		n/a						
78.18	67.22	91.42		n/a		0%-0.8%	0.8%-1.6%	1.6%-2.4%	2.4%-3.2%	3.2%-16%

TABLE 8-5   What to Look for in a New Community (and to Recheck
            Your Present Area For)

Climate and environment: temperature range
Accessibility: highways, railroads, airlines, bus
Population: of local town and nearest major center. Up? Down?
Character: stable government; well maintained public areas such as streets, municipal buildings, parks
Recreational facilities: close by and inexpensive—unless you can afford the privacy of a club— for golf, tennis, bowling, swimming, fishing
Health services: convenient, well-equipped hospital, clinic, ambulance and groups of physicians, dentists, and other practitioners.
Transportation: buses, taxis and special mini-buses for elderly
Houses of worship: keyed to your interests. If you're a Unitarian, you may not be happy in a community dominated by fundamentalists.
Educational institutions: universities, colleges for courses, lectures and seminars; technical schools for learning new skills
Cultural opportunities: local or visiting orchestras, ballet companies or, if you want to be involved, a local band, chorus, Little Theatre.
Group activities: at clubhouse, senior center, AARP chapters.
Restaurants that serve the kind of food you like and offer Early Bird specials.
Shopping: within walking distance, a small center with a convenience store, hairdresser and cleaner. Within easy driving distance, shopping centers with a supermarket, bank, drugstore, card store (to keep in touch with the family and friends), cobbler and post office, department and specialty stores to shop for clothing and gifts, and entertainment for yourself and visitors.
Housing: priced within your budget range; special units for retirees, singles and couples. Remember, the less expensive your new housing is than your old housing, the more cash you'll have for your retirement when you sell your old home.
Volunteer Opportunities: a chapter of RSVP (Retired Service Volunteer Program) so you can keep busy and help those less fortunate than you
Future changes: will new highways spur developments that can impact on traffic, housing, recreational opportunities?
How do planners (and knowledgeable friends) project the community to look in 10 to 15 years?

Checklist for Moving

To make a move to another community smoother:

• Close out all checking and savings accounts. If a CD has time to maturity, arrange for the proceeds to be forwarded to your new address. Early withdrawals may be subject to penalties.

• Clean out your safe deposit box and separate items in plastic bags with labels.

- If you plan to keep the same broker, notify the broker of your address change. If you start anew, have the account transferred to a branch of the same firm or to the new broker.

- Pay all outstanding bills: charge accounts at department stores, for utilities, water/garbage service, local/state taxes.

- If you move to another state, get the name of a local lawyer and have your will rewritten to conform to the laws of the new state.

- Have your insurance cancelled or transferred. For auto coverage, check to see if you need to add to your coverage to comply with state laws. For life insurance, be sure to give the insurance company your new address. For home insurance, maintain coverage until the old house is sold. Schedule your new insurance to start when your ownership or occupancy begins.

- Transfer or cancel membership in any organization for which you pay dues.

- Collect deposits for utilities, and for security on apartment/condominium.

- Send change of address cards (available from the local post office) to your bank, thrift or credit union so that you will receive year-end tax information; to companies from which you receive dividends or interest; to credit card companies; to department stores with branches in the new community; to Social Security; to the bank/employer responsible for pension checks; and to the regional IRS office.

- Leave forwarding address with your employer, broker, insurance agent and a close-by neighbor.

Retiring Abroad

Retiring abroad is an appealing choice for many retirees. Currently, Social Security checks go to some 340,000 retirees living outside the USA. Once you qualify for Social Security benefits, you are entitled to receive monthly checks anywhere in the world except in legally banned countries such as Afghanistan, Albania, Cambodia, Cuba, East Germany, Soviet Union and Vietnam.

Retiring abroad has many attractions, especially for those who have family or friends in foreign countries. That $1,000 a month in Social Security can be a small fortune in the mountains of Greece, the lakes of Scotland or the hamlets of a South Sea island. However, there can be drawbacks to living abroad:

(1) you probably will no longer be covered by Medicare and, except in countries like Canada, will have to pay for your health services;

(2) when death occurs abroad, there can be problems as to whether your will can be probated plus extra taxes and hassles on the distribution of property (check the consular office for rules);

(3) you may not have the protection of a legal system that recognizes your right to control your assets;

(4) living costs depend more on the type of community than the country and will of course, reflect the value of the dollar. Rapid changes in currency values can make anticipating future living costs difficult.

TABLE 8-6   Living Costs Around the World

The first column in this chart shows average monthly costs for modest apartments in major cities around the world. The spaces are comparable but the amenities— furniture, appliances, safeguards—will be different. The second column gives a weighted index—using New York as a base with a value of 100—of other living costs.

City	Average Monthly Rent*	Cost of Living Index**
New York	617	100
Tokyo	552	203
London	430	109
Brussels	340	104
Dublin	340	107
Zurich	310	123
Paris	280	109
Montreal	244	101
Copenhagen	240	120
Tel Aviv	130	123

* All rent figures are for 1982, except Montreal (1981).

** All cost-of-living figures are for 1988.
SOURCE: *The Book of World City Rankings*. Macmillan, Inc.
Business International Corporation

In foreign cities, as shown by Table 8-6, apartments in Tokyo and Hong Kong were more expensive than in New York but those in Mexico City rented for about one third as much. These comparisons are misleading because furnishings, services and amenities in many foreign countries are significantly different than those of the USA.

You may be able to hire servants in Portugal but your appliances will be limited and electricity may be available only intermittently.

To check living costs abroad, contact such international organizations as the National Council of Churches, United Nations Development programs and major corporations with worldwide interests.

You are considered a U.S. citizen unless you renounce this privilege (and vote in the foreign country). Since you will probably want to retain your U.S. citizenship, taxes should be considered. You will be subject to U.S. income taxes regardless of where you live or earn wages/salary. Some countries have tax treaties with the USA so a portion of your taxes may be deductible from your federal return. Write IRS for Publication #54: *Tax Guide for U.S. Citizens Abroad.*

WHAT TO LIVE IN

Your housing should be realistically designed for your retirement years. You'll want housing with few or no steps because of the *probability* that one spouse will have to use a cane or be confined to a wheelchair. The interior should be organized for convenience and comfort (particularly during periods of ill health) rather than for style and display. Also look for housing that will require minimal maintenance. When you have arthritis or a bad back, you will have to hire help and this can dent your fixed budget.

For about $1,500 to $2,500 per unit, these features—recommended by the Florida Housing for the Elderly Committee—can be included, or planned for, in all types of senior housing to make life easier, safer and more comfortable:

- One level, or short steps convertible to ramps

- Bright, cheery rooms: bedrooms, preferably two to allow privacy and sick care, close to bathroom; one large enough for twin beds, two dressers and small cabinets

- Non-skid floors in living and bathroom areas; firmly anchored rugs and carpets

- Doorknobs with levers and easy-to-find keyholes

- Lighting: adjustable, and three times as bright as those designed for younger families; uniform coverage because dark spots can look like obstacles when eyesight is poor

- Night lights between bedroom and bathroom with an electric photocell activated when someone passes

- Switches located outside doors, low enough to be reached in wheelchairs

- Electrical outlets at least 18 inches from the floor in every room and hallway

- Windows low enough to see out to a garden, but high enough to discourage intruders; double-glazed and insulated to save on heating and cooling; wide, water-impervious sills for safety and to accommodate planters and flower pots

- Doors and hallways wide enough for a wheelchair (not always a problem as new designs permit narrowing with levers); about $15 more

- Mirrors tilted so that you can see yourself when in a wheelchair or bent over

- Bathtub with step-in feature, shower, grab bars ($55 more), seat ledges and non-slip stripping ($35 extra)

- Toilets at least 18 inches high or, when low, with extensions that can be raised

- Faucets: levers rather than those that must be grasped strongly for turning ($15 to $55 more)

- Ample-size medicine chest (you'll be surprised at how many pills and lotions you'll acquire)

- Kitchen: closed-in sink that is convenient to a person in a wheelchair; lazy Susans in corners of cupboard; countertop ranges with dials in the front and, preferably, with panels that tilt: labor/step-saving items such as a self-cleaning range; round-corner cabinets to avoid bruises from bumping; expect these items to cost about $1500; a non-skid floor will cost another $120

- Garage with automatic door opener; entry to home via wind/rainproof passage to the house; a covered porch ($615 extra)

- Ample space for garbage, papers, collections of old clothes for Salvation Army; storage area for garden tools and supplies

- Hobby/work area: well ventilated and lighted; non-skid floors, ample storage area and electrical outlets; overhead lighting that throws no shadows

- Safety features: smoke detector; fire alarm and automatic dialing system on the telephone to summon help if needed

More Comfortable Homes

One advantage of building your retirement home is that you can take advantage of new techniques and designs that can make living more comfortable and convenient. When included at construction, these user-friendly features are relatively inexpensive. Ask your architect and builder about the items listed below:

Feature	Added Cost When House Is Built
KITCHEN	
Custom-made pantry	$149
Single-lever faucet	15
Non-slip floor	120
BATHROOM	
Grab bars for tub/toilet	55
Non-skid floor	35
Single-lever faucet	55
Extra-wide door	15
ENTRANCE/OUTDOOR	
Non-slip concrete sidewalk	25
Covered porch	615
Package shelf at door	40
Extra-wide door	56
Lever/deadbolt locks	212

Other items that seniors find useful include

- electrical outlets 24 inches high

- easily accessible and well-lighted closet space

- car storage area that is visible from house windows

- house windows that are low enough to look out of, yet high enough to discourage intruders

- handrails at stairs and landings

- photocells to illuminate entry areas

If you choose an apartment/condominium, here are some other items that can make your life easier and more secure:

- highly visible entrance

- well-maintained building (inside and out)

- wide, well-lighted foyer/hallways

- elevator (preferably two)

- laundry room that is conveniently located so you won't have to carry washing very far

- accessible long-term storage bins/rooms

- parking lot: well-lighted, convenient, safe

- superintendent who lives in; readily available handyman

- building phone system for visitors and locked-outs (memory falters with age)

- pets permitted within reasonable limits

Although you may initially find ornate, crowded, conventional housing more attractive than more well-organized, functional quarters that may appear bleak and sparse, keep in mind what you might need (rather than want) if you ever become infirm.

Apartment. Apartments offer the advantage of freedom to live pretty much as you want. With competent management, there should be few headaches because the landlord will handle maintenance, repairs and painting; clear the parking lot; provide security, etc. Money which would be required as a down payment on a purchase can earn extra income for you. Rents can be projected by leases with escalation clauses. If you aren't happy, you can move when the lease expires. Apartments are good for those who don't want to be bothered with details, and can be an excellent choice for people living alone.

If you decide to live in an apartment, make sure that you have protection if the owners decide to convert it into a condominium and you must buy your unit or move out.

Condominium. Condominiums are long-term investments. You don't have the option of moving out at the end of a lease, and if you don't like a condominium after you move in, you could lose money selling it. Maintenance is usually handled by an individual or firm, paid for by a monthly fee. Costs of replacing major items (such as a roof, furnace, air-conditioner) are paid for through special assessments. Usually, there will be special facilities for recreation and entertainment.

When you live in a condo, you're involved in a joint venture with many others. Condominiums are resident-managed, so to protect your interests and your investment, you should plan on joining in activities and participating in meetings.

Condominiums have the potential of offering financial benefits. Interest on a mortgage to purchase a condominium is tax-deductible. The condominium may appreciate in value. However, given the fact that (a) your tax bracket will probably be low, and (b) you may not have reason to sell your condominium while you are living (and so will not benefit personally from any appreciation in price), consider whether these features will benefit you.

When budgeting for a condominium, allow for increasing maintenance payments over the years and special assessments. As a building gets older, equipment is more likely to break down, and these costs are more likely to rise. Before buying, check the trend in special assessments to get a handle on what they are likely to cost in the future. Remember, if you're unable to pay for these fees, you will forfeit your condominium interest.

Warning: when a condominium offers extra services (such as a bus), be sure that these costs are included in the assessment. Otherwise, if too many people who do not pay for the service use it, the service will eventually be discontinued.

For more information, get *Questions About Condominiums: What to Ask Before You Buy,* #567L, Consumer Information Center, Dept. K, Pueblo, Colo. 91009.

Retirement Community/Development?

Retirement communities offer pleasant (if small) living areas; no worries about maintenance; opportunities for companionship and involvement; and over the long term, predictable costs.

The tradeoff for these features is a controlled environment where you might be forced to conform and accept the mores, prejudices and routines of your neighbors. You will be expected to participate in planned activities and must, to some degree, lose outside contacts. As one person, who has lived in his project for a decade, explains, ''You have to weigh the benefits of total care/involvement with mandatory association with a small number of peers against the freedom of choice and movement that is available with regular housing. There are times when I cannot stand another birthday party or listen to the same stale arguments between almost senile neighbors.''

When making a choice, remember that what seems attractive today may not suit your needs or lifestyle tomorrow. In the early years, you may want to set your own pace, make your own friends and retain privacy. In community living, this can be difficult. As you grow older, however, you may appreciate the prepared schedules, the organized events and structured lifestyle. Such security can be especially welcome when one partner becomes ill and, later, when there's one survivor.

Lifecare Housing: Expensive But Comfortable

These are similar to retirement communities in that they permit only senior residents but, usually, they are smaller developments consisting of fewer housing units. You can choose between pay-in-advance centers and rental units. Pay-in-advance centers generally feature an entry charge of $40,000 to $80,000, plus a monthly fee of $400 to $1,000 for meals, maid service, maintenance, activities, etc. Rental units can cost from $1,200 to $1,800 per month for a small unit and two meals a day, plus extra charges as used for transportation, group recreation, limited health care and outside entertainment.

Who Will Be Your Neighbors?

No matter how joyful you may believe life in a specific community will be, always check on the compatibility of you and your new neighbors, with special attention to their lifestyle.

For example, if most of the residents of a community bought their homes when the section was opened, 10 years ago, they will have set lifestyles based on cliques, church affiliations and interests that may seem narrow to a younger newcomer. Moving into another environment, with neighbors that you have more in common with, may be more rewarding.

Lifecare housing is still in an experimental stage and few have been operating long enough to determine resident wishes and investor profits. To stay ahead of competition, developers are expanding services, such as special rooms and staff for temporary medical/nursing care for those returning from a hospital, or for a single resident who is confined to bed for a short time. Another option that may be offered is long-term care insurance. For example, a person might pay a one-time $10,000 premium to assure lifetime residence. If that person needs to move to more extensive, expensive facilities, the policy will pay the extra cost.

Checklist for Lifecare Housing. You should thoroughly investigate lifecare housing operations before paying a fee or advance rent for a lifecare unit. Ask these questions:

- Are the sponsors and administrators qualified and experienced? What are their credentials? Have prior projects been successful and attractive?

- What does the residency agreement cover in its financial provisions, fees, deposit, and refunds? What happens when your money runs out?

- Who will be responsible for financing losses, the owner or the tenant?

- What are the sources of operating income? Is there a cap on rents? Will increases be subject to review, and, possibly, veto by the residents?

- With units requiring endowments (pre-payments), what are the choices if one partner dies, or the enterprise goes bankrupt?

- Are there provisions for a partial refund if the property is sold at a profit?

- Are the units well-built; do they carry a warranty?

- Is there full security with competent police and fire departments and access to an ambulance service?

- Are the recreational facilities and community centers complete and paid for so that the future costs of membership and maintenance will continue to be reasonable and under the control of the residents, not of the developer who could sell the units to a promoter able to charge what he wants?

- Will there be continued maintenance (by the development or the local government) of common areas such as streets, meadows, and ponds?

- Who will be the ultimate manager? In new developments, all of the services and expenditures will be controlled by the developer but, when the majority of units have been sold, the Homeowners' Association takes over. Have your lawyer check this management agreement. Be prepared to become personally involved in the Homeowners' Association. Before you make a substantial investment, be sure that you're willing to accept this responsibility.

Types of Congregate Housing

Adult Congregate Living Facilities (ACLFs). These are boardinghouses which, in most cases, are regulated by the state. They provide shelter (usually, your own room) and such personal services as assistance in eating, bathing, dressing or supervision of self-administered medication. They range in size from homes serving half a dozen elderly who create their own lifestyle, to major projects with 100 or more tenants with extensive services, transportation, organized recreation, exercise classes and so forth.

Don't Overlook Manufactured Housing

If you will be purchasing a new home for your retirement, manufactured housing is an option that you should consider. If you have not seen the latest models, visit a dealer for a real surprise. They are smart looking, comfortable, inexpensive, available in a variety of styles, often designed for senior citizens and can be located almost anywhere—with some zoning restrictions.

Prices start as low as $30,000 but there are also striking designs with three and four bedrooms, cathedral ceilings, tiled bath, walk-in closets and garages. Some can be erected on your lot; others are prefabricated and trucked to your site—a leased or owned lot that can be part of a cooperative, professionally managed development with recreation center, pool and so forth. Or, if you prefer isolation, the ready-to-move-in structure can be hauled to a remote location. The drawback with this option is that builders, carpenters, and electricians can be difficult to hire.

ACLFs can be very good for singles and couples who need support or enjoy helping others, provided the proprietors are caring, competent and honest. Look for these qualities when examining an ACLF. By law, there can be only limited-to-supervision health care but, in Florida, the state is recognizing the need for services halfway between those of an ACLF and a nursing home: shelter, food plus basic medical care.

Share-A-Home. These are good for seniors who do not need supervision and who can afford to pay a reasonable rental, typically the Social Security payment of the primary wage earner. Similar to ACLFs, groups of unrelated individuals share a single family house, usually owned by a community organization, similar to a co-op. Each person has a room and shares common areas such as bathrooms and living and dining areas. Cooking and cleaning chores are shared or, in some cases, handled by a manager.

Home Sharing. At its simplest, this involves taking in one or more boarders. For a single survivor with a large house, this provides extra income, help with household tasks, companionship and security. Ideally, there should be one or two ''guests'' about the same age as you are, with similar backgrounds and interests. In college communities, however, the visitor can be a student or students. They will brighten the home and, hopefully, will be willing to lend a hand with the lawn, garden, window cleaning and other chores that are difficult for the elderly.

If you have a large house, try to work with an organized group such as a church or senior center to help in screening residents and developing house rules.

Accessory Apartment Also known as Granny Flats or ECHO (Elder Cottage Housing Opportunity), there are two types:

(1) a single family dwelling conversion into two or more individual units with kitchen and bath;

(2) a detached, small home on the edge of a large lot of a single family house. Typically, this is a prefabricated unit that permits the senior(s) to live independently. When the resident dies or moves, the temporary quarters can be removed.

When constructing an accessory apartment, be sure that the zoning laws permit such construction and habitation.

In some communities there are Senior Housing Information Centers which help to match homeowners and dwelling-seekers. Some of these offer counseling and help both parties to explore their concerns, expectations and hopes, and suggest specific arrangements.

For information, check your Area Agency on Housing, or write for a directory: Shared Housing Resource Center, 6344 Green Street, Philadelphia, PA 19144.

IF YOU OWN YOUR OWN HOME

What You Can Afford

Whether or not you decide to move, if you are going to own your own home, you have to determine how much you can afford to spend. Generally, plan to spend about 25% of your sure income on housing. Do not plan to spend more than 30% of your sure income. If your income cannot support paying for the house you want without exceeding 30% of your sure income, first try to use the savings or profits from the sale of your home to make up the difference. If you plan to purchase a new home, look at lowering the down payment (so you will have more money to earn income), or stretching out the terms of the mortgage from a 15-year mortgage to a 25- or 30-year loan.

Whether to buy or rent depends on available cash, assured income and lifestyle. Ownership will provide:

(a) a sense of security;

(b) relatively fixed costs in that mortgage payments can be set for many years;

TABLE 8-7   Housing Costs

Interest Rate	Monthly Mortgage Payments per $1,000	
	15 years	20 years
10%	$10.75	$ 9.65
11	11.37	10.33
12	12.00	11.01

Total Loan	Mortgage (15 Years/12%)	Annual Costs*	Total	Income Needed**
$50,000	$6,000	$4,800	$10,800	$43,200
40,000	4,800	3,600	8,400	33,600
30,000	3,600	3,000	6,600	26,400

* Annual Costs: Utilities, Insurance, Taxes, Maintenance
** based on total housing expenditure = 25% of income

(c) possible monetary benefits from deductions of payments for interest and property taxes;

(d) in many states, homestead exemption (in Florida, $25,000) or tax breaks for those over 65 and veterans;

(e) for householders, 55 years or older, a one-time exclusion, up to $125,000, of the capital gains from the sale of the home;

(f) hopefully, appreciation which will benefit the surviving spouse and, eventually, heirs.

With all housing that you buy, keep a 10-year frame in mind. For most dwellings, that's about the time when appliances will need repairs, plumbing will leak, the air conditioner or heating unit will conk out and the roof will begin to sag. These extra expenses will, inevitably, occur just when you've taken the last installment from your pension plan or savings account.

Table 8-7 shows that, with a 15-year loan of $50,000 at 12% interest, the mortgage payment will be $500 per month ($6,000 a year) plus costs, for utilities, insurance, taxes and routine maintenance of $400 per month ($4,800 a year). This total is $10,800 annually, so, to fund this expenditure, you would need a yearly income of $43,200. Remember, older people want greater comfort (higher heat in winter, cooler air conditioning in summer, and prompt, frequent repair service) so operating costs projections have to be generous. Maintenance, repairs and replacements will require substantial outlays.

If your mortgage is fixed, your payments will remain flat; but keep in mind that your total payments will rise because of higher local taxes, appreciated value and special assessments. For example, in some fast-growing Florida areas, taxes increase 5% annually. Compounded, that's an increase of 63% over 10 years! In more stable regions, without pressure for roads, schools, hospital care, etc., you can easily project a 30% increase in property taxes while you both live.

Now, let's try to forecast the future. You want to be sure that your housing costs in 15 years are still about 25% of your income. You can expect costs (including taxes and maintenance) to increase 5% annually. In the 15th year of the mortgage,

Total Loan	Mortgage (15 Years/12%)	Annual Costs	Total	Income Needed*
$50,000	$6,000	$9,984	$15,984	$63,936
40,000	4,800	7,488	12,288	49,152
30,000	3,600	6,240	9,840	39,360

* based on total housing expenditure = 25% of income

But don't panic. The inflation that pushed up your costs has eroded the cost of your future mortgage payments in today's dollars. Assuming a 5% inflation rate, here's what your year 15 outlays will be in today's dollars:

Total Loan	Mortgage (15 Years/12%)	Annual Costs	Total	Real Income Needed*
$50,000	$6,000	$4,800	$10,800	$43,200
40,000	4,800	3,600	8,400	33,600
30,000	3,600	3,000	6,600	26,400

* based on total housing expenditure = 25% of income

As you can see, therefore, despite rising costs, your total housing outlay will decline in real dollars as time goes on. The key for you will be to make sure that your income doesn't decline as well.

The best approach is to work backwards:

(a) choose a reasonable term for the loan, preferably related to the life expectancy of the primary wage earner: at age 65, 15 years for the male; 19 for the female;

(b) calculate total costs;

(c) use as much cash as you can spare;

(d) to keep total housing outlays to 25% of sure income: $5,000 for $20,000 a year. You can always raise this percentage with economies in other areas.

If you choose a good house in a good location, its value should appreciate so that you can recast the loan or take out a reverse annuity mortgage. If interest rates drop 2% in the future, refinancing may create a better cash flow. And if one spouse dies, that spouse's life insurance should provide an extra cushion to replace inflation-eroded income. *Be conservative:* lengthen the payout only when the income is sure. After the spouse's death, Social Security may be one-third less!

If you are close to, or over, the limit, and you plan to live in your old home, consider selling or taking in boarders.

Always review future housing costs. Don't go overboard with a new house, just because you are retired and want to make all your dreams come true immediately. Remember, if things are tight at the start, they will seldom ease over the years. If problems develop, you may have to get a job. That's not what most retirees want to be forced to do.

Paying for Retirement Housing

There are several ways to pay for a home you purchase for your retirement. You could take out a mortgage. You may also want to consider other less-conventional means of paying for housing. These often allow you to pay less each month by paying only for the value of the shelter that the house provides, while equity growth goes to another investor who shares payments. See page 218 for details.

There are several sources for mortgage funds. Mortgage money can be obtained from commercial or savings banks, savings and loan associations, life insurance companies, and other lenders, such as relatives or other individuals.

You must shop around for a mortgage to get the best deal. Today, rates, types of mortgages, and terms vary between different banks. Be aware, however, that some banks will lend only to their customers. If you do not have account with such a bank, you will not get a loan, regardless of your credit rating or earnings.

Conventional mortgage. With a conventional, or fixed-rate, mortgage your monthly payment is fixed throughout the life of the loan, which may run to 25 or 30 years. At the beginning of the loan, most of the payment is interest charges; at the end of the loan, most of the payment is principal.

Example: You get an $80,000, 30-year mortgage at 15%. Your monthly payment (principal repayment and interest) is $1,012; over $960 of the first payment is interest.

TABLE 8-8   30-Year Monthly Mortgage Payments at Varying Rates

Mortgage Amount	$10^1/2\%$	11%	$11^1/2\%$	12%	$12^1/2\%$	13%	$13^1/2\%$	14%	$14^1/2\%$	15%	$15^1/2\%$	16%	17%	18%
$ 10,000	$ 91	$ 95	$ 99	$ 103	$ 107	$ 111	$ 115	$ 118	$ 122	$ 126	$ 130	$ 134	$ 143	$ 151
$ 12,000	110	114	119	123	128	133	137	142	147	152	157	161	171	181
$ 16,000	146	152	158	165	170	177	183	190	196	202	209	215	228	241
$ 20,000	183	190	198	206	213	221	229	237	245	253	261	269	285	301
$ 24,000	220	229	238	247	256	265	275	284	294	303	313	323	342	362
$ 28,000	256	267	277	288	299	301	321	332	343	354	365	377	399	422
$ 32,000	293	305	317	329	341	354	366	379	392	405	417	430	456	482
$ 36,000	329	343	357	370	384	398	412	427	441	455	470	484	513	543
$ 40,000	366	381	396	411	427	442	458	474	490	506	522	538	570	603
$ 44,000	403	419	436	453	469	487	504	521	539	556	574	592	627	663
$ 48,000	439	457	475	494	512	531	550	569	588	607	626	645	684	723
$ 52,000	476	495	515	535	555	575	595	616	637	658	678	699	741	784
$ 56,000	512	533	555	576	598	619	641	664	686	708	731	753	798	844
$ 60,000	549	571	594	617	640	664	687	711	735	759	783	807	855	904
$ 64,000	585	610	634	658	683	708	733	758	784	809	835	861	912	965
$ 68,000	622	648	673	699	726	752	779	806	833	860	887	914	969	1025
$ 72,000	659	686	713	741	768	796	824	853	882	910	939	968	1026	1085
$ 76,000	695	724	753	782	811	841	870	900	931	961	991	1022	1084	1145
$ 80,000	732	762	792	823	854	885	916	948	980	1012	1044	1076	1141	1206
$ 84,000	768	800	832	864	896	929	962	995	1029	1062	1096	1130	1198	1266
$ 88,000	805	838	871	905	939	973	1008	1043	1078	1113	1148	1183	1256	1326
$ 92,000	842	876	911	946	982	1018	1053	1090	1127	1163	1200	1237	1312	1387
$ 96,000	878	914	951	987	1024	1062	1099	1137	1176	1214	1252	1291	1367	1447
$100,000	915	952	990	1029	1067	1106	1145	1185	1225	1264	1305	1345	1426	1507

NOTE: All figures have been rounded to the nearest dollar.

Adjustable-rate mortgage (ARM). The interest rate on the mortgage fluctuates according to an index tied to either U.S. Treasury securities, money market rates, the Federal Home Loan Bank Board's average for mortgage rates, or another index. How often the rate can be adjusted will vary from state to state and whether the bank is governed by federal regulations. The change in rates may translate into an adjustment in monthly payments or it may affect the outstanding loan balance. A borrower may find that ARMs are being offered at a slightly lower initial rate than a conventional mortgage or with fewer points. Check on the limits to which interest and/or monthly payments may be raised.

Graduated-payment mortgage (GMP). Monthly payments increase according to a schedule set at the beginning of the loan. This type of mortgage is designed to make financing more affordable by keeping monthly payments low in the first few years of the loan. The price of this reduction to the home buyer may be negative amortization. That is, instead of reducing the outstanding principal, the borrower may be increasing it for the first three, five, or even ten years. This means that if a house bought with an initial $50,000 mortgage is sold after two years, the borrower would have to repay more than $50,000. Retirees normally shouldn't take out a GMP; the higher mortgage payments will occur in later years, when the homeowner is more likely to be financially strapped.

Rollover mortgage (ROM). The mortgage looks like a conventional mortgage as monthly payments are fixed for the life of the loan. However, there is this catch: a ROM must be refinanced every few years, often three or five, at the then-prevailing interest rate. In fact, monthly payments are set only until refinancing is required. Again, retirees will probably want to avoid these.

Renegotiable mortgage or balloon-payment mortgage. This loan is similar to a ROM in that the principal must be repaid at the end of a set term by refinancing. However, unlike the ROM, there may be no guarantee of refinancing. These are particularly risky for retirees.

Federal Housing Administration mortgage. An FHA mortgage is obtained from a private lending institution, but the FHA insures the lender against loss in case of the homeowner's default. Because of this guarantee, some lenders may be willing to accept smaller down payments and a lower interest rate, and may lend their money over longer periods. However, when mortgage money is tight, lending institutions are less inclined to handle loans insured by the FHA. FHA charges a low insurance premium on the unpaid balance, included in the monthly payments called for by the mortgage. There is a dollar limitation on the value of the homes for which the FHA will provide mortgage insurance.

If you apply for an FHA-insured mortgage, the FHA will make a complete review of your ability to meet the mortgage obligations even after the bank has run its credit check and approved you for the loan. In addition to appraising the property, the FHA will consider your estimated prospective monthly housing expenses and estimated living costs, debts, and other financial obligations. Thus an FHA mortgage will take more time for approval than a conventional one.

Veterans Administration mortgage. If you are a veteran, you should check with the local VA branch regarding eligibility and opportunity for a VA-guaranteed mortgage. Generally, a VA mortgage will run for a longer term, may have lower interest rates, and require a smaller down payment, or none in some circumstances. As with FHA loans, those insured by the VA are only granted for property meeting rigid standards.

Straight or Adjustable Rate Mortgage?

For most retirees with essentially fixed incomes, a level interest rate is the safest. Adjustable rate mortgages usually start with a lower interest rate but there's no guarantee that you won't have to pay more. The same caveat goes for other special types of loans: graduated payment, indexed rate and so forth.

Creative financing. This is a catch-all phrase for combining a variety of financing techniques to cover the purchase price. One device is for the buyer to assume the seller's outstanding mortgage. The buyer takes over the mortgage and continues to pay off the lender. The buyer pays the seller the difference between the price of the house and outstanding balance of the mortgage. They are best to use when you sell your old home.

Another device is the purchase-money mortgage. If you cannot get financing to buy the house you want, the seller might take a mortgage on the house if he or she is not in immediate need of funds to buy another residence. The purchase-money mortgage may be for the entire cost of the home in excess of a down payment or in addition to a mortgage secured through a bank or other institution. Sometimes, a purchase-money mortgage requires a balloon payment shortly after the sale. For example, you may buy a $100,000 house by putting $10,000 cash, obtaining a $77,000 mortgage from the bank and getting a purchase-money mortgage from the seller for $15,000. This loan may contain a clause that the $15,000 is due 12 months from the date of sale. If you do not come up with cash or refinance, the seller may foreclose on the house. Generally, retirees want to avoid situations involving balloon payments.

Another financing arrangement sometimes accompanying new home purchases is a "buy down," in which the builder pays the lender a lump sum to lower the buyer's monthly payments for the first few years of the mortgage.

Shared equity is a program where two (or more) people join forces to buy a house. One becomes the Owner Occupant; the other, the Owner/Investor. Owner occupied loans require only a minimum down payment, seldom over 10%, but investor loans usually require a down payment of 20% or more.

The percentage of the original investment sets the schedule for all costs, benefits, and proceeds. Each person pays his/her share of the mortgage payments and operating costs, according to the percentage of interest owned. But the occupant pays rent to the investor on the portion of the property not owned. Each partner files separate tax returns and, as tenants in common, the property will pass to each individual's estate.

The occupant gets to deduct his or her share of interest and real estate taxes, and accumulate equity. The occupant also benefits from affordable payments, and is protected against mismanagement of the property. The investor gets to share in the ownership of well-managed, well-maintained property, with regular rent payments, and enjoys tax breaks and equity with potential for appreciation.

Example 8-1 shows the payments each party would be responsible for in a 50-50 deal on a unit where the mortgage payment is $868 per month.

Example 8-1

Property price: $110,000; down payment: $11,000; mortgage, $99,000 at 10%. *Monthly payments:* mortgage: $868; taxes: $100; insurance: $44: total $1,012 or $506 each.

Shared Equity Per Month
Income/Payments

	Owner Investor	Owner Occupant
Principal/Interest	$434	$434
Taxes	50	50
Insurance	22	22
Rent	+350	−350
Total	$156	$856
Deductions		
Interest	$425	$425
Taxes	50	50
Insurance	22	
Depreciation	337	
Write-off	$834	$475

Source: Karen DeVost Rollings, American Venture Realty, Silver Spring, MD. 20901.

These deals are complex, so consult a real estate lawyer before you set one up.

Using Your Home's Built-up Value

If your home has appreciated significantly, it represents a significant financial asset that you can use. If you don't use it, you're effectively deciding to just turn it over to your heirs. There's nothing wrong with this if you can afford it, but if you're strapped for funds, you may want to tap your home's value.

There are many different sorts of home equity loans and second mortgages that you can take advantage of.

All of these special loans involve risks. Some seniors may be confused, some lenders may be dishonest, and because the arrangements can be complex, there may not be adequate protection under some state laws. Retirees should only sign an agreement after all documents have been checked by an experienced attorney and all contingencies have been discussed with concerned outsiders such as relatives, social workers and financial advisers.

Home Equity Loans

A home equity loan is a line of credit, secured by a home. Interest is paid periodically, and the loan is repaid at some future date. With a house bought for $50,000 now worth $150,000, and a mortgage paid down to $30,000, you can borrow up to about $85,000 at an interest rate that is lower than that of credit cards, a personal loan, or a second mortgage.

The terms can be flexible: monthly payments to fit your budget (often, interest only for several years); repayments periodically or in full from the proceeds of the sale of the property; fixed or variable interest rate and, generally, tax deductions for the interest.

Although ads boosting home equity loans sound like a good deal, in most cases they are best for those who don't need them and dangerous for those who do. Still, under certain conditions, home equity loans can be useful when limited in size, subject to scheduled repayments and, for older retirees, used to supplement income.

As with all debts, the worth of a home equity loan depends on what you do with the proceeds and how much the payment of interest and amortization will impact your assets and income. One of the best uses of a home equity loan is for a bridge loan to build your dream house.

Points to Consider

In reviewing any type of home equity loan, project the worst possible scenario. Assume that, at some point, because it's so easy to write another check, the original loan will swell to double its initial size. Suddenly, you lose your job and there's a recession so that the value of your home drops and is now only a bit more than the debt. To stay afloat, you will have to sell your home and, in retirement, will probably have to rent because you do not have enough cash to make the down payment on a new home. Too tragic? Maybe, but this sad set of events occurs every day, and there's no guarantee that it couldn't happen to you.

Still, a home equity loan makes sense when:

- The property appreciates rapidly so that the loan represents an ever-smaller portion of total value.

- The proceeds of the loan can be used profitably with minimal risk: to buy shares of company stock at a discount or to acquire real estate at a super-bargain price.

Checkpoints

In selecting a lender, chances are that you will want to do business with the firm that holds your first mortgage. Bargaining may save you money. These loans can be sufficiently profitable to justify concessions such as no interest for the first three months, reduced up-front fees or the opportunity to revise the terms periodically.

- With a variable rate, you may pay less at the start but take the risk of a rising cost of money. This floating rate is usually keyed to the prime rate with a maximum limit to change of 2% to 3%. There can be problems if the interest rate soars, especially when you have adjustable rates with both the mortgage and the home equity loan.

- Choose the type of interest rate best suited to your financial abilities, both now and in the event of financial calamity. A fixed rate may be more expensive at the outset, but it shifts the risks of higher interest rates to the institution. You always know your commitment.

- Establish a sensible repayment schedule. Without amortization or a preset payment date, it's a perpetual loan. With monthly installments of 1.25% of the balance of a $10,000 home equity loan at 10% interest, it will take 29 years and $24,300 for repayment. Try to have the full debt repaid one year before retirement.

- Make sure that the interest rate is locked in. Lenders have been known to advertise a low rate that was in effect for only three months, after which the rate rose annually by 1% to a maximum of 6% above the headlined rate.

- Check your tax adviser to learn whether the interest can be deducted. If you have substantial debts, you may lose this tax benefit.

- Is the lender allowed to call the loan? A lender with the right to call a loan can make you pay all you owe if you skip a couple of payments. This could lead to foreclosure and a forced sale of your home.

- Beware of a balloon payment. In a balloon payment arrangement, you have to pay off the balance of the loan at a set future date. This might make sense if you can look forward to an inheritance, but do not make this sort of a financial commitment if it must be met later than one year after retirement.

- If you do agree to a balloon payment arrangement, make sure the bank agrees, in writing, to give you the option to refinance the loan when the balloon payment comes due.

- Make certain that the lender does not insert, in small print, a right to cancel or alter terms retroactively. For instance, make sure the lender can't demand full repayment if the legislature changes the maximum interest rate that can be charged.

- Keep the total debt modest. Once this equity has been tapped, you no longer have these assets for a real emergency.

- Make sure that you cannot owe more than you borrowed and that there is no penalty for prepayment.

- Watch ALL closing costs. For example, an upfront fee of 1% to 2% of the maximum credit will cost you from $500 to $1,000 (plus annual levies between of $15 to $100) whether you take out $10,000 or $50,000. Also look out for extra charges such as a mortgage tax, fees for application, appraisal and county clerk, and the cost of title search and insurance, recording fees and legal counsel. Closing costs of $640 boosts the true interest rate of a loan with an interest rate of 10.25% to 14.4% for a five-year loan.

Special Mortgages for Retirees

Reverse Annuity Mortgage (RAM). This is a for-seniors-only form of a home equity loan. With the home as collateral, the lender makes a monthly payment to the retiree, who can use the money to use as he or she sees fit.

A RAM can be valuable for those who are house-rich and cash-poor, by providing income for a stated period or, if so desired, for as long as you or your spouse stays in the house.

A RAM should be a supplement to, not a substitute for, income. The payouts are not overly generous because the interest is compounded and there must be provision for payments of premiums for an annuity in case the borrower lives too long. With an $80,000 loan, at 9%, the monthly benefit is $491 for 10 years; $211 for 15 years. But, with a RAM, the owner can stay in his or her home!

Federally Insured Home-Equity Conversion Mortgages

The Federal Housing Administration has plans to insure equity-conversion loans from approved mortgage lenders. The mortgages will be available to homeowners over 62. There will be three different forms:

- Tenure mortgages, where homeowners receive monthly checks so long as the house is their principal residence

- Term mortgages, which set a specific repayment date for all money paid out, such as 10 years after closing

- Line-of-credit mortgages, permitting homeowners to draw out cash as needed.

As we go to press, this is an experimental FHA program, but it is expected to become adopted nationally. Call the FHA for details. Several states, such as Maine and Connecticut, have initiated projects and, in California, New Jersey and Pennsylvania, RAMs are being offered by private investors.

Older Homeowners Line of Credit. This is a form of a RAM sponsored by the United Seniors Health Cooperative in Maryland. (For information, write to them at 1334 G Street, NW, Washington, DC 20005). The details are still under development, but, in general terms, the criteria are:

- Applicants must be age 54 with annual incomes of under $30,000.

- The amount of the loan is tied to the age of the applicant. The older the home owner, the higher the loan as a percentage of home equity.

- Flexibility on drawdowns: no need to take money until needed, but a maximum annual payout of one-third of the credit line.

- No requirement for repayment until the borrower dies, moves voluntarily from the house or has to go to a nursing home. At that point, the loan is paid back from the proceeds of the sale of the home.

Transferring Property to Your Children

If you want to transfer property to your children, you must be aware of the tax ramifications. There are three ways to transfer property to your children: you can sell it to them, you can give it to them while living, or will it to them after you pass.

If you sell it for more than what you paid, you'll be subject to taxes just as with any other sale. If you sell it for less than the going price, gift tax may be assessed. If you sell it on an installment plan, charge the going interest rate, or else the IRS will tax you as if you'd received the going interest rate in income. And if an installment sale house is sold within two years, any capital gain you realized will not be spread out over years, but will be lumped together in your income at the time of the second sale.

One way around these problems is to will the house to your children, avoiding income tax problems and capital gains. But if your estate is over $600,000, there may be estate tax problems. And if estate taxes are owed, the house may have to be sold to pay those taxes. Also, if the house is in your name, and you require expensive long-term care (such as nursing home care) the house may have to be sold to pay for that care.

Sale-Leaseback. Here, an investor/relative buys the senior's home and leases it back at a predetermined rental. The buyer assumes all costs, such as real estate taxes, major maintenance, insurance, etc. The seller pays normal upkeep and can stay in the house for life. The seller also receives payments via a hefty down payment and interest-bearing installment notes satisfied by monthly checks. This can be a good deal when everyone is honest and the terms are fair, and is an excellent alternative for children who want to help their parents and still have a profitable investment.

Granny Mae (Golden Rule Annuity Mortgage Association). In this variation on the sale-leaseback theme, you sell your home to a child or outside investor and buy a lifetime annuity, leasing the home back at a rental based on fair market value. The annuity provides that, in the event of early death of both you and your spouse, your estate will receive the monetary difference between the projected payments and the value of the home from the insurer.

Example: Suppose you own a $100,000 home. You pay $2,000 per year for property taxes and insurance. You could sell it to your children for $95,000 and buy an annuity that would yield $12,000 a year. They could then rent back the house to you at $6,000 a year. You get $6,000 in extra income, and save $2,000 in expenses, for a total of $8,000 in extra income, each year, for life.

IF YOU SELL YOUR HOME

Taxes on Sale of House

At any time, when buying a house more expensive than that sold, you can defer the taxes of the profit if the new home is bought within two years after the sale. For instance, if you paid $40,000 for your first house and sold it for $100,000, you won't have to pay tax on any of the $60,000 gain if you buy a new house for at least $100,000 within two years. And when you are age 55 or older and have lived in the house three of the last five years, there's a once-in-a-lifetime exclusion of the first $125,000 capital gain.

What if you don't want to use this tax credit when you sell the house? There may be other financial factors at the time or you may want to hold it for some years after retirement when the property will, presumably, be much more valuable. Here are some ideas to consider:

(a) Buy a smaller house on a large plot of land, where the house is worth less, but the land is worth more. Later, subdivide the acreage and sell off the building plots as you need money. (Profits from the sale of these plots will be taxable).

(b) Rent the family mansion and enjoy the extra income. At death, the house will become part of your estate with no federal taxes until assets are more than $600,000. The property will pass to heirs at its then current value.

(c) Consider an installment sale by taking back a mortgage so that the gain will be spread over many years.

Watch out if you buy and sell several houses over the years. The taxable profit is cumulative. Suppose, in 1960, Chauncey bought a house for $45,000; in 1978, he sells for $100,000 and buys a new one for $200,000. He sells this for $300,000. The taxable gain is $155,000: $55,000 on #1; $100,000 on #2. And remember that you cannot defer a tax if, within two years before the final sale, you deferred the tax on a profitable sale of another principal residence.

Taking Back a Mortgage

Usually, a second mortgage is too risky an investment for your retirement savings. If the buyer needs to refinance the primary mortgage, but interest rates rise, refinancing may be more than the buyer can handle. Then, you will have to extend the loan or start costly, irritating foreclosure proceedings. If you need to extend a second mortgage to sell your property, look at selling the second mortgage to a finance company. To do this, you'll have to sell at a hefty discount, probably about 20%.

USING YOUR VACATION HOME IN YOUR RETIREMENT YEARS

A vacation home—cottage, house, or condominium—can be a wise investment for retirement but must be carefully chosen. Too often, what may be a profitable property will prove to be a poor place to live year-round. For vacations, most people look for a change from normal living: quiet, privacy, a hideaway to get away from people and pressures.

Such isolation may be OK in the early years when you are healthy and can drive a car. But later, you will need

- neighbors—to talk to and to help in emergencies

- convenience—a walk or short drive to stores, health care facilities and services

- comfort—that seashore cottage that is so delightful in July can be cold and dreary in January.

If you do opt to use a vacation home, plan to make this the first of two after-work moves.

These considerations are even more important with land. The lot that will be an excellent investment will probably be unsuited for retirement; otherwise, it probably would not still be vacant.

Avoid buying or renovating a vacation home for retirement housing if there aren't other retirees in the area with similar interests and need for services. Visit the area during the off-season to make sure that the priorities and interests of the neighbors don't conflict with your own. A cabin on the lake that is superb in the summer may be too isolated in the winter. Be sure that you won't be too far from stores, health care services and public transportation.

Vacation Property: Watch the Tax Limits

A house, cottage, condominium or mobile home used for vacations can be an excellent investment, especially when you plan to move there, or use it frequently, after you quit work. However, there are limits to tax deductions.

You can still deduct the interest on the mortgage up to the original purchase price plus the costs of improvements. But when you rent it out for more than 14 days, IRS rules take over. You must pay a tax on that income but you can now write off rental expenses proportionately. Thus, if you occupy the house for 20 days and rent it out for 60 days, you can claim 75% of use and expenses. The depreciation starts after deductions for interest, taxes, insurance, etc. See your attorney or real estate agent to work out the most tax-beneficial rental agreement.

Be careful with the title when the vacation property is in a state other than the one which you claim as principal residence. At death, the home state tax collector can consider this part of your taxable estate or vice versa. This will probably be more important at the second death because of the tax-advantaged transfer of the assets of the first to die to the spouse.

ADJUSTING TO YOUR NEW ENVIRONMENT

The key to adjusting to a new environment is to minimize stress. Never forget, stress kills. And any radical change (including those you initiate, but especially those imposed upon you) is stressful.

Renting Your Cottage or Condo

If you own a second home and are counting on renting it for extra income and tax deductions, check with your tax adviser. The IRS has strict rules that could affect what you realize from these rentals.

Under current law, you do not have to report the income from, and can deduct the mortgage interest and property taxes for, rentals totalling fewer than 15 days a year. For longer leases, you must report all income to the IRS and then can deduct expenses, maintenance, depreciation, interest and taxes within limits.

Ease into your new environment. If you belonged to national social, fraternal, or service organizations and clubs, join the local branch. Attend local religious services (even if you don't ordinarily go) and introduce yourself to the priest, minister, rabbi, or imam. They'll help you to meet your new neighbors.

As you engage in activities you've participated in (for example, golf, tennis, cards), you'll come to meet others with the same interest. Go to the local public recreation facilities to get started.

If you feel homesick, don't fight it. Call friends often. Invite them to visit you, and visit them yourself.

As for adjusting to everyday life in your new environment, don't expect to carry over the everyday routine you followed before you moved. If a certain routine feels uncomfortable, change it! And if you have a mate, make sure that he or she is also adjusting to the new environment. (This is critical: if one of you is happy and the other isn't, soon both of you will be unhappy.) Soon, you'll settle into a lifestyle that fits both your new environment and you.

Private Annuity

This can be an excellent idea when you have good property—a house or income-producing building—that is attractive to your children. The goal is to use this asset as the basis for a private annuity to assure regular income as long as you or your spouse lives. The child buys the property from the parent with regular payments, of interest and principal, under IRS tables. The buyer pays all taxes; the seller has a lifetime right to occupancy and is responsible for maintenance/repairs. With a $500,000 property acquired by a 25-year-old son, the monthly payment would be about $3,000.

This must be a legal transfer with no strings attached. There will be taxes to pay but a smart lawyer can show you how to reduce them by taking advantage of the annual $10,000 gift exclusion ($20,000 for a couple). Be sure that the payments will be made on time and that you will need the income. Otherwise, you'll be building your own estate and, probably, subjecting your heirs to extra taxes.

A variation of this annuity is the sale of a house under an installment plan: for a modest cash payment and a long-term mortgage that will provide regular income. This idea had merit in the past but is not so attractive under new tax rules. Time was when a retiree could sell his house, bought for $30,000, for $170,000: $30,000 cash plus a 10-year note for $140,000 at, say 10% interest. By taking advantage of the $125,000 exclusion for over 65s, the tax base would be $15,000.

No more. Now, that $140,000 is considered a note and the profit is immediately taxable.

Where to Get Additional Information

Directory of Life Care Communities, Nora E. Adelmann, H. W. Wilson.

Retirement Edens: Complete State by State Guide to Retirement, Peter Dickinson, E. P. Dutton.

The $100,000 Decision: The Older American's Guide to Selling a Home and Choosing Retirement Housing, Robert Irwin, McGraw-Hill.

Guide to Retirement Living, Rand McNally.

Unlocking Home Equity for the Elderly, Kenneth Scholen and Chen Yung-Ping, Ballinger Press.

Where Will You Live Tomorrow? Michael Sumichrast, Dow Jones-Irwin.

Woodall's Retirement Directory, Highland Park, IL.

CHAPTER 9

Moving into Retirement

Now that you know what to expect after work, let's go back to the preparations that will make the switch smoother and sessions with your attorney and financial adviser more productive.

It's helpful to set up: (1) a special file for papers/records/policies that will be needed; (2) a wish/check list in a separate envelope into which you can slip clippings of what seem like good ideas. Over 10 years, you'll be surprised at how these subjects change.

Table 9-1 lists which records should be kept, where and for how long. It applies to pre- and post-retirement. For hoarders, here's advice from a former probate judge: "In over 30 years of dealing with estates, I remember only two situations where the items on this list, and their destroy dates, were not applicable. [Don't] worry about throwing away old papers, unless they involve taxes."

Retirement Checklist

The Retirement Checklist (Worksheet 9-1, at the end of this chapter) is a companion item that provides a frame of reference for your files and discussions. When discussing retirement plans with your spouse, it is valuable primarily to suggest areas for which there should be projection and broad decisions. You should start using it after age 55 and update it annually thereafter. Add your own items for special plans. After a couple of planning sessions, you will probably want to make revisions to fit your own ideas and time frame.

Moving After Retirement?

If you're going to move after retirement, three months before the date of your retirement, get a copy of Moving Expenses (Publication 521, IRS), and make a list of

TABLE 9-1   Which Records to Keep, for How Long and Where

Item	*Original*	*Copies*	*How Long*
Marriage/divorce papers	Safe deposit		Permanently
Birth certificates	Safe deposit	Home file	Permanently
Citizenship papers	Safe deposit		Permanently
Military records	Safe deposit		Permanently
Deeds/title policies	Safe deposit		Permanently
Mortgages/leases	Safe deposit		When current
Stocks/bonds	Safe deposit	Broker	As long as held
Valuable jewelry	Safe deposit		As long as owned
Notes: you owe or are payable	Safe deposit	Home file	6 years after paid
Auto titles		Home file	As long as owned
Tax returns		Home file	6 years
Tax estimates		Home file	Annually
Records of tax payments	Safe deposit	Home file	3 years (home) 6 year (safe deposit box)
Canceled checks	Safe deposit	Home file	6 years (key payments only)
Records of major financial transactions		Home file	6 years or longer
Bank books		Home file	While current
Bank statements		Home file	6 years
Records of costs of home improvements		Home file	Until house sold and taxes paid
Wills	Safe deposit	Lawyer	Permanently, but destroy old one
Powers of attorney	Home file	Lawyer	While viable
Safe deposit key	Home file	Lawyer	As long as rented
Insurance policies		Home file	While current

everyone to be notified: bank, brokerage firm, insurance agent, attorney, accountant, physicians, dentist, creditors, stores, credit card companies, government agencies such as Social Security, IRS, county tax collector; subscription departments of magazines, clubs, college, trade and professional associations.

One month before moving:

- Send change of address cards
- Select a new bank and open a checking account
- Transfer title to cars
- Get credit history for future use
- Check will, medical records, employment records
- Cancel electricity, gas, telephone, charge accounts

One week before moving, be sure to:

- Close out bank accounts
- Pick up clothes at the cleaner
- Return books to the library
- Refill prescriptions
- Notify the post office
- Clean out safe deposit box

WORKSHEET 9-1

Target date for retirement   1. _____ 2. _____

Preparation: location of all important documents:

☐ will	☐ securities
☐ insurance policies	☐ deeds to house and other property
☐ birth certificates	☐ mortgage records
☐ military discharge papers	☐ shares of mutual funds
☐ bank accounts	☐ tax returns for past five years

Names, addresses and phone numbers of relatives, business associates, close friends, insurance agent, lawyer, accountant, broker and tax adviser.

Are both wills up-to-date? _____

Which life insurance policies do you plan to drop? _____

Or do you prefer to roll over into an annuity? _____

Financial focus: estimate of money available in retirement from:

Social Security: single _____ couple _____ after first death _____

Employer pension: annuity for both _____ after first death _____

Personal pension plans: maximum _____ minimum _____

Purchased annuities _____

Deferred compensation _____

Savings/investments _____

Options for work after retirement: consultant _____ part-time _____

own business _____ other _____

Anticipated NET income (after reduction in Social Security when earned income is over $8,800), withholding and Social Security taxes, etc.

Health insurance: will the company continue payment of premiums? _____

How long? _____

Will we have to pay all or part of the cost? _____

With Medicare, what benefits will be paid? _____

WORKSHEET 9-1 *(cont.)*

Which supplementary coverage will provide the broadest benefits? _____

   At what cost? _____

Housing: do we want to stay in the same community? _____

Why? _____ At what cost? _____

In a smaller dwelling: house, apartment, condominium? _____

Possible retirement locations: (1) _____ ( ) _____

Permanent? _____ Part-time? _____

How does each rate for personal pleasure now? _____ after retirement? 5 years _____

   10 years _____

What are probable costs of: moving _____ furnishings after moving _____

What are the attractions of each area? Recreation _____

Cultural _____ Educational _____ enjoyable living _____

Location: convenient to family? _____ friends _____

Interesting activities _____

Future prospects for both old and new location:

Taxes: higher _____ about same _____ lower _____

Increase in property value _____

Possible changes in area/community _____

Health/fitness

	Spouse 1	Spouse 2
Instructions from physician after last check	_____	_____
Weight	_____	_____
Eating habits	_____	_____
Target weight	_____	_____

WORKSHEET 9-1 *(cont.)*

	Spouse 1	Spouse 2
Physical: regular exercise	_____	_____
Why not?	_____	_____
Medicine: up-to-date on preventive medicine?	_____	_____
understand drugs and dangers of misuse?	_____	_____
Leisure time		
How much spare time per week?	_____	_____
What present activities will we want to continue? If we stay here	_____	_____
If we move	_____	_____
What hobbies/interests will we pursue?	_____	_____
If they require training/knowledge, where can we learn	_____	_____
Should we take early retirement?	_____	_____
Why?	_____	_____
Why not?	_____	_____
Should we postpone retirement?	_____	_____
Why?	_____	_____
Why not?	_____	_____
How do I define a joyous retirement?	_____	_____

CHAPTER 10

Using Your Time—Making the Most of the Opportunities That Retirement Offers

Your goal in retirement living should be to make every day as enjoyable and fulfilling as possible. Too many retirees fail to realize, let alone take full advantage of, the opportunities that retirement offers. You will soon recognize that, without the structure of work, there are opportunities to expand old interests and find new ones. Indeed, experimenting can be half the fun. Retirees usually enjoy good health, an assured income, and time to do whatever they want. If you ever wanted to write the Great American Novel, sail across the Atlantic, ski for days on end or surf the endless summer, now's your chance!

But retiring happily on your own terms does not just happen. The better you plan while working, the greater the likelihood of success. Savings are essential but your personal preparations for living in retirement are just as important.

Realize that retirement is not "a week of weekends." If you live your retired life this way, your life will soon become boring, as your older friends will tell you. Also keep in mind that, after retirement, you are not the same person.

PRE-PLANNING LIFE IN RETIREMENT

At least three, and, preferably, five years before quitting work, start a series of discussions with your spouse and family on what, when and how you plan to do things in retirement. Although your goals will have to be consistent with your personal financial framework (you can't have caviar dreams on a tuna-fish budget), emphasize dreams and hopes rather than the needs and routines of daily living. Once you have developed broad outlines, start filling in the details.

Table 10-1 gives you an idea of what items to consider and how you can hope to initiate or expand after-work projects. Keep the list wide open; try asking your grandchildren for ideas. Gradually, narrow the choices to: (1) what you'd like to do; (2) what you think you can do; and (3) how each choice will affect both partners and the family.

TABLE 10-1   Looking Ahead to Retirement

If, While Working	You Need	Consider
You had little opportunity to be creative	Opportunity for self-expression; to tap creative skills	Painting, photography, landscaping, growing flowers, writing, theater
You feel regimented, told what to do, seldom allowed to do what you prefer	To be in command; to find activities where you set the rules and time schedule	Look for areas where you can do what you want to do when you want to do it: collecting, playing a musical instrument, hiking, swimming, bicycling
You regard much of your life as a failure	Feeling of achievement in areas in which you are not supposed to be competent	An unusual project: learning to speak a foreign language, mastering a craft, becoming knowledgeable on local or family history
You faced considerable tension and frequent exasperation	To relax and, on occasion, to waste time and energy	Active sports such as tennis, working out at health clubs, chopping wood
Life was dull and routine	To look for adventure, to find a challenge	Mountain climbing, scuba diving, exploring historic areas, finding a need and trying to make a difference for others
You spent too much time caring for others	To be selfish; to do what you want with no apologies or explanations	Go back to school to learn something you're missed; to do something of unusual interest: bird watching, kite flying

Next, put down special "hope" projects: an African safari, sailing along the Maine coast, etc. Then, calculate the costs of each and set priorities according to their importance, time and money. Unless you are both in excellent health and have ample savings, 10 years is about as far out as you should go. Due to changing finances, work opportunities and family and community responsibilities, planning beyond this point is usually fruitless.

ADJUSTING TO RETIREMENT

Retirement can mean a loss of identity when you're no longer Jane Doe, CEO of Megacorp, but simply Jane Doe, retiree. And this can be a more serious problem with people who sacrificed family life for career, such as professionals. When both partners are professionals, there's no reason why both should quit work at the same time. Try to work out a compromise, not only in time but also in a way that can maintain each other's position and pride.

Don't kid yourself that all days will be spent in golf, swimming, fishing and lounging. If you have made any sort of mark in your job or community, do-little projects will seldom be enough.

The switch should be fairly easy for singles used to independence. With couples, however, this new lifestyle can range from discomfort, dismay, and disillusionment to the joy and excitement of freedom and new challenges.

For most active couples, the biggest problem involves TOGETHERNESS: spending 24 hours a day with one person. One solution is to discuss each partner's responsibilities at the outset, given the change in each partner's ability to execute those responsibilities. Make a chart to show which portion of the household chores each will be responsible for. One (or both) of you may have to learn to start picking up after yourself; the excuse of "I've got to get to work" won't wash anymore.

Set down, almost hour by hour, what you plan to do and discuss, with your partner, how this schedule will affect your life together. If one spouse has always been at home while the other worked outside the home, consider how the daily presence of the latter spouse will affect the stay-at-home spouse. For example, if an executive stays home, will he or she decide to rearrange the cupboards that the spouse has managed for 30 years? Will he or she draw up a time/motion schedule for the spouse to handle the washing? Don't try to "boss" your spouse around, now that you're at home. And look to read more, because you both will have a lot of time for conversation.

It's great to think in terms of joint activities but be careful not to plan programs that don't allow for personal interests. Everyone needs time for individual chores, pleasures, and responsibilities. Make a considered effort to respect the other's point of view and established routines. If the wife plans to play bridge on Wednesday afternoon, the husband should arrange his schedule to be busy at that time. If the husband plays golf on Tuesday morning, the wife should not plan to use the car.

Be prepared to handle your spouse's responsibilities in the event that that spouse becomes incapacitated. Start a FORMAL training course in household economics. Each week, set aside two days when the spousal roles will be reversed. Each spouse should learn from the other how to handle these household chores.

Laundry

- buying soap, detergent, starch and softener
- sort clothes for the washer
- add the liquids or powders and set the wash cycles
- transfer the bundle to the drier
- iron handkerchiefs and blouses, fold towels and sheets and store them in the closet at the bottom of the pile for easy rotation.

Food

- buying the food
- planning meals
- cooking—soups on the stove, frozen foods in the microwave

Household Maintenance

- fixing the toilet
- checking the fuse box
- repairing frayed electrical wiring

Household Finances

- reviewing income tax returns
- setting up an understandable record of receipts and expenditures that will satisfy the IRS.

Make this training a regular, serious commitment. You can have fun but the benefits will be limited until you both go the course. As my widower friend laments, ''If I had spent a little time learning how my wife ran the house, I could have skipped burnt fingers, eliminated indigestion, saved on laundry, cleaning bills and not be ashamed of the condition of the house. Being alone is hard enough. It's worse when you become frustrated because of unnecessary ignorance.''

Living Together

Most people spend their lives with dreaming that, after work, they will have greater freedom, fewer responsibilities, and more time to share with their mate. This may be true in the early years but, with more people living longer, the twosome may swell to accommodate elderly parents, troubled children, and lonesome grandchildren.

Don't forget that your children are now adults and have rights to their own lives on their terms. Your responsibility is to build personal and conjugal independence: to establish your own social life; to earn your own extra money; and to find and foster your own support systems. As retirees, you both should be the ones hard to get, so busy and so involved that you can refuse invitations from your children. Such independence will not only enhance your pride and sense of well-being but will also free your son and daughter of a sense of guilt for not calling you more often.

You waited a long time for this leisure and have the right to enjoy it under your own terms. Being independent does not mean that you cannot love, admire and enjoy your children (and vice versa). Think of them as ''best friends'' who know you well, understand your moods and interests and are there when you need them.

Living Alone

There is an excellent chance that, at some point during your retired life, you will be living alone. Two-thirds of all retirees will be living alone for three or more years; at age 60, 40% of women are divorced and 50% are living alone. By age 65, over 50% are receiving some sort of governmental assistance: food stamps, rent subsidy, Medicaid, etc.

You should have planned for the financial ramifications of living alone (discussed in Worksheet 1-1, page 20). But you should also be prepared for the emotional aspect. Single people, whether unmarried, divorced or widowed, have special problems in retirement planning and living. Compared to married couples, their taxes are greater and their benefits, from both private and government programs, are smaller. When troubles start, they may not have adequate reserves or support systems.

The loss of a partner will be traumatic and, for most, will require a difficult adjustment. If death comes after illness, there may well be a sense of relief. However, the ensuing lack of responsibility and loneliness may create a vacuum in your life that can give rise to depression. To prepare for this, try to develop other interests, primarily those which you can control and which you enjoy. Then, when faced with personal crisis, you can use these interests to lend some stability to your life when other aspects undergo upheaval.

If you lose a spouse or longtime partner, you'll naturally focus on your loss. That's normal; that's part of adjusting. But don't expect others to also focus on your lost loved one. Even though your grief will probably not be felt as deeply by anyone else, however, take all the time you need. If single members of the opposite sex make overtures that awaken no response in you, it's just a sign that you're not yet ready to begin another relationship. Eventually, you will go on to build new relationships in which you will feel needed and loved.

Second Marriage

Marriage is a serious step at any time; in retirement, it's more so because the goal is seldom to build a life together but, more likely, to create a happy and, hopefully, loving companionship for relatively few years.

There is no reason why an older person, now single because of death or divorce, should not seek happiness with a new companion. The decision for a second marriage should:

(1) Consider the children but not to the extent that their wishes take precedence over the individual's future;

(2) Recognize that each is an individual with a more or less set lifestyle, definite views, prejudices, routines, different friends and, most important, relatives, some of whom will have qualms about what they may consider an intrusion;

(3) Realize that even those mutual interests may not always be viewed the same way;

(4) Understand that being lonesome, by itself, is not a valid reason for a new partnership.

Here are guidelines digested from comments by family counsellors:

• Know each other well under several different situations: in the home community; on a trip involving pleasures both anticipate will continue; visiting old friends; a weekend at a resort; at a convention which either, or both, have enjoyed before.

- A feeling that the other person's life is useful and important and that, to a degree, each can share those roles. Companionship must be more than physical.

- Think twice before living in the same house where either lived for a long time. The ghost of the past can put a severe strain on the new deal and it's inevitable that each will be compared to the other's previous spouse.

- Make no commitment until both partners have completed, and accepted, grieving for the deceased. This does not mean blotting out those years but it does require that attention be focused on the present and future.

Caring for Parents

With more people living longer, a family can include two generations which are drawing Social Security. In fact, one third of all retirees have a living parent and one out of every two of these elders receives financial support from the son or daughter.

Over one million Americans provide direct physical care for a parent, and many more help support a parent. When planning retirement, account for the possibility of needing to care for an aging parent. You should have already planned for the financial effect of this (see page x-ref), but keep in mind that when there's a need for personal attention, such as a parent living in your home or requiring frequent care, there can be severe strains. If you have to care for someone requiring constant care, look for a senior day-care center, or some other alternative that will allow you occasional respite from your duties to look after your personal business. Also look for support groups. One of the largest, Children of Aging Parents, may be contacted at 2761 Trenton Rd., Levittown, PA 19056 (215-945-6900).

The timing of this phase of preparation depends on the projected health of the father or mother. There's no reason to panic and start building an extra bedroom on the ground floor of your house. However, you should have candid discussions of whether and how you both can cope with such a situation: what services will be needed; how much they will cost; and what will be the specific responsibilities of children and parent. Once you and your partner have developed a viable framework, include your parents in the discussion. Remember that, at appropriate times, outsiders such as a physician, lawyer and social worker might be able to make a valuable contribution.

In these reviews, be realistic. You want to do the best you can for your loved ones but only within the reasonable limits of your resources. Do not be carried away by your emotions or what you imagine other people will think or say. Keep in mind these two points:

(1) The majority of all care for the elderly is furnished within the family;

(2) Most professionals believe the most humane and economical way to help individuals is to help them stay in their homes and out of nursing homes. For example, Community Care for the Elderly costs about 10% of the cost of a nursing home: $1,300 a year versus $13,000 (or more).

For more information, read *Caring for Your Aging Parent,* Robert T. Cadmus, Prentice-Hall or *Your Aging Parent,* Maxine Dowd Jensen, Zondervan.

AVAILABLE ACTIVITIES AND PURSUITS

Here are some ideas that can make life in retirement more enjoyable, save money and avoid financial rip-offs.

Consider A Pet

Pets can add joy and provide therapy for loneliness or depression. Although fish can be colorful, and a bird can add a cheerful note, your best choice is probably a dog or cat. These animals can be companions, someone to talk to and to keep the owner active and involved because they require attention: feeding, grooming, and, often, walking.

If you don't have such a friend, visit an animal shelter. Usually, you will have to pay only for a medical checkup and license. To avoid even those costs, if you live in one of 70 participating cities, join the *Pets for People* program. To be eligible, you must be over 60 and pass the local shelter's screening procedures. Ralston Purina, the sponsor, will provide a free checkup including shots, spaying or neutering plus a pet care starter kit. For information: Pets for People Program, Ralston Purina Co., Checkerboard Square, 6T, St. Louis, MO 63164.

Before you choose any pet, make certain that you and your spouse understand the responsibilities. You are adding a new member to your family and must be willing to accept fleas, illness, special diets, veterinary bills and, eventually, the tragedy of death. If you own a pet when you move, make sure that the pet is allowed under the rules of the new community or home.

The Importance of Support Systems

Almost everyone who lives to be an Old Old (OO) will need help in living a reasonably healthy, comfortable life. Four out of five retirees call on support services in one way or another. There are two basic sources of aid: family care and community services.

Family Care. Traditionally, this has been furnished by some relative: a spouse, child, in-law or cousin. Nowadays, seniors may call on friends as well as relatives. However defined, family care accounts for the great majority of all help to seniors. However, this sort of personal care is decreasing because of divorce, remarriage, single parenthood, job responsibility and distance. That means that aging retirees must start to build support systems before reaching a dependent status.

Community Services. These are available from both private, for-pay agencies and, for those over age 60, from public agencies at no cost for those who cannot afford to pay, at modest fees for those with limited incomes, and for all with a request for voluntary contributions.

Typically, a social worker will visit the home, assess the need for help and recommend those services that will help the senior to remain independent, and at home, for as long as possible.

The scope of community services varies widely. In some areas, the key force is the United Way; in others, help may be obtained from state agencies, or from citizens working through local groups.

The primary coordinating group is the Area Agency on Aging (AAA) set up under the Older Americans Act to provide help to senior citizens. Usually, the AAA covers a governmental district. Funded by federal, state and local governments, the AAA provides information and referral for senior citizens. They contract out services that range from free or low-cost transportation, congregate and home-delivered meals, programs at senior centers, home-care assistance, help with housing, and other services. Some AAAs limit their roles to funding and supervision, while others take leadership in advocacy for seniors through their boards of volunteers.

Because of the large number of retirees in the state, Florida has developed programs that are expected to be adopted by other states in the next century. Here are some of the major types of support programs:

In-Home Services—
Community Care for the Elderly (CCE): designed to help keep seniors out of nursing homes. Services furnished include personal care, homemaker service, home-delivered meals, medical transportation, respite care and similar services. This is the core program for the elderly in Florida; the cost of CCE is about one-tenth of the cost of nursing home care.

These services may be part of CCE, or provided separately—
Home Care for the Elderly. A trained social worker takes over to help the individual stay at home.

Homemaker Services: handling housekeeping duties such as meal planning and preparation, shopping assistance, and routine household activities such as dusting, cleaning, washing dishes, and laundry.

Home Assistance: usually help from groups such as Scouts, Future Farmers, church teams and neighborhood groups, to help shovel snow, rake leaves, and remove trash.

Personal Care to assist functionally impaired elderly with bathing, dressing, housekeeping, emotional security, eating, supervision of self-administered medication, etc.

Meals on Wheels. Nutritious, ready-to-eat meals delivered daily or, when frozen, weekly in a package that can be heated or boiled when needed.

Respite Care. A trained companion stays with the homebound patient while the caregiver shops, conducts business and relaxes.

General Support Systems

For those able to move or be moved, Senior Centers are places where the elderly can gather for companionship, exercise, learning, socializing, and community service projects. These centers range from a room at a church to specially designed buildings with kitchens, auditoriums, library, craft rooms, and medical facilities.

Usually managed by a professional, they offer such services as:

Adult Day Care. These are places for the elderly to be involved in activities suited to their energy levels, abilities, and interests. Some are part of publicly financed senior centers, while others are for-pay units, often with additional facilities and staff for rehabilitation and medical supervision. You can come in for a few hours or stay all day. They're great for companionship and security, and they're a welcome respite for caregivers.

If you're still active and eager, volunteer to provide transportation, teach classes and organize games. If you are beginning to falter, investigate and find the center that's convenient, friendly and provides the programs you may need. For information, check the Area Agency on Aging, Health Department, or United Way.

Recreation. Activities such as exercise classes, dancing, sports, games, art, painting or ceramics, etc.

Education. Classes ranging from nutrition, personal finance, beauty tips and cooking to history, languages, poetry and needlework.

Transportation. Regular and mini-buses to shopping centers, hospitals, medical offices and, at an extra cost, to attend concerts, games, plays and exhibits.

Congregate Meals. Served five days a week, usually at noon. There's no charge but the greater the voluntary contributions, the more people can be served.

Another plus: people who are familiar with support services, as volunteers or as observers, are more likely to use them for their personal or family benefit. The elderly who have never visited a senior center wait too long before asking for help. By then, their health may be too tenuous to respond to ordinary care, their income too depleted to hire competent assistance and their depression too severe to permit them to continue to stay in their own home.

The role of the family support should be discussed with your children and relatives. When there are special problems, such as health care or finances, get input from your physician, lawyer and financial adviser. There's no reason to panic but the scenario should be realistic. No matter how loyal your daughter, if you live in North Carolina and she works in Boston, her help must be advisory and vocal . . . neither of much value to a bedridden OO.

Consider, too, that relatives may be caring and anxious to be involved but their support may be limited by available time, other responsibilities, skill, strength, mental attitude or lack of training. In such a situation, it is better to hire a professional or to rely on your family for respite care. Let them take over for a weekend or vacation so that the caregiver can get relief, have the opportunity to handle personal chores and, in many cases, to enjoy a few nights of uninterrupted sleep.

Do not be embarrassed about trying to establish a family support system when you are both active. You never know when there will be an accident or illness. There are two approaches: as a volunteer and as an observer.

Examples: Join an organization such as HELPING HAND. This started in a Florida condominium and has spread rapidly to other housing units. In this organization, the younger retirees (trained at a nearby senior center) join together to help their older neighbors.

Each morning, the volunteers make reassurance phone calls to their "clients." Once a week, they drive some OOs to the center for an hour of exercise and talks on health and nutrition followed by a full-course congregate meal and an hour of recreation and companionship. Every few weeks there are group trips for shopping, visits to the physician, dentist, chiropractor, etc. If there's no such service near you, why not start one?

To learn about available services, visit a senior center, attend lectures at churches or hospitals and serve as a volunteer through RSVP or a United Way agency. Approach this seriously. Visit a congregate-meal site one or two days a week, learn the scope and availability of programs and personnel. When your partner or a friend needs help, it can make a big difference when you know the agency director, understand how the system works and are able to ask for the most beneficial services.

Travel: One of the Great Joys of Retirement

Key your travel to your physical and financial fitness. In planning for travel in retirement, schedule the most rigorous and expensive journeys soon after quitting work: the first BIG trip while you are eager, vigorous and flush with cash from your final paycheck. Later, when you become interested in specific regions, you can be more leisurely, staying a week or two at a gracious inn, castle, resort, following up earlier interests and, always, always, relaxing.

Help for Parents (and When You Grow Old)

If you are not able to keep in close touch with your aging parents, there are special services that will do this for a fee. On the West Coast of Florida:

Family Partners, Inc. For $100 per month, they will visit the client's home twice, call the client twice a week, arrange for necessary service and write a monthly report to the family.

Drymon-Stumbo Management handles finances, settles estates, pays bills, acts as guardian, and provides financial counsel. The fee is negotiable.

This type of service replaces the role of the small banks which have been merged with holding companies who are not structured to deal with difficult individuals.

With travel, more than with most areas of retirement, do not become locked into routines. Experiment; try something new every year or so:

At home: take a steamboat ride down the Mississippi; charter a yacht in the Caribbean; spend 10 days in Washington;

Abroad: cruise British waterways or French canals; take the luxury boat trip on the Rhine and Danube; play the golf courses in Scotland; and, while you're still agile, bicycle through Brittany.

Always view travel as recreation. When it becomes a bore, stay home!

Choosing a Travel Agent

If you need help, ask travel-wise friends, your banker or automobile club secretary for travel agency references. Then ask questions like these:

- Is the firm affiliated with respected organizations: ASTA (American Society of Travel Agents); International Airlines Travel Agent Network (IATAN); or Airlines Reporting Corporation (ARC)?

- Where do you bank? locally? or in the Cayman Islands?

- Are you designated as a special agent by any major tour company?
  Then, to determine competency and compatibility:

- What is your definition of a "nice" hotel and "reasonable" prices?

- Do you have a computer to get the best air fares?

- How are refunds handled if there is a cancellation?

- What are the options with air travel: commercial? charter? economy class in USA? abroad?

- Are special fares good only for certain months and days or times? If there are future changes, what could the costs be?

- Who confirms reservations? how? when?

- Has a principal of the firm traveled in that country? Taken this trip? If so, can you have a briefing first?

Take your time. Be wary of special deals until you are certain of what you are getting as described in *printed* form; get the names of hotels where the group will stay and check them with Frommer's travel guides.

If you enjoy the trip or tour, thank the agent and ask him or her to advise you of similar opportunities in the future.

A warning here about travel swindles. Swindlers often send retirees phony discounts on travel. They may tell you, by mail or by phone, that "You Have Just Won a Prize": a coupon that entitles you to a free week at a posh resort, a super-discount on a tour to Waikiki Beach or a luxury suite on a cruise ship for the price of a third-class cabin. "All you have to do, Mrs. Gracious Lady, is to send in $$$$ and we will do the rest." In fact, this is just a phony come-on to get your money.

Before sending your money to ANY business that you're unfamiliar with, check with your local Better Business Bureau. And don't stop there—ask for referrals from satisfied customers. Ask your lawyer to read the fine print, and check the business' credit references. This may seem like a lot of trouble, but thousands are swindled every year, and these steps could have saved a lot of people a lot of money.

Tips on Planning That BIG Trip

- Research the countries you plan to visit in your local library. Look at travel magazines, brochures from tourist bureaus, and historical books (to get an idea of the background, culture and traditions). Make a list of items of special interest, such as desirable attractions, hotels, restaurants and locations. Look for dates of special activities such as pageants, plays, exhibits or competitions.

- Decide your travel style: (1) with a tour, which will be less expensive but restrictive; (2) type of group: college alumni association, local museum or art center or AARP chapter; (3) escorted service: expensive but convenient, especially when there's heavy luggage; (4) solo where (a) you personally select destinations, set the itinerary and pay for hotels in advance or (b) work with a travel agent on the transportation and accommodations.

- Confirm (or have confirmed) all reservations: for airline tickets, hotels, rental cars and special events. If you need a special diet, give the airline at least 24 hours notice. For a double check, use the toll-free 800 number available for many hotel chains, car rental companies and country-sponsored travel bureaus.

- Health check: get vaccinations for cholera and yellow fever, if required, and for polio and tetanus if you have not had them recently. Review all drugs or pills with your pharmacist to be sure they are fresh and safe.

- Travel documents: passports, good for 10 years, and visas, legal for shorter periods, can be obtained from federal offices in major cities directly or by mail or through your travel agent. These require small-size photos so have a couple of extras made for your traveling wallet.

- List the clothing needed, preferably washables, and, a month before, examine every item for loose buttons. Try on shirts, dresses and trousers to be sure they still fit! Be sure to include a raincoat and, if you like to walk, rubbers.

- Housekeeping: ask the post office to hold your mail; stop delivery of newspapers; arrange for a neighbor to pick up packages and throwaways. Double check your home: by testing locks, alarms, timers to turn on and off lights and radio; make sure someone will shovel the snow from the driveway or mow the lawn and reserve a kennel for your dog or cat. If it's a long trip, arrange for payments of bills for the mortgage, utilities and insurance premiums.

- Prepare a detailed itinerary with names, addresses and phone numbers of hotels and American Express offices. Leave a copy with a relative or friend.

- Relax for one full day before the trip begins, especially if the first leg involves a long air flight.

Tours: Be Choosy

Tours become more attractive as you age because they eliminate the inconvenience of having to make reservations, to check and carry luggage and to get tickets to festivals and theatres. But they are communal entities that require conformity and discipline and leave little time for your personal browsing.

Tours come in a variety of types and price ranges, so it pays to shop (and I mean *really* shop) at agencies, airlines, alumni associations and senior organizations to find the package that appears to be best for you. Since most retirees can travel when they want, the most attractive deals will probably be off-season: in the spring and fall.

Be wary about joining neighbors in a tour, especially those in your retirement community. You see enough of these folks during the rest of the year. Often, since you are presumed to be an ''old friend,'' you will be expected to nurse the ill, comfort the bored and calm marital disputes. Do not let the bargain price or local pressures overcome your personal pleasures. You are traveling for relaxation, not to continue your regular lifestyle.

Don't overlook smaller, specialized trips to one area, such as the British Isles, ancient Mediterranean cities or Inca ruins. These luxury tours, usually sponsored by a college or museum, generally are headed by a professor familiar with the history, culture and highlights of the countries visited. The pace is leisurely and your companions will be new people with educational backgrounds and interests similar to yours. They're well worth the extra costs.

Packaged plans that cover transportation, hotels and car rentals might be for you. You can set your own time frame so can revisit favorite spots, stay as long as you want and travel your way. The major drawback: flights go from and to only one or two major airports. If you have to backtrack, say from Paris to London, it can be expensive.

Travel Insurance

Since trips are so important to retirees, you may want to take out insurance to cover the costs of cancellations, medical emergencies and loss or theft of personal effects. For information, ask your travel agent.

Life on the Road

One of the fastest-growing and most popular areas of travel in retirement is the RV (recreational vehicle) life. Many RV owners are relatively affluent and like to do what they want to do when they want to do it. Some like the solitude; others enjoy the companionship through clubs, caravans and conventions. Almost all of the time, they feel free and enjoy an unique status that allows them to choose destinations and friends.

Special Deals for Singles and Pet Owners

With most packaged tours and cruises, single travelers must pay extra. To serve these individuals, specialized agencies find compatible same-sex partners for travel and thus save money and provide companionship:

Travel Partners Club, Box 2368, Crystal River, FL 32629. Keyed to widows and widowers over age 50. Membership is $40 a year and includes newsletter and profiles.

Singleworld, 444 Madison Avenue, New York, NY 10022: broad coverage for singles of all ages and almost all destinations.

Travel Companion Exchange, Box 833-M, Amityville, NY 11701: specializes in the independent traveler, from those who want to travel to popular countries and places to the adventuresome who prefer African safaris, exploration of South African ruins or raft trips down the Colorado rapids.

For those who travel by automobile with a dog: a directory of hotels/motels that welcome pets plus an explanation of how to park the pooch at the Gaines-sponsored pet care center at Disneyland or DisneyWorld. Contains discount coupons for Gaines products, so well worth the $1.50 price: *Touring with Towser,* P.O. Box 877-M, Young America, MN 55399.

This companionship often centers around organized groups such as the Good Sam Club with over half a million members whose median age is 63 and rising as more older travelers take to the road. One of the most dramatic examples of the popularity of such "friendship" is the gathering at the annual Rose Bowl Festival in Pasadena, CA. Thousands of RVs line the route for weeks ahead, often parked by states and always with outdoor grills, lounging chairs and "Welcome To" signs.

The modern RVs are true homes with cellular phone, microwave ovens, gas ranges, double beds, closets and cable TV. They cost from $40,000 to $300,000. Small trailer units which can be hitched to your automobile (with a special locking device) are available for as little as $20,000.

Before you buy any type of RV, rent several different models, make trips involving varied driving conditions, times of year and geographic areas. Then, make sure that both partners are physically able to handle the driving and that both of you are prepared to "enjoy" the close proximity day after day.

Costs and Adjustments

Financially, after the original investment, RV life can be inexpensive living. Count on spending $1,000 to $1,500 per month in total RV-connected costs. Commercial campgrounds will cost $15 to $25 per night ($250 to $300 per month for longer stays). These sites provide hook-ups for water and electricity, a pool barbecue area and, often, a clubhouse for recreation, rallies and lectures.

Other typical monthly expenses, outside of food, clothing and health care, include $375 for gasoline and propane gas, $150 for maintenance, and $200 for insurance.

RVs involve adjustments that can be difficult for some. Psychologically, you have to adapt to a vagabond lifestyle. And financially, you have to master the tricky logistics of keeping accounts, bills and investments while in transit. You can handle some things yourself: have pension, Social Security and dividend checks automatically deposited in your bank. Also, arrange your itinerary to visit your physician's office regularly.

It may help to have a child, other relative, or friend to help manage your affairs while you are on the road. That person can collect all your mail and forward bills, letters and pertinent publications to you in a weekly package sent to a recreation park or General Delivery at a nearby post office. The person (who should be someone you can trust) should have power of attorney for emergencies, and a major credit card for advances of $300 to $400. To avoid interest charges, have an equal-sum check sent to the credit card company.

Bed & Breakfast Places

With hotel/motel prices soaring, you can save money and enjoy the friendliness of a family host by stopping at Bed and Breakfasts (B&Bs): individual homes which are opened to tourists for an evening and breakfast for about half the price of regular lodgings.

The best recommendations will be by word of mouth, but if you do not have such resources, write to the Chamber of Commerce along your route or check directories like these:

National
Bed and Breakfast Reservation Services Worldwide, Inc.
P.O. Box 14797,
Baton Rouge, LA 70898

Boston
Bed & Breakfast Associates, P.O. Box 166,
Babson Park
Boston, MA 02157

Bed & Breakfast Brookline/Boston, Box 732,
Brookline, MA 02146

New York
Bed & Breakfast, 35 West 92nd St.
New York, NY 10025

City Lights B&B, Ltd., P.O. Box 20355
Cherokee Station, New York, NY 10028

Urban Ventures, P.O. Box 426,
New York, NY 10024

Washington
Bed & Breakfast League, Ltd., 2639 Van Ness St. N.W.,
Washington, DC 20008

Bed 'n Breakfast Ltd., P.O. Box 22011,
Washington, DC 20005

Chicago
Bed & Breakfast Chicago, P.O. Box 14088,
Chicago, IL 60614-0088

Dallas
Bed & Breakfast Texas Style, 4224 West Red Bird Lane,
Dallas, TX 75237

San Francisco
American Family Inn, P.O. Box 349,
San Francisco, CA 94101

Los Angeles
Bed & Breakfast of Los Angeles 32074
Waterside Lane
Westlake Village, CA 91361

Elderhostels: for an Educational Holiday

These can be among the most exciting and rewarding experiences of retirement. Every year, more than 100,000 men and women over age 60 flock to college campuses in the USA and, increasingly, abroad, to study everything from genetic engineering to Japanese art. A few adventurers travel to Great Britain to learn about Romans in Wales; others drive to the mountains of Colorado to live in rustic cabins and study geology; and still others study computers, wood-carving or gourmet cooking.

These courses are available on campuses in the USA and abroad through Elderhostel, a network of more than 800 colleges. They are open to anyone older than 60 or accompanied by someone over that age.

In America, most classes are for one week, mainly during the summer but, often, throughout the year. Abroad, the sessions last one to three weeks and may include a stay with a local family.

This type of learn-while-you-travel is not for everyone because, usually, you have to become a student again: live in a cramped room, sleep in rickety beds, use a communal bathroom, eat in a cafeteria, sit in straight-backed chairs and, occasionally, listen to a rambling discussion by an ill-informed, trying-to-be-important boor. However, a friend who has attended a score of classes rates the instructors as "Good to Excellent" in most cases.

The subjects are taught (in English, abroad) by professionals including retirees; the visit permits the use of the library, gym, golf course and other facilities. There are no exams, no grades, no homework, and, in most classes, you are encouraged to participate. Best of all, you meet interesting people.

The costs are low: in the USA, the typical charge is $205 for six nights of lodging; five days of meals and classes. You furnish your own transportation.

Overseas, the fees are all-inclusive: air fare, travel within the country, local excursions, room and board and tuition. For Europe, these range from $1,200 to $1,650; for Australia and Asia, up to $3,600.

For information, write: Elderhostel, 80 Boylston Street, Boston, MA 02116.

Money Savers

Once you receive your Medicare card (age 65) or, in some cases, when you pass age 60, you are eligible for special treatment by business and professional organizations and by governments: discounts, free admissions, extra benefits and so forth. Find 'em; use 'em; enjoy 'em.

Some require membership in an organization such as American Association of Retired Persons (AARP), National Association of Senior Citizens (NASC) or a local retirees association; others involve participation such as maintaining a savings account in a financial institution. Here are typical ones:

Banking Services: free checkbooks and no service charges, usually when you maintain a minimum balance.

Silver Pages Telephone Book: these list stores, companies and services that offer discounts to seniors and provides all sorts of valuable information. You'll find a Community Resources Section with names, addresses, telephone numbers of agencies and services providing health care, nutrition, employment, housing, transportation and so on.

Senior Festivals, usually sponsored by a major corporation, such as a utility, with cooperation from the Area Agency on Aging. These have free health tests, samples of foods, talks on health, finance and nutrition plus all sorts of entertainment by seniors. Fun, informative and a good way to spend an enjoyable afternoon.

Golden Passport: for seniors over age 62, these provide 50% discounts of admission fees to national parks. Get your card from the Department of Interior or Forest Service; no charge.

Food and Travel Discounts: Seniors can often get 10% off the price of rooms at hotels/motels and 25% savings on Amtrak round-trip rail fares. Also look for low-cost tokens or tickets on bus systems, and 10% to 25% savings on admissions to amusement parks.

Early Bird Specials: Many restaurants (chain and local) give elderly diners who eat before 6 p.m. (and sometimes later) regular meals at lower prices.

Airline Bargains: special tickets for seniors, usually when over age 62. Typically, the flight must be in the middle of the week or on Saturday, with reservations made at least six days before the travel date. For example, at this writing Delta Air Lines offers four flights to any one of over 100 destinations for $368. For comparison, two round trips from West Palm Beach to Boston and back would cost a younger passenger from $465 to $1,105, depending on the restrictions. And, with the Eastern Passport, a senior can fly to any domestic city as many times as he or she wishes for $1,299. Flights must be between noon Monday and noon Thursday or on Saturday. If you retire to Maine and your children live in California, this can be a terrific deal. (Check around; some airlines may offer better deals for you, while other programs may have been discontinued or changed).

Frequent Flyer Discounts. For each flight on a company's plane, the traveler earns points that can be used for travel. This membership also assures discounts on rooms at major hotels, car rentals, etc.

Special Employment and Volunteer Opportunities

After the euphoria of travel, recreation and "freedom," many people feel the need of some sort of schedule, the opportunity to give orders to someone other than their spouse and to be important again. If money isn't the aim, employment may be for

> *Challenge:* to tackle a new career or expand a hobby into a money making project. Typically, this will involve realization of an earlier dream so that money is secondary. For example, if you were a radio announcer in college or have training in public speaking, you might be successful as a substitute radio announcer. Similarly, a former dietitian, whose hobby is gourmet food, may prepare and serve gourmet parties for family birthdays and anniversaries.

or for

> *Pleasure:* usually, this type of work involves a hobby or an extension of work interests. Examples include the commercial artist whose watercolors are good enough to be exhibited in art galleries; the toolmaker who carves duck decoys; the market researcher who digs out family genealogy from museums and historical societies from Salem, Mass., to San Francisco. Not much money but enough to pay expenses for vacation trips.

There are also rewarding volunteer opportunities available. In my research, I started to look for projects that could appeal to retirees, especially those who are in good health, have no financial problems and are willing to accept a challenge. When I included religious-related activities, the list became too long and too specialized to be useful. So here are three typical areas of opportunity: one foreign, two domestic. For more information, check your religious center, the United Way, public library and the Area Agency on Aging.

International Executive Service Corps—for retirees who have had hands-on management experience in business or government, are willing to live abroad and can afford to be away for six months or more. These volunteers act as advisers to private enterprises in developing countries.

Currently, some 9,000 men and women are listed and there are over 600 active projects around the world: poultry breeding, construction, hotel management, printing, manufacturing, administration, food processing, retail business and even archeological digs.

Volunteers receive no pay but get travel expenses (for spouse, too) plus a per diem based on the cost of living in the country of assignment which permits comfortable living. Knowledge of a foreign language is helpful and specific skills will be a plus.

Applications are reviewed by qualified volunteers to match qualifications with specific needs. Send resume to: International Executive Service Corps., 8 Stamford Forum, Stamford, CT 08902-2005.

Foster Grandparents—a program to encourage seniors, 60 years or older, to spend four hours a day with children who suffer sight or hearing impairments, language difficulties, learning disability or who are mentally or physically handicapped.

The seniors get a modest, non-taxable stipend, an annual physical exam, a daily hot meal and transportation to and from the site. The children benefit from TLC and the old folks feel young again.

Retired Senior Volunteer Program (RSVP). This is a national project funded by the Federal Government that has offices throughout the 50 states. A paid director enlists and directs volunteers who must be over 60 years of age. There's no remuneration but you may get mileage reimbursement.

These volunteers serve in scores of different jobs: aides in hospital, interviewers in social agencies, researchers in departments, tutors in schools, guides in museums and so on. Fun, rewarding, and making a difference.

Tips for Extra Pleasures

Remember, and keep reminding yourself and spouse: life in retirement should be fun or, at least, interesting. Forget about routines and standardized, acceptable conduct:

- Make it a point to do one new thing each week or approach the old routine differently.

- Visit a museum or art show and try to understand what the artist was trying to say. You may get an idea worth pursuing.

- Attend a lecture or concert with a friend and, on the way home, discuss the performance at a cafe.

- If it's a lovely day, pack a lunch and picnic in the park, at the shore or at a resort center.

- Make love in the afternoon. You won't have to worry about pregnancy and you can have plenty of time to make the liaison meaningful. Afterwards, take a nap and dress for a special cocktail.

- For a day or two, or even a week, forget about friends and neighbors and do exactly what you want to do.

- Play games. Minutes after your husband leaves for golf, set the table so that, when he comes home, he'll think you are preparing dinner just for him.

- Do put frosting on the cake: an annual party to celebrate the birthday of an old friend; a family gathering when you visit the children for a wedding or graduation of grandchildren.

When both can be involved:

- Do chores first, play later. Otherwise, the house can become sloppy.

- On a rainy day, do extra planning for the future: listing possible areas for future cutbacks such as selling one car, dropping memberships in clubs or associations, cancelling subscriptions or eliminating gifts to charities in which you are no longer involved.

- Recognize that togetherness has risks as well as rewards. It's wise to team on family projects such as budgets, vacations, community investments but try to establish routines that will maintain individual independence. If a couple shares every experience, there's not much to talk about.

Practical Points

Life in retirement requires greater patience, tact and understanding, both with each other and within the family, than while busy with work. Pressures and irritations which would have been forgotten during the day away from home can fester and get out of hand. And family relationships can become more stressful when several generations are involved or there's need for assistance and constant care.

To set a firm foundation of understanding, for others and yourself, write down a series of basic rules like these and review them when there are troublesome periods.

Basic Rules After Retirement

- DO remember that you are retired so there's no need to rush, to finish each task the same day you started it. Hopefully, you have another 20 to 25 years to go.

- DO recognize that 40% of normal worries do not happen; that, of these concerns, 30% are things that can't be changed, 22% will be petty and only 8% will be legitimate. So, why waste energy on 92% of nothing?

- DON'T interrupt your spouse when he or she is busy doing something else, unless the house is on fire.

- DO share financial responsibilities: paying bills, handling checkbooks, preparing income tax returns, etc. The best deal for each partner is to have a separate checking account; each with his or her own receipts from Social Security, pension and dividends or interest.

- If your spouse hasn't handled the family finances up to now, DON'T shelter that spouse from financial facts. If your spouse outlives you and does not know and understand family finances, there can be severe problems. If that spouse is unwilling or unable to accept such responsibility, designate an executor or adviser to take charge.

- DON'T assume that you will be protected after your spouse's death by money in a checking account (your own or a joint one), by continuation of your spouse's pension, and by the terms of the will or a trust. In the event of divorce or separation, you could be caught short.

- DO take advantage of the benefits of being a senior citizen: discounts for car rentals, drugs, hotels/motels, air travel, entertainment and educational opportunities.

- DO get out of step with the working world: shop between 10 AM and 3 PM; travel Monday through Thursday; vacation off-season.

- DO become a good shopper: watch for special sales; use coupons for items you need; stock up with staples when there's a super-sale; drop by fleamarkets; have repairs made by retirees recommended at senior centers.

- DO paste this at the top of your mirror and read it every morning: TODAY IS THE FIRST DAY OF THE REST OF MY LIFE!

Index

Annuities, 105–7, 227–28
Apartments, 188, 206, 211
Assets, 38–42, 54–57, 186. *See also* Net worth

Bonds (bond funds), 78–82

Cancer, 143–45
CDs, 86–87
Charitable gifts/trusts, 112–13
Children, 223, 227–28, 239, 241–42, 246. *See also* Estate planning
Civil Service Retirement System (CSRS), 62–64
Community property, 113–14
Condominiums, 188, 206–7
Congregate housing, 209–11
Congregate meals, 244
Crummey Trust, 110

Death of spouse, 118–20, 239–40. *See also* Widows/widowers
Death payment, Social Security, 5
Deferred Compensation, 70
Defined–benefit pension plans, 13, 15, 64, 65, 69
Defined–contribution pension plans, 13–14, 64
Diabetes, 154–56, 162
Diet, 127, 128, 131–34, 146–53, 155
Disease prevention, 124–25
Divorce, pension plans and, 69–70
Doctors. *See* Physicians
Drug abuse, 125–27

Early retirement, 4–5, 45–50
Embolism, 151–52
Emergencies, health, 162–64
Employer-funded pension plans, 1, 12–14, 46–47, 50, 60–64
Employment, 43–44, 70. *See also* Post-retirement employment
Estate planning, 95–120
  annuities, 105–7
  community property and, 113–14
  documents needed for, 96–97
  joint ownership and, 114–15
  joint purchase and, 115
  lawyer fees and, 95
  life insurance and, 101–5, 107
  transferring property, 223
  trusts, 107–13
  will and, 97–101

Estate taxes, 116–17
Exemption-equivalent Trust, 110–11
Exercise, 129–31
Eyesight, 157–58, 178

Fannie Maes, 84
Fat, dietary, 131–32, 150–51
Federal Government CSRS (Civil Service Retirement System), 62–64
Food, 244. *See also* Diet
Foot discomfort, 161–62
Foreign country, retiring to, 201–3
Financial planning, 27–50, 119
  assets and savings and, 38–42
  budgeting, 30–33, 43
  debt retirement, 32, 42–43
  for early retirement, 49–50
  housing costs and, 31
  income and, 43–44
  inflation and, 34–38
  meeting expenses, 38–42
  for Old-Olds, 27–29
  taxes and, 32
401(k) plans, 13, 29, 67–68
403(b) plans, 13, 68

Generation-Skipping Trust (GST), 110
Granny Mae (Golden Rule Annuity Mortgage Association), 223–24

Health (health care), 121–86. *See also* Diet; Health insurance
  age and, 38, 121–23
  alcohol abuse and, 123
  avoiding quacks and frauds, 164–65
  cholesterol level and, 146–48
  diet and, 131–35
  disease and, 142–54
  early retirement and, 48
  emergencies, 162–64
  exercise and, 129–31
  family and, 243
  home care, 177–78
  home tests and, 143
  hospice care, 181
  information on, 165–66
  in–home services, 243–44
  maintaining, 123–24
  nursing homes, 183–86
  physician and, 127–29

prevention of disease, 124–25
recurring (chronic) problems, 142, 154–62
sexual, 135–36
stress and, 136–42
Health insurance, 169–86. *See also* Medicaid; Medicare
Health Maintenance Organizations (HMOs), 129, 178–81
Hearing loss, 160–61
Heart disease, 145–48
High blood pressure (HBP), 149, 152, 154
Home equity loans, 219–22
Home health care, 177–78, 243–44
Home ownership, 89, 186–88, 211–28
  costs of, 211–14
  estate planning and, 113–15
  home equity loans and, 219–21
  mortgages, 214–19, 221–25
  private annuity and, 227–28
  second, renting, 227
  selling your home, 224–25
  transferring to your children, 223
  vacation home, 225–26
Home sharing, 210
Hospice care, 181
Household tasks, training in, 238–39
Housing, 187–228. *See also* Home ownership
  adjusting to new environment, 226–27
  costs of, 31
  living alone, 239–40
  living with other family members, 239
  moving and, 200–1, 229, 231
  neighbors and, 208
  types of, 187–89, 203–7
  where to live, 187–203

Income, 43–44. *See also* Retirement income
Individual Retirement Accounts (IRAs), 13, 29, 66–67, 69, 70
Inflation, 34–38
Investment, 57–95
  bonds, 78–87
  common stocks, 71–78
  mutual funds, 82–87
  pension plans, 60–70

real estate, 89–93
supplementary/alternative
  retirement benefits, 70–71
Irrevocable Trust, 109

Job training for retirees, 21–22,
  24–26
Joint ownership of property,
  114–15, 117
Joint purchase of property, 115

Keogh plans, 12, 61, 64–65, 69

Life after retirement, 229–58. *See
  also specific topics*
  adjusting to, 237–39
  checklist for, 229, 232–34
  household tasks and, 238–39
  living alone, 239–40
  living with other family members,
    239
  pre–planning, 235–37
  projects for, 236–37
  support systems and, 242–45
Lifecare housing, 208–9
Life expectancy, 27, 40, 41
Life insurance, 101–5, 107, 117
Living Trust, 109
Living will, 182
Loans, 68, 219–22

Managed Funds, 78–79
Marital status, 2–4. *See also*
  Spouse; Widows/Widowers
Meals, services providing, 244
Medicaid, 169, 170
Medicare, 169–74
Medication, 125–27, 155–56,
  181–82
Medi-gap insurance, 174–76
Menopause, 156
Mental health, 158–59. *See also*
  Stress
Menus, high fat/low fat, 150–51
Military pensions, 62
Money Market Funds, 86–88
Mortgages, 214–24
Moving, 226, 229, 231
Municipal bonds, 80
Mutual funds, 78–79, 82–87, 91

Neighbors, 208
Net worth, 51–57. *See also* Assets
Nonresident aliens, 9–10

Nursing care insurance, 185–86
Nursing homes, 183–86
Nutrition. *See* Diet

Old-age, survivor, and disability
  insurance (OASDI), 13
Old-Olds (OOs), 27–29, 242–45

Parents, caring for, 241–42, 246
Pension plans, 1, 12–21
  divorce and, 69–70
  employer-funded, 1, 12–14,
    46–47, 50, 62–64
  401(k) plans, 13, 29, 67–68
  403(b) plans, 13, 68
  government, 14, 62–64
  IRAs, 66–67
  Keogh and Professional
    Corporation, 12–13, 61, 64–65,
    69
  loans from, 68
  OOs and, 29
  personal, 1, 13, 66–67
  Simplified Employee (SEP), 13,
    29, 67
  widows/widowers and, 13
  withdrawals from, 14–15, 68–69
Pets, 242, 250
Physicians, 127–29
Post-retirement employment, 1,
  7–8, 21–26, 38, 255–56
Prenuptial agreements, 112
Private annuity, 227–28
Professional Corporation plans,
  12–13, 61, 64–65, 69
Prostate problems, 156–57

Q–Tip Trust, 109

Rabbi Trust, 70
Railroad Retirement benefits, 9–10
Real estate, investing in, 89–93
Real Estate Investment Trusts
  (REITs), 91
Record keeping, 5–6, 96–97, 230
Respite care, 244
Retirement checklist, 229, 232–34
Retirement communities, 189,
  207–8
Retirement income, 18–21. *See also*
  Financial planning; Pension
  plans; Social Security
RV (recreational vehicles), 250–51

Savings, 38–42
Second marriage, 240–41
Sexual health, 135–36
Share-a-home, 210
Singles, 239–41, 250. *See also*
  Death of spouse;
  Widows/widowers
Skin protection, 162
Smoking, cigarette, 144, 145
Social Security, 1–12
  early retirement and, 4–5, 45, 46,
    50
  taxes on benefits, 32
Spouse, 112, 237–38, 240–41. *See
  also* Death of spouse
State taxes, 117, 194–99
Stocks, common, 70–78, 87–89
Stress, 47–48, 136–42, 226
Stroke, 148–49
Support systems, 242–45

Taxes
  annuities and, 106–7
  estate, 116–17
  home ownership and, 224–27
  IRAs and, 66–67
  joint ownership of property and,
    117
  life insurance and, 117
  on Social Security benefits, 8–12,
    32
  state, 117, 194–99
  transferring property and, 223
  trusts and, 107–8
Tax–exempt bonds, 80–82
Travel, 246–54
Trusts, 107–13

Uniform Gift to Minors Act
  (UGMA), 108
Uniform Transfer to Minors Act
  (UTMA), 109
Unit Trusts, 78

Vacation homes, 225–26
Veterans' benefits, 176–77
Volunteering, 255–56

Widows/widowers, 13, 140
Will, 97–101, 182
Working after employment. *See*
  Post–retirement employment
Workmen's compensation, 9